W9-AED-256

PURITY AND POLLUTION
IN ZOROASTRIANISM

Purity and Pollution in Zoroastrianism

Triumph over Evil

By Jamsheed K. Choksy
Foreword by Richard N. Frye

 University of Texas Press, Austin

Copyright © 1989 by the University of Texas Press
All rights reserved
Printed in the United States of America

First Edition, 1989

Requests for permission to reproduce material from this work should be
sent to Permissions, University of Texas Press, Box 7819, Austin, Texas
78713-7819.

The publication of this book was assisted by a grant from the Andrew W.
Mellon Foundation.

LIBRARY OF CONGRESS CATALOGING-IN-PUBLICATION DATA

Choksy, Jamsheed K. (Jamsheed Kairshasp), 1962–
    Purity and pollution in Zoroastrianism : triumph over evil / by
Jamsheed K. Choksy ; foreword by Richard N. Frye.
        p.   cm.
    Bibliography: p.
    Includes index.
    ISBN 0-292-79802-4
    1. Purity, Ritual—Zoroastrianism.   2. Zoroastrianism.   I. Title.
BL1590.P85C46   1989
295'.38—dc19   88-22725
                                                                        CIP

TO MY PARENTS

. . . for as long as a man's father and mother live, he is like a lion in the jungle that has no fear of anyone at all.

—ĀDURBĀD Ī MĀRASPANDĀN
ZOROASTRIAN HIGH PRIEST FOURTH CENTURY C.E.

CONTENTS

FIGURES

TABLES

ABBREVIATIONS

Ar.	Arabic
Av.	Avestan
D.	Dari
Gk.	Greek
Heb.	Hebrew
L.	Latin
N.P.	New Persian
O.P.	Old Persian
P.Gj.	Parsi Gujarati
Phl.	Pahlavi
Pth.	Parthian
Pz.	Pāzand
Skt.	Sanskrit

FOREWORD

RITUALS AND beliefs on purity and pollution may appear to be curious relics of the past for many contemporary observers. Although unimportant and neglected in the Christian tradition, ritual purity remains central to the lives of the followers of such faiths as Zoroastrianism, Judaism, and Islam. The Zoroastrian tradition has elaborated and preserved many features of the religion's early rules of purity and pollution. These purity codes played an important role in the history of religions by influencing Jewish and Islamic practices. Little has been written about Zoroastrian concerns for the maintenance of purity since the first decades of this century, and these works have long been out of date and out of print. The present study, which focuses on the aspiration for purity and the fear of pollution as central aspects of the Zoroastrian cultus, is both needed and welcome.

Jamsheed Choksy is well qualified to write the present work. He is a Zoroastrian, and for this work he has studied the relevant texts in the languages in which they were written centuries ago, recorded contemporary practices and beliefs, and pursued a rigorous methodology in the study of religion, as well as philology, with commendable objectivity. He analyzes fundamental aspects of the notions of purity and pollution in Zoroastrianism, traces these notions over the faith's long history, and demonstrates the interrelationship among doctrine, ritual, and mythology. Choksy carefully investigates development and variation in the ritual practice and elucidates the ramifications of social change on the lives of devotees. The book's special significance lies in its combination of a study of the past with contemporary observance and practice, in addition to a critical application of modern scholarship on religions, societies, and ritual studies. Furthermore, comparisons with other religions and rites of purifications in other cultures enhance the value of the work.

The present book is unique in its focus on major rituals of purification and the pursuit of purity in daily life. The reader is shown the importance of both ritual purification and physical cleansing in the communal and individual lives of Zoroastrians, with parallels being drawn to Judaism, Islam, and Hinduism. Likewise, the work uses the Zoroastrian example to argue that the study of ritual must be based upon and integrated with the devotional tenets and eschatological aspirations of societies. Choksy establishes the close relationships among religious values, ritual practices, and eschatological myths and utilizes these interconnections to ascertain the cultural importance of purity and pollution for Zoroastrians past and present.

Zoroastrianism shares a common cultural background with many other faiths of the Near East. It is likely that the study of purity and pollution in such a religion as Zoroastrianism, which is conservative in the preservation of ancient beliefs and practices, can shed light on Judaism, Islam, and even Christianity. A book on such an important aspect of Zoroastrianism, especially when it is as well written and readable as the present study, will provide an impetus for further elucidation of a fascinating religion's spread and influence on the world.

Richard N. Frye
Aga Khan Professor of Iranian
Harvard University

PREFACE

THE CONCEPT of this book began several years ago while I was at Columbia University. I gratefully acknowledge the guidance, inspiration, and comments provided by Professor Richard W. Bulliet, Associate Professor James R. Russell, and Professor Ehsan Yarshater on chapters written while I was at Columbia. Research on contemporary beliefs and practices was conducted among the Zoroastrians in India, Pakistan, and Sri Lanka between 1984 and 1988. In India, Dastur Dr. Firoze M. Kotwal, high priest of the Wadia Ātash Bahrām, guided me through the intricacies of Zoroastrian rituals. Ervad Rustom N. Panthaky and the students of the Athornan Boarding Madressa repeatedly performed these rituals for my edification. Without their instruction this project would not have been possible. Likewise, the many Irani Zoroastrians, both recent immigrants and trainee-priests, whom I met in India provided valuable information on contemporary beliefs and practices in Iran. Mr. and Mrs. Erach F. Cooper, Mr. and Mrs. Framroz E. Cooper, Ervad Ramiyar P. Karanjia, Mr. Malcolm Metha, Mr. Khojeste P. Mistree, and friends at Zoroastrian Studies must be thanked for their assistance in India. A Columbia University research grant funded my initial research in India. Mrs. Aban Kabraji, Mr. Khurshed Marker, and Ms. Meher Marker were particularly helpful in Pakistan. My gratitude is also extended to the other Zoroastrians in Pakistan who provided me with details of their own practices. In Sri Lanka, Ervad Aspi D. Daruwalla willingly shared his time and knowledge, for which I am most grateful.

At Harvard University this study greatly benefited from valuable insights contributed by Professors Richard N. Frye and Carl C. Lamberg-Karlovsky, who encouraged me to publish it. Professor Gernot L. Windfuhr of the University of Michigan gave valuable advice for the manuscript's improvement. Thanks also go to Professor Emeritus Mary Boyce, Assistant Professor William R. Darrow, Professor Emeritus Cyrus R. Pangborn, and Dr. Denise A. Spellberg for their helpful comments. Mr. Noshir M. Desai kindly provided the photograph published as figure 5. Mrs. Elise D. Green and Mr. Stephen Green skillfully prepared the manuscript. Above all, special thanks go to my parents, who have constantly supported my endeavors.

Chapter 1 and a section of chapter 3 are based on articles published in the *Mankind Quarterly* and the *Journal of Ritual Studies,* respectively. I thank the editors of these journals for permission to make use of these materials in their modified forms. The transcription of Avestan, Pahlavi, Pāzand, New Persian, and Parsi Gujarati texts that deal with purity has been restricted to short phrases in order to avoid the printing of long passages. Unless otherwise noted, all translations are mine.

This book is intended for an audience of scholars and students of Near Eastern and Asian religion, history, anthropology, and ritual—nonbelievers and believers alike.[1] It is hoped this study will reveal that the promise of religious history lies in both specialized research and interdisciplinary inquiry. Indeed, theories proposed by historians, specialists in Iranian religions, scholars of comparative religion, and anthropologists are utilized, manipulated, and often fused. I believe that the interdisciplinary fusion of these ideas greatly aids elucidation of the origins, development, symbolism, and social function of the Zoroastrian doctrines and rituals of purity and pollution.

Society of Fellows
Harvard University

INTRODUCTION: ANALYSIS OF BELIEFS AND PRACTICES

The main context, though not the only one, in which religious symbols work to create and sustain belief is, of course, ritual.

—CLIFFORD GEERTZ

ZOROASTRIANISM AND its adherents' notions of purity and pollution can be traced over the span of history. The modern scholar has, of course, no direct entrée to the past, and his or her knowledge of it must be based on vestiges of past beliefs and practices. A scheme of events has to be reconstructed to account for the intentional and unintentional traces of the past garnered through research. The same is usually true for documentation and analysis of contemporary beliefs, practices, and occurrences, for often a scholar is neither a believer nor a practitioner of that which is studied. The unique task of a scholar in fields of history, religion, and anthropology is, therefore, not only to recover beliefs and practices of past eras, but also to determine why these were accepted and propagated. In addition, he or she has to correlate the conclusions obtained from study of the past with evidence from the present, that is, data on current doctrines and rites.[1] Notions of purity and pollution are expressed chiefly through ritual. Clifford Geertz has argued that most rituals embody symbols that reflect religious beliefs (1971: 100). Since purification rites often command each devotee's attention, it is necessary for scholars to ascertain whether such rites possess symbolic valence.

Zoroastrianism, a faith based upon the revelations of the prophet Zarathushtra, was a major religion in ancient and medieval Iran and the Near East. During this period it greatly influenced Hellenic, Roman, and Jewish beliefs and philosophies. After the Arab conquest of Iran by 651 C.E. (Common Era), Zoroastrianism gradually lost many of its adherents. In the tenth century C.E. many Zoroastrians migrated to Gujarat in India, where they formed the Parsi community. Zoroastrians continued to dwell in Iran, and a large community survives to the present day in Yazd. Zoroastrians also dwell in other cities and towns of Iran, such as Tehran, Shiraz, Isfahan, Karaj, Ahwaz, Maryam-Abad, Taft, Mehdi-Abad, Khorramshahr, and Ahrestan (Parsiana 1987: 17). In India, they are found in most major cities, such as Bombay, New Delhi, Calcutta, and Hyderabad. Zoroastrian communities even exist in Pakistan, Sri Lanka, Australia, New Zealand, England, Germany, a few other places in Europe, the United States of America, and Canada (Choksy 1988). Both the modern Irani and Parsi Zoroastrian communities continue many of the beliefs and practices of their common ancestors, particularly those relating to purity and pollution.[2]

There is, unfortunately, a dearth of detailed studies on Zoroastrian doctrines and rites relating to purity and pollution in the fields of Near Eastern history, religion, and Iranian studies. The difficulties posed by languages and doctrines have resulted in little attention being paid to this important and long-lived faith by anthropologists and scholars of comparative religion. In addition, the laws of purity and pollution, under which all non-believers are regarded as unclean and capable of polluting religious sanctuaries, have limited the access of scholars to ritual practices, especially the rites of purification. Although a few non-Zoroastrian scholars have been granted access to these rituals in Iran, they have not been permitted to participate in the rites or to have direct contact with the participants and sacred implements. For example, in 1963 and 1964 Mary Boyce was permitted to observe the rituals, but only from a distance (1977: 119, 128). As both a scholar and a member of the Parsi Zoroastrian community, I was not governed by these restrictions and had unlimited access to all aspects of the faith, including actual performances of the purification rituals. This book is thus based on the analysis of a chronological sequence of religious and secular writings and the correlation of written evidence with my observations of and participation in actual modern practices.

Early studies of purity and pollution in Zoroastrianism were based on late-nineteenth- and early-twentieth-century notions of physical hygiene and pathology. Consequently, James Darmesteter regarded purification as a theory of hygiene (1892: x–xii, 146–147). Sorabji E. Dubash, in his analysis of purification laws and rituals among late-nineteenth-century Zoroastrians, interpreted all beliefs and practices as a sanitary code (1906). Dubash concluded that the ancient and medieval Zoroastrian clergy was aware of microscopic organisms, contagious diseases, and causes of infection (1906: 21, 39, 72–73, 86–91, 144). The source of pollution, according to Dubash, was "nothing more than the contagion or specific germ of a contagious or infectious disease" (1906: 20). The only detailed scholarly description of Zoroastrian beliefs and practices dealing with purity and pollution was compiled by Jivanji J. Modi (1922). In his book on Parsi ceremonies and customs, Modi documented the purification rituals and rites as they were practiced during the early twentieth century C.E. His descriptions are a unique account of Zoroastrian rituals during the early modern period of the faith. But Modi, too, was greatly influenced by modern science and analyzed these ritual practices in terms of quarantine and the spread of infectious diseases (1922: 87–90, 103–106, 157–161).

There is, however, no evidence that the ancient and medieval Magi, as Zoroastrian priests are called, possessed scientific knowledge of pathology. To the innovators and practitioners of Zoroastrian purity rites during the ancient and medieval periods, pollution was not caused by germs but by spiritual, supernatural forces that arose directly from evil. Hence, demonology, and not hygiene or health, was the basis of Zoroastrian attempts to comprehend and categorize the material and spiritual universe. In recent years Boyce has directed the attention of scholars to the importance of purity codes in Zoroastrianism. Several of her valuable studies on the faith contain discussions of purity and pollution (1975, 1977, 1979, 1982). She has been a pioneer in attempts to interpret Zoroastrian laws of purity in terms of religious doctrine (1975: 294–324). Boyce also carefully recorded the rites of purification practiced by Irani Zoroastrians during the early 1960s (1977: 92–138).[3] However, only limited attention has been paid by Boyce to the symbolic importance and function of purity rituals (1975: 294; 1979: 94, 128). Additionally, there is an occasional tendency on her part to regard physical cleanness as the most important function of purification and to view the main purificatory substance as a disinfectant (1975: 310; 1979: 6). For Zoroastrians physical cleanliness is, indeed, essential because there is no religious dichotomy between matter and spirit. The primary focus of purity and purification, however, has always been on the spiritual universe and not on the material world. Finally, no scholar has previously elucidated the elaboration and variation of purity laws and purification rites within a chronological framework that spans the faith's history, although Boyce has recognized that the rites did change over time (1975: 294–295; 1977: 92; 1979: 43; 1982: 189–190).

Geertz has suggested that "the essential vocation of interpretive anthropology is . . . to make available to us answers that others . . . have given, and thus to include them in the consultable record of what man has said" (1973a: 30). Geertz's recommendation must not be limited to anthropology but should be extended to the historical study of religion. This book originated in an attempt to elucidate and interpret the historical development of purity codes in Zoroastrianism within the context of the changing votive and social circumstances of the faith's adherents. The chapters are structured to progress from an informative introduction on the study of ritual to the doctrinal basis of purity and pollution in Zoroastrianism and a historical clarification of the major, minor, and daily rituals of purification. The nature and causes of the gradual elaboration and recent decline of these rites are examined, and ultimately these beliefs and practices are argued to be central to the cosmology and eschatology of the faith. Further, by means of presentation, argument from Zoroastrian examples, and assertion based on analysis, it is demonstrated that ritual should not be studied in vacuo. Zoroastrian beliefs and practices are documented in terms of historical elaboration and variation in order to preserve, disseminate, and examine these data. The ancient and medieval versions of ritual acts are elucidated from religious and secular writings. Modern rituals are then analyzed in relation to their older versions. Information on contemporary doctrines, beliefs, and rituals is based largely on research conducted in India, Pakistan, and Sri Lanka. The accounts of the modern rites of purity and purification have been derived chiefly from my fieldnotes, personal observations, and direct participation. Data on Zoroastrian beliefs and practices in Iran, which have been inaccessible to scholars since the Islamic revolution in 1979, were obtained from Irani Zoroastrian trainee-priests in India.[4] The contemporary data, although collected in person, are not presented as an ethnographic description based on having "been there" (cf. Geertz 1988: 4–17). No impressionistic scenes of pious devotees performing arduous rites under a relentless noonday sun will be evoked. The relevant information on present-day rites is adduced to illuminate variation in performance and function of rituals. It is not intended to form a narrative landscape upon which an ethnographer serves as the tour guide on a quest for exotic practices. Nor is this book an exercise in philological or textual problems, because the doctrines, ritual practices, and historical development of purity and pollution in Zoroastrianism are aspects of the faith that are clearly documented and carefully preserved in the faith's literature.

First, extant Zoroastrian liturgy, literature, and priestly traditions in Avestan, Old Persian, Pahlavi, Pāzand, New Persian, and Gujarati are used to establish and analyze the doctrinal basis of purity and pollution. Next, these sources are utilized in tracing the extension of the doctrines and laws from the earliest period to their final codification in the medieval period. The doctrine by which the various sacred material creations—metal, earth, water, fire, plants, animals, and human beings—are believed to be under the protection of the gods and beneficent immortals is investigated. The means by which these creations are protected from pollution and impurity are studied in a religious, symbolic, and historical context. Thereafter, the causes of ritual impurity are established, and the purification rituals used to ensure and regain ritual purity are examined. For purposes of this study the history of Zoroastrianism is divided into three eras: the ancient period, which extends from the earliest years of the faith until the end of the Parthian dynasty (ca. 1200 B.C.E–224 C.E.); the medieval period, which encompasses the Sasanian and Islamic centuries (224–1700 C.E.); and the modern period, which covers the past three centuries (1700–present C.E.).

The purification rituals are grouped into three categories. The most important category involves the purification of both body and soul through the Barašnūm ī nō šab, which should be undergone by every devotee at least once during his or her lifetime. The next category comprises three rituals: the Pādyāb, which is performed several times each day and ensures purity for daily activities and simple devotional acts; the Nāhn, which has two versions and provides purification during rites of passage and after occasional contact with carrion; and the Rīman, which was developed by the Parsis to fulfill the original functions of the Barašnūm ī nō šab. The final category includes all minor purification rites. These minor rites regulate aspects of daily life and ensure purity of every devotee and the entire community. The development of these rituals and minor rites is traced, and the significance of each is elucidated within the context of Zoroastrian beliefs and cross-cultural parallels. During the nineteenth and twentieth centuries, the role of increased interaction between Zoroastrians and non-Zoroastrians in the decline of these ritual practices is also analyzed.

In conclusion, the interaction of purity, symbols transmitted in purification rituals, and eschatological beliefs is examined. The role played by this interaction in Zoroastrians' perception of evil, life, and social order will also be determined. It is demonstrated that the precise symbolism of purification rituals can be related to religious beliefs and utilized in revealing the spiritual functions attributed to purity by devotees. The importance accorded by Zoroastrians to maintaining ritual purity and undergoing purification is linked to the fate of each individual soul at death and in the afterlife. Finally, the eschatological function of purity in ensuring the expulsion of evil, impurity, and pollution from the universe will be interpreted in conjunction with the cultural role of religion.

The study of religious beliefs and practices in ancient and even contemporary societies is an analytic problem numerous scholars have attempted

to solve. Religious beliefs, and the ritual practices associated with such beliefs, appear to be widespread in both past and present cultures. Despite
the vast attention paid to religious communities, there is little consensus
within the disciplines of anthropology, comparative religion, and history
on the nature and function of religious beliefs and practices. Hence, it is
first necessary to briefly examine the nature of religious beliefs and practices and the concepts of ritual purity and pollution. Such an examination
will aid the analysis of Zoroastrian notions of purity and pollution.

Religious Beliefs and Ritual Practices

Émile Durkheim, in his pioneering study on the nature of religion, concluded that religious belief consisted of two categories: belief in good
supernatural beings and forces that produce beneficial effects and belief in
evil beings and forces that produce harmful effects (1957: 409). He argued
that religious beliefs presuppose a classification of all things, real and ideal,
into two classes or opposed groups, the sacred and the profane (1957: 37).
For such researchers as Jack Goody (1961: 155, 157) and Melford E. Spiro
(1966: 91), the core of religion has consisted of belief in superhuman beings and the power of such beings to assist or harm humans. But neither
Durkheim, Goody, nor Spiro perceived any distinct dichotomy of superhuman beings into the categories of good and evil. In Zoroastrianism
there is, indeed, a clear dichotomy of the entire universe, both material and
spiritual, into the realms of good and evil, sacred and profane. This dichotomy is formulated in a doctrine of cosmic and ethical dualism, a universal
battle between the forces of good and evil from which there will be no
respite until all evil is neutralized and defeated. However, contrary to Durkheim's hypothesis, this dichotomy of sacred and profane is not merely a pre-
supposition, but an intrinsic part of the faith itself. It is both the cause and
the result of the religion's fundamental tenets.

Yet, is not religion more than merely the belief in beneficent and malefi-
cent spiritual entities superior to human beings? Indeed, religious beliefs
form a cognitive system, a set of explicit and implicit propositions con-
cerning the spiritual world and humanity's relationship to it. This results
in a unified system of beliefs and practices (cf. Spiro 1966: 101). Religious
phenomena may be arranged, for convenience, into two fundamental categories: beliefs and practices (Durkheim 1957: 29–30, 36, 47). In many religions, including Zoroastrianism, the entire cosmos is regarded as an ar-
tifact of a god or gods. Because it is believed to be of divine origin, the

world came to be regarded as sacred in nature and function, and the creation of the world was thought to have laid the foundation of all human behavior and every social institution. Hence, human beliefs and practices are held, by such religions, to belong to sacred history (Eliade 1975: xi).

Definitions of religion are numerous, but few address the majority of features encompassed by belief, and fewer still successfully relate beliefs and practices to human experience. Yet, a comprehensive definition of the term "religion" is essential for any study of religious doctrines and rites. Within the framework of human history, religion may be regarded as "a perspective, a standpoint, in which certain dominant images are used by its adherents to orient themselves to the present and the future. It may be understood as a way of looking at experience as a whole or, better, as a way of interpreting certain elemental features of human existence" (Harvey 1966: 258–259). Van A. Harvey's definition stresses the cultural and collective aspect of religion. The cultural features of religion cannot be overlooked, for the perfect and eternal concepts in a religious system unite with myth, cosmogony, and eschatology to describe and reshape the lives of human beings in conformity with models believed to be immutable and sacred. In such a system, the importance of beliefs and ritual practices lies in their ability to shape and endow daily life with meaning. Indeed, viewed from the perspective of a believer, Zoroastrian doctrines and laws become personal and collective, mythical and factual, historical and acutely contemporary. The beliefs and practices create a dynamic relationship of ritual continuity between the past, with its authority based on cosmogony and revelation, and the future, with its power to transform matter and spirit and thereby alleviate human suffering. As a result, the past is not historical in the Zoroastrian world view, but is ever present. Only with knowledge of the past, as preserved and transmitted through religion, can Zoroastrians succeed in the present and future battle against cosmic evil.

The challenge to a scholar of religious beliefs and practices lies in attempting to document and analyze the expression of ethos through symbol systems propagated in rituals. The history of a religion, with its precepts and rites, cannot be separated from symbolism. The elaboration, propagation, and modification of ritual practices over time must be elucidated in order to comprehend fully the symbols and values attached to beliefs and practices. In other words, doctrines and rituals should be studied within a historical context, because peoples and cultures cannot be separated from their heritage. It would be foolish to deny the importance of past experience, both individual and communal, on perception and faith.

Hence, this book is an attempt to decipher Zoroastrian beliefs and practices relating to purity and pollution within a historical context that spans nearly three millennia.

The problems of suffering and death are possibly the most complex of the personality tensions, within both individuals and societies, that religions attempt to treat. As Albert Camus observed with reference to Christianity: "For twenty centuries the sum total of evil has not diminished in the world. No paradise . . . has been realized. An injustice remains inextricably bound to all suffering, even the most deserved in the eyes of men" (1975: 267–268). Camus' statement need not be limited to Christianity, for the dilemma of evil confronts every religious system. Talcott Parsons, following Bronislaw Malinowski, saw religious beliefs as symbolic resolutions of this dilemma (1949: 58–59). Human beings face the inescapable fact that the greatest material rewards do not always come to persons who most carefully follow the codes and rules of society. Often, righteous and just individuals suffer and fail while unrighteous and unjust people prosper. The suffering of humans and the presence of evil in the universe are thus basic religious problems that, if left unanswered, disrupt integration of the individual into the general social order.[5] In order to counter this threat, every religious system formulates, by manipulation of symbols, an image of genuine cosmic order that accounts for the paradoxes of life. The response from within the ancient Zoroastrian world view was to formulate a doctrine of moral dualism, one that absolved the gods from all evil. The locus of evil became the demons, and the function of creation came to be perceived as the progressive elimination of evil, death, and suffering from the universe. Ritual purity, in belief and practice, was developed as a means by which the religious goal of expelling evil could be achieved.

Faith is sustained in the world by ritual practices, symbolic arrangements, and social structures that enable comprehension of belief. The specific content of a religion is incorporated in the images and metaphors used by its followers to define reality. The function of rituals and symbols lies in their relationship to individual and communal beliefs, practices, and social status. As Geertz deduced, the main context in which religious symbols operate to create and sustain belief is ritual (1971: 100). It is through religious law and the performance of rituals that symbols serve to formalize belief and social order in human societies.

While the importance of ritual is undeniable, perfect definitions of the term are elusive. Indeed, what is a ritual, what is the nature of the ritual field, and at whom is the rite aimed?[6] In general, it can be argued that each ritual is a stereotyped sequence of activities, involving words, gestures, substances, and objects, often performed in a sequestered location and designed to influence the gods. Such a ritual may be contingent, performed in response to an individual or collective crisis (Turner 1977*a*: 183). Within the Zoroastrian community, pollution is one such crisis for the unclean individual and all his or her contemporaries. Arnold van Gennep has classified rituals of passage into rites of separation, transition, and incorporation (1960: 10–11, 21). He designated these three categories of rites as preliminal, liminal, and postliminal, respectively, with the concept of liminality referring to thresholds in spatial, temporal, corporeal, and spiritual terms. All three categories are present in Zoroastrian purification rituals and are interlaced by religious symbolism.

Yet, how do all the features of a ritual relate to each other and to the religious community? The answer to this question lies in the realization that each ritual is an expression of the religious and social beliefs, desires, and needs of its participants and observers. Rituals express the religious beliefs of a society and can therefore provide insights into these beliefs. Further, rituals preserve a notion of the sacred and serve as a means for sustaining religious devotion (cf. Eliade 1976: 164). Each ritual is also a conglomerate of enacted symbols. Indeed, rituals maintain and reestablish the sacred order of the world through symbols. But, as Victor W. Turner has demonstrated, rituals are not merely concentrations of symbolic referents about beliefs, values, and norms (1977*a*: 189). They also represent a fusion of the powers believed to be inherent in the deities, persons, objects, events, and spiritual relationships symbolized in the rituals. Thus, rituals may be defined as consecrated actions in which the corporeal world is fused, via symbols, with the religious universe and then clarified and reinforced for the believer.[7]

Like all other religious concepts, ritual imagery possesses its own justification. Images and symbols expressed through doctrines and rites are both authoritative and persuasive for the believer. As a result, the coalescence of beliefs and world view is often mediated by images and symbols (cf. Geertz 1971: 110). Enactment of rituals reinforces acceptance, by the populace, of the authority that underlies the religious perspective embodied by these rituals. Through ritual actions, religious concepts are disseminated beyond their specific contexts and serve to provide a general framework of beliefs and practices. In Zoroastrian purification rituals a symbolic relationship is established among the actions, words, objects, and substances used in these rites and the religious universe itself. This relationship transmits the beliefs that underlie ritual practices to the participants in terms of the faith's fundamental tenets (cf. Douglas 1973: 41–42). Indeed, the revelatory encounter with symbols, although present in everyday life, occurs most forcefully within the religious and social parameters of ritual practices. Hence, the laws of purity and pollution, and the rituals of purification, are important conduits for the transmission of religious beliefs by means of symbols.

Concepts of Purity and Pollution

Purity and pollution are paired concepts that play extremely important roles in religious activities, with purity linked to sanctity, and pollution to impurity, irreligion, and danger. Personal and communal activities are carefully regulated by rules and rites designed to protect the individual believer, the religious community, the deity or deities, and even the world itself from the impurity caused by pollution. These two concepts arise from within the context of the religious world view, often having demonology as the determining factor. Thus, modern notions of hygiene and disease that appear to be reflected in these religious rules and rites bear only accidental correspondence (cf. Douglas 1969: 35). Purity and pollution in a religious system are usually not based on physical cleanness and uncleanness or contamination, but on ritual purity and the loss of this purity through transgressions that render the believer ritually unclean or polluted, thereby excluding him or her from partaking in the activities of the community. The emphasis is, therefore, on ritual purity and not physical cleanliness or purity. In order to comprehend the concept of ritual purity, it is necessary to elucidate the principles that regulate fear of pollution and impurity.

The concept of impurity and the fear of pollution are the result of a systemic ordering of the religious cosmos. They involve the specific rejection of all inappropriate elements, especially disorder. As convincingly demonstrated by Mary Douglas, reflection on pollution involves reflection on the relation of order to disorder, being to nonbeing, form to formlessness, and life to death (1969: 5). Pollution is equated with disorder and becomes associated with nonbeing and death. The problem of impurity and pollution passes easily into the problem of evil, for, if pollution is severe enough, it usually is equated with moral disorder caused by the forces of evil. Thus, the sacred must be protected from defilement. As a result, holiness and impurity come to be located at opposite poles within the religious universe (cf. Douglas 1968: 338; 1969: 7).

This division of all things along lines of purity and pollution, order and disorder, the sacred and the profane, life and death does conform in its general outlines to the Durkheimian view of religion. It is important to note, however, that the religious basis of this classification is usually founded on an elaborate hierarchy of ritual values. The categories of social structure that result from this classification embrace the universe in a single, symbolic whole, within which devotees are required to orient themselves toward purity. Instances of pollution are regarded as invasions into the sacred by the profane and require that the sacred be purified. In addition to rituals for purification, taboos and prohibitions arise to prevent pollution from occurring. A taboo (*tabu*) is essentially a social mechanism of obedience that has ritual significance. It enforces restrictive behavior in situations that pose a threat to the religious world. Hence, taboos deal with the sociology of danger and are concerned with the protection of devotees who, if exposed to danger, threaten society (Steiner 1956: 20–21). A ritual prohibition, however, is a rule of behavior associated with the belief that an infraction will result in the loss of the religious status of anyone who fails to obey the prohibition (Radcliffe-Brown 1952: 43).

Zoroastrian prohibitions are based on moral codes and serve to protect the believer from harm caused by the demons, whereas in Polynesian societies taboo does not imply a moral quality but merely expresses a connection with the gods.[8] Things that are *tabu* are sacred in Polynesian society; in Zoroastrian society things that are prohibited are never sacred and are always impure and polluting. Indeed, the Polynesian violation of the *tabu* does not cause pollution by evil but brings the wrath of the gods upon the violator. But a Zoroastrian who violates a ritual prohibition is exposed to impurity and pollution. It would be appropriate, therefore, to define Zoroastrian edicts that seek to prevent pollution as ritual prohibitions rather than as taboos (cf. Mistree 1982: 61). Further, in Zoroastrian practice, prohibitions are inviolable laws, not negative rites. Separation of the pure from that which is polluted is based on the religious dichotomy between the sacred and the profane, between good and evil. This dualism is central to an understanding not only of purity and pollution but also of the entire religion. Thus, the study of purity and pollution provides valuable insights into the beliefs, practices, social order, iconography, cosmogony, and eschatology of Zoroastrianism and Zoroastrian communities.

Purity and Pollution in Zoroastrianism

Numerous methodological problems exist in the interpretation of purity laws and rituals, particularly in relation to emic and etic analyses and the significance of belief systems associated with purification rituals.[9] The

problems of emic and etic analyses arise, of course, from attempts by observers to elucidate both the manner in which members of various groups
or communities define themselves and the beliefs that form the bases of
ritual acts. Yet, such interpretations are themselves "second and third order
ones to boot. (By definition, only a 'native' makes first order ones: it's *his*
culture)" (Geertz 1973*a*: 15). As a result, Geertz questions: "If we are going
to cling—as, in my opinion, we must—to the injunction to see things
from the native's point of view . . . what happens to *verstehen* when *ein-
fühlen* disappears?" (1976: 222).

For Zoroastrian beliefs and practices of purity and pollution, the answer to Geertz's question is found in the concept of cultural relativity anticipated by Lucien Lévy-Bruhl and proposed by Franz Boas.[10] Beliefs and
rituals are both personal and social phenomena and should be examined
within the context of the values and meanings assigned to them by adherents of the religion. If a documentation, analysis, or interpretation is
separated from its specific context, it is rendered meaningless (Goody 1961:
157; Geertz 1973*a*: 18; 1983: 44). Consequently, a proper analysis of Zoroastrian rituals must be rooted in concrete examples and in the beliefs and
symbolism elicited. An analysis should never be construed as separate and
apart from the domains it serves to integrate. Nor should an analysis be
considered in vacuo as Claude Lévi-Strauss does in several studies of myth
and religion (1963, 1968, 1987).

Malinowski (1948: 1–71), Turner (1968: 578), and Douglas (1969: 49;
1963; 1968; 1976; 1985; 1987) have emphasized that it is necessary to study
purification and all other rituals within the context in which they occur.
Each specific ritual must also be examined as one component of a total
system of religious beliefs and practices. Further, symbols and rites must
be related to those found in other aspects of the religion. In addition, as
Fitz J. P. Poole has poignantly observed, studies of religion and ritual often
devote scant attention to the historical context in which beliefs and practices developed (1986: 412). Many significant aspects of meanings are neglected if the history of a faith's doctrines and rituals is not determined.
Therefore, the study of purity and pollution in Zoroastrianism should integrate beliefs and symbols with the specific behavior patterns generated
by beliefs over the course of time. This complex integration of data elicited
from historical and contemporary sources, and observed in person, is, in
essence, what Geertz named "thick description" (1973*a*: 27).

In Zoroastrian belief, pollution and all other forms of evil are seen as a
single metaphysical absolute, not a relative state or continuing dialectical
process. The distinction between good and evil forms the central dualism

of the faith, with purity symbolizing all that is good and sacred, and pollution symbolizing everything that is evil and profane. The symbolism of evil as defilement, and not sin or guilt, is linked to a ritualistic world view in which evil is an external pollutant (cf. Ricoeur 1969). The sacred is viewed as the source of all existence, reality, and purity (cf. Eliade 1965: 11–13). By adhering to the doctrines, laws, and ritual practices of purity and pollution, Zoroastrians believe that they can comprehend the purpose and significance of the religious cosmos. Through devotion and ritual practice, the world becomes full of meaning and, consequently, intelligible to the faithful.

More important, evil and pollution provide the means by which each Zoroastrian becomes the central protagonist in the myth of creation, the linear progression of history, and the cosmic struggle between good and evil in the material world (cf. Ricoeur 1969: 162–163). Transgression of cosmic law and order, through violation of purity, results in a Zoroastrian's breaking the primeval covenant between the creator god and the devotee's immortal spirit. Because an act of pollution breaches the relationship with the divine and furthers the cause of evil, it becomes a sin. Purification rituals and acts of penance must then be undergone because, unlike in Muslim, Hindu, and Buddhist belief, purity and purification can be used to negate impurity and defilement. The Hindu, Buddhist, and Jain penances (Skt. *tapas*) do not negate impurity and defilement caused by loss of ritual purity through contact with an external pollutant. They are undergone as a form of repentance, not purification. Impiety and sins, not acts of voluntary or involuntary pollution, are expiated (Obeyesekere 1984: 53). The same is true for self-flagellation and acts of penitence undergone by Shīʿī Muslims, particularly during the month of Muharram. These acts involve themes and acts of suffering and pain to provide expiation of sin (Fischer 1980: 175–176). Zoroastrian rites of purification do not serve to expiate personal sins but rather function as means of ensuring personal and communal purity.

PURITY AND POLLUTION
IN ZOROASTRIANISM

1 LAWS OF PURITY AND POLLUTION

We hold, then, that God is a living being, eternal, most good; and therefore life and a continuous eternal existence belong to God; for that is what God is.

—ARISTOTLE

THE ANCIENT Indo-Iranian tribes developed a complex system of religious rules regulating purity and pollution, with ritual purity being important in the service of the gods and as a safeguard against evil. Among other practices, the purity of the sacrificial ground on which worship was performed and of all sacrificial instruments was ensured. Many of these Indo-Iranian codes and rites of purification were inherited by Zoroastrianism and were preserved by the Iranian peoples as their tribes migrated onto the Iranian plateau. Available evidence indicates that the prophet Zarathushtra (Av. Zaraθuštra; Phl. Zarduxšt), or Zoroaster (lived ca. 1200 B.C.E.) as he is commonly called, had been trained as a priest in the cult of his tribe.[1] He knew, therefore, many of the Indo-Iranian laws and rites that regulated ritual purity and incorporated these into the faith he preached. Zoroaster regarded the divine creator as eternal and supremely good, just as Aristotle would centuries later (12: 7.9). The spread of Zoroastrianism onto the Iranian plateau and its acceptance by numerous Iranian peoples granted the faith an important position in the ancient Near East. With the rise to power of the Achaemenian (549–330 B.C.E.), Parthian, or Arsacid, (247 B.C.E.–224 C.E.), and Sasanian (224–651 C.E.) dynasties and the spread of the political influence of these empires throughout the Near East, Zoroastrianism reached its zenith as one of the major religions of the ancient world. The doctrines and practices of the faith were enforced throughout the empires, particularly under the Sasanians. Zoroastrian purity laws were strictly adhered to, and purification rituals were widely practiced.

The Doctrinal Basis of Purity and Pollution

The concepts of religious purity (Av. *yaožda-;* Phl. *yōǰdahrīh*) and pollution (Av. *irimant-;* Phl. *rēmanīh*) in Zoroastrianism are based on the fundamental cosmic and ethical dualism between the truth, or righteousness (Av. *aša-;* Phl. *ardā*), and the lie (Av. *drug-;* Phl. *druǰ, druz*) preached by the prophet. This dualism between righteousness and wickedness, truth and falsehood, order and disorder was personified by Zoroaster in a pair of primal spirits: the Beneficent Spirit (Av. Spənta Mainyu; Phl. Spēnōg Mēnōg) and the Destructive, or Evil, Spirit (Av. Aŋra Mainyu; Phl. Ahreman, Gannāg Mēnōg). Spənta Mainyu is the hypostasis of the Lord Wisdom (Av. Ahura Mazdā; Phl. Ohrmazd), the supreme creator deity of the Zoroastrian pantheon. Zoroastrians, consequently, refer to themselves as Mazdeans or Mazda-worshippers (Av. *mazdayasna-;* Phl. *māzdēsn*). According to Zoroastrian doctrine, these two spirits are irreconcilably opposed to each other. The earliest portion of the Zoroastrian scriptures, or Avesta, "Pure Instruction" (Bailey 1985: 9–14), are the Gāthās, "Hymns" or "Songs," believed to have been composed by Zoroaster himself. The term Avesta (Phl. *abestāg*) is, however, of early medieval origin and refers to the received tradition, as distinct from the Zand (Phl. *zand*), or established exegesis, which gradually arose after the Avestan texts were compiled. It is possible that the terms *abestāg* and *zand* were calques on Greek *epistēmē* and *gnōsis* (Windfuhr 1984: 134). The prophet proclaims in one of the hymns of the Gāthās: "Now I will speak of the two spirits of whom, at the beginning of existence, the holier one thus spoke to the evil one: 'Neither our thoughts, nor our teachings, nor our wills, neither our choices, nor our words, neither our deeds, nor our consciences, nor our souls are in accord'" (Yasna 45: 2). This irreconcilable opposition stems from the choice between good and evil made by these two spirits at the beginning of time:

> Then, in the beginning, these two spirits, who are twins, revealed themselves in a vision. They are in thought, word, and deed, the better and the worse. Between these two [spirits] the wise choose rightly, not so the unwise. And when these two spirits came together, in the beginning they created life and nonlife, so that at the end will be the worst existence for the followers of the lie, but the best mind for the righteous ones. Of these two spirits, he who was of the lie chose the doing of the worst things, [while] the holiest spirit, who is clothed in the hardest stones, chose righteousness, as

do all who satisfy Ahura Mazdā through good deeds. Between these two spirits the demons did not choose rightly, for as they deliberated delusion came upon them so that they chose the worst mind. Then, they rushed together to wrath through whom they afflict the life of man. (Yasna 30: 3–6)

The first hymn expresses the relationship of one spirit to the other in terms of "the holier one" and "the evil one," while the second passage does so by the semantic antonym "the better and the worse." The use of comparative terminology in these passages expresses a dynamic asymmetry of dualism in which Ahura Mazdā was regarded, by Zoroaster, as fundamentally superior to Aŋra Mainyu (Windfuhr 1984: 150–151, 160–162). It is possible that by invoking this comparative asymmetry Zoroaster was objecting to a more simplistic view, presumably held by his contemporaries or adversaries, of mere opposites in the spiritual realm.[2] During the centuries after the prophet, however, a gradual transformation of the Zoroastrian world view occurred from the dynamic asymmetry of the Gāthās to the rigid cosmic dualism first visible in the Vidēvdāt, "Law against the Demons." Such a transformation in ethos would explain both the rise in importance of physical purity and the preoccupation with purification rites visible in the texts that were compiled into the Vidēvdāt.

According to Zoroastrian doctrine, Ahura Mazdā, the righteous creator, is by definition a perfect, good, rational, and omniscient being from whom no evil can proceed, however indirectly, because it is believed that a perfect being cannot originate imperfection. This belief, gradually elaborated in the following centuries, was clearly stated in the Škand Gumānīg Wizār, the "Doubt-Dispelling Explanation," a ninth-century C.E. Pahlavi or Middle Iranian text:

Thus, it is explicitly revealed that there are two first principles [and] no more; and also this, that good cannot arise from evil, nor evil from good. From this it is possible to understand that something which is completely perfect in goodness cannot produce evil. If it could [produce evil] then it is not perfect, because when a thing is described as perfect there is no place [in it] for anything else. And when there is no place for anything else, nothing else can emerge from it. If god is perfect in goodness and knowledge, ignorance and evil cannot be known from him. If it is possible, then he is not perfect. If he is not perfect, it is not possible to praise him as the god who is perfectly good. (8: 101–110)

As a result, Zoroastrians hold that good and evil, purity and pollution, life and death all proceed from two distinct loci and that Ahura Mazdā created the spiritual and material worlds completely pure. According to the ninth-century C.E. Dēnkard, "Acts of the Religion," "the creator [is] the origin of all goodness and no evil proceeds from him" (251 ll. 12–13). Hence, in Zoroastrian ethos, all the spiritual and material creations were made perfect and pure; sin, irreligiosity, pollution, dust, dirt, stench, excrement, disease, decay, and death are perceived as weapons brought into material existence (Phl. *gētīg astišnīh*) by Aṇra Mainyu when he invaded the world as part of his universal attack on Ahura Mazdā (Vidēvdāt 20: 3, 22: 2; Bundahišn 3: 12–14).[3] This dualism was summarized in the Čīdag Handarz ī Pōryōtkēšān, "Select Counsels of the Ancient Sages," another ninth-century Pahlavi text:

> One is the path of good thoughts, good words, and good deeds, of heaven, light, purity, and infinity, [which are] of the creator Ahura Mazdā who always was and will always be. The other is the path of evil thoughts, evil words, and evil deeds, of darkness, finiteness, all kinds of affliction, death, and evil which belong to the accursed Evil Spirit who once was not in this creation and again will not be in the creation of Ahura Mazdā, and who will be destroyed in the end. . . . There are two first principles, the creator and the destroyer. The creator is Ahura Mazdā who is all goodness and light. And the destroyer is the accursed Evil Spirit who is all evil, full of death, the lie, and the deceiver. (ll. 10–14)

Evil is not merely psychological, nor is it directly created at an individual level. It originates from the Evil Spirit, who is the antithesis of the Lord Wisdom. In Zoroastrian belief, paralleling the conclusions of Aristotle, evil does not exist apart from matter and by its very nature cannot survive as mere potentiality in the corporeal universe (9: 9.1–3). Because they afflict the pure creations of Ahura Mazdā, the afflictions produced by Aṇra Mainyu are believed to pollute the creations and, through this pollution, render the creations ritually impure. As a result, matter is said to be in a state of mixture (Phl. *gumēzišn*) of good and evil.

The Lord Wisdom created six beneficent immortals (Av. *aməša.spənta-;* Phl. *amahraspand*), a category of spiritual beings, to assist him in protecting the material creations. These spiritual beings are said to be

of one mind, voice, and action; whose thought, speech, and deed is
the same; whose father and ruler is one, namely, the creator Ahura
Mazdā. Who behold each other's soul, thinking of good thoughts,
good words, and good deeds, and of paradise. Whose paths are
radiant as they descend for the sacrifices. Who are the creators,
fashioners, makers, observers, and protectors of Ahura Mazdā's
creations. It is they who will restore the world . . . and the demoness will perish . . . in accordance with the will of the lord. (Yašt 19:
16–20; cf. Wizīdagīhā ī Zādspram 35: 1)

Ahura Mazdā, himself, has been regarded as the seventh beneficent immortal. In response, Aŋra Mainyu produced numerous demons (Av. *daēva-;*
Phl. *dēw*), including those that cause pain, suffering, pollution, and death,
to attack the spiritual and corporeal worlds.

Zoroastrianism holds that human beings were created by Ahura Mazdā
as allies in his cosmic struggle against Aŋra Mainyu and that humans con-
sented to enter into physical existence to further this battle. It is written in
the Bundahišn, "[Book of] Primal Creation," a Pahlavi text dating from
the ninth century C.E.:

Ahura Mazdā deliberated with the perceptions and immortal souls
of mankind, and having brought omniscient wisdom to all mankind, said: "Which seems more useful to you, that I should create
you into corporeal form, so that incarnate you will battle the lie
and vanquish it, and that I should resurrect you perfect and immortal at the end, and re-create you in corporeal form, and that you
become immortal, unaging, and without enemies forever; or is it
necessary always to protect you from the adversary." The immortal
souls of mankind saw, through omniscient wisdom, that the evil
from Aŋra Mainyu would arrive into the material world and [saw
also] the final nonopposition of the adversary. They agreed to enter
the material world to become perfect and immortal in the final
body up to eternity and eternal progress. (3: 23–24)

As a result of this covenant, the religious function of each person is to aid
the increase of righteousness and combat the forces of evil through every
action performed during his or her lifetime. The theological linking of the
spiritual and material aspects of the universe present in the Gāthās indi-

cates that righteousness and good actions by people in the material state aids individual and cosmic triumph of good over evil on the spiritual (Av. *mainyava-;* Phl. *mēnōg*) level. Therefore, maintenance of ritual purity through the protection and purification of the seven holy creations in the material world (Av. *gaēiϑya-;* Phl. *gētīg*) furthers the victory of good over evil (Boyce 1975: 294). This victory, in turn, will aid the separation (Phl. *wizārišn*) and expulsion of evil and the final renovation of the universe (Av. *frašō.kərəti-;* Phl. *frašagird*). Purity thus became a means of expressing cosmic order, while pollution was perceived as disorder (cf. Douglas 1969: 3). Because this basic doctrine involves every member of the Zoroastrian community in combating evil through the ordinary tasks in life, all actions are strictly regulated by rules and rites for maintaining ritual purity.

The Zoroastrian religious mind perceived, and still perceives, humanity as poised, individually and collectively, midway between all good and absolute evil, between the sacred and the profane, purity and pollution, light and darkness, life and death, immortality and nonexistence. A free-willed choice between the gods and the demons was made at the beginning of time by human spirits. As a result, everyone was expected to fulfill the covenant with the gods. The humans were required to tilt the balance toward the gods in order to ensure the success of both the gods and themselves. During the early modern period, however, Zoroastrian beliefs gradually changed from the original dualism based on polytheistic pantheons and pandemoniums to a quasi monotheism in which Ahura Mazdā is regarded as God and Aŋra Mainyu has become the Devil. European missionaries played a pivotal role in this transformation of Parsi and, later, Irani beliefs (cf. Boyce 1979: 202–204, 207, 220, 225–226). The deities of the original pantheon have been accorded a variety of statuses, usually equivalent to angels, and are regarded as the creations of Ahura Mazdā. The creatures of the original pandemonium have become minor evil spirits and ghouls produced by Aŋra Mainyu. Yet, most Zoroastrians continue to believe that human beings serve a vital function in the struggle between God and the Devil. They regard purity as an essential feature of righteous living and divine will and consider it essential for final salvation; human beings must be pure in soul and body in order to combat evil. Hence, the battle against cosmic evil was, and still is for devotees, the purpose of humanity's twelve-thousand-year odyssey through space and time.[4] William Shakespeare wrote, "All the world's a stage, and all the men and women merely players" (*As You Like It* 2: 7). Shakespeare's observation is apt for the Zoroastrian ethos, in which life is a drama, where humans are the chief actors and the world is the setting or stage for the cataclysmic struggle between good and evil, which will determine the entire universe's fate. In the Avestan texts from the religion's earliest days, doctrine offers no conclusions on whether the battle will be won or lost. But no religion could survive without extending to its adherents some hope of salvation or immortality. Hence, by the medieval period, the Pahlavi texts herald the forthcoming triumph of good over evil and the salvation of humanity.

The Elaboration of Purity Laws

The doctrines of purity became widespread as generations of Zoroastrian priests, or Magi (O.P. *magu-*; Gk. *mágos*; L. *magus*; Pth. *maybed*; Phl. *mowbed*; N.P. *mōbad*; P.Gj. *mōbed*), extended the codes that regulated ritual purity. The priestly terminology of the Avesta mentions only the terms *zaotar-* (Av.) "one who offers libations [to the deities], priest," and *āϑravan-* (Av.) (Skt. *atharvan-*) "one who tends the fire, priest." Yet, it was the Magi who have been recognized as the priests of the faith in recorded history. Little is known for certain about the rise of the Magi to the status of the Zoroastrian clergy.[5] Herodotus mentions that the Magi were the sixth tribe of the Medes (1: 101) and noted that no sacrifice or other rite could be performed without the presence of a Magus; members of this tribe were essential for all religious and ritual acts (1: 132). He also listed practices peculiar to the Magi, such as the exposure of corpses to birds of prey and dogs and the slaughter of insects and reptiles (1: 140). The Magi became the sole priestly group among the Medes, were soothsayers and priests at the Median royal court, and later served as clergymen to the Achaemenian monarchs. Although the exact events are unclear, it appears likely that the Magi associated themselves with the worship of Ahura Mazdā and other deities of the Zoroastrian pantheon after the faith gained adherents on the Iranian plateau and in the Achaemenid court. In time, the Magi claimed that the prophet Zoroaster had been a member of their tribe. Magian propaganda proved to be highly effective, for by the fourth century B.C.E. even Plato referred to Zoroaster as "the Magus" (1: 121). Later, Iranian myth even placed the prophet's homeland in the northwestern province of Azerbaijan, where the Magi claimed to have dwelt in antiquity.

The ascendence of the Magi to the rank of sole priests of Zoroastrianism closely corresponds with the elaboration and dissemination of the faith's ritual codes, particularly the laws and rites of purity attested in the Vidēvdāt. It is possible that the Magi elaborated and exploited ritual law to entrench themselves as indispensable to the laity. Their influence in Iranian society extended over the years. By the middle of the Sasanian period, the Magi had firmly established themselves as the priests of the state church and had possessed an elaborate hierarchy headed by the Priest of Priests (Phl. *mowbedān mowbed*). They preserved, performed, and transmitted the laws and rites of purity with constant elaboration and rigid enforcement until the Arabs conquered the Sasanian empire between 633 and 651 C.E. The conquest installed Islam as the religion of the new state. Loss of royal patronage resulted in the gradual decline of the Magi and the entire Zoroastrian community during the late medieval and early modern eras of the faith's history (cf. Choksy 1987*b*: 17–18). Just as the rise of the Magi facilitated the expansion, propagation, codification, and practice of Zoroastrian purity laws and rituals, the decline of this priestly sect has contributed to the gradual erosion of purification rites.

As a result of the nexus between the Magi and Zoroastrian rituals, although the more ancient portions of the Avesta, namely, the pre-Achaemenid Yasna and Yašts, reveal few traces of purity laws and rites, subsequent books in Avestan and Pahlavi display an ever-increasing concern with problems of purity and pollution. Enforcement of these codes gained overriding importance during the reign of the Sasanian dynasty and in the early years of Muslim rule. Indeed, many Pahlavi texts from the late Sasanian and early Islamic periods deal with the maintenance of ritual purity. The laws of purity also created a barrier that often segregated Zoroastrians from all non-Zoroastrians (Boyce 1975: 294).

This separation of believers from nonbelievers persisted after the Arab conquest of Iran in the seventh century C.E. (Choksy 1987*b*: 24–25). According to the Persian Rivāyats, which dates from the fifteenth to eighteenth centuries C.E., it was believed that "a non-Zoroastrian is not naturally fit for observing the precautions about carrion" (85, l. 3). Nonbelievers came to be regarded as naturally unclean, and numerous rules existed for the regulation of interaction between Zoroastrians and nonbelievers. Sexual intercourse with non-Zoroastrians was prohibited, as was the common use of bathhouses and the consumption of food prepared by them.[6] Nonbelievers could even be bound and chained, if necessary, to prevent them from polluting the sacred elements. Every action came to be regarded as either opposing the Evil Spirit or aiding him, for it was dictated that all acts and deeds were either meritorious works or sins, with there being no neutral functions (Pahlavi Rivāyat of Ādurfarnbay and Farnbaysrōš 29: 2). According to religious law, therefore, a Zoroastrian cannot remain neutral in the conflict between Ahura Mazdā and Aŋra Mainyu. It is believed that individuals who stay neutral, or whose good and wicked deeds are equal, will be subject to the heat and cold of the Place of the Motionless Ones, or limbo (Phl. *hamēstagān*), without savoring the rewards of heaven (Av. *garō.dəmāna-;* Phl. *garōdmān, wahišt*) or suffering the trials of hell (Av. *drujō.dəmāna-;* Phl. *dušox*) after death (Ardā Wīrāz Nāmag 6: 1–12). According to the religion, a continuous battle must be waged by all Zoroastrians against the Evil Spirit and his demons, because the forces of evil never relinquish their struggle to overpower human beings (Dēnkard 532, ll. 3–5).

The main Avestan source on purity and pollution is the Vidēvdāt, or Vendīdād, the "Law against the Demons" or "Code for Abjuring the Demons," with its Pahlavi commentary (Phl. Zand).[7] The Vidēvdāt is a collection of prose texts in twenty-two chapters and deals mainly with the laws of purity. Some of the contents of the Vidēvdāt had their origins in pre-Zoroastrian and early Zoroastrian times, but much of the ritual stipulations can be attributed to the Magi. Furthermore, the extant redaction of the Vidēvdāt is believed to have been codified only at the beginning of the Parthian period (247 B.C.E.–224 C.E.). Additional material on purity and pollution is present in the Pahlavi books composed during the Sasanian era (224–651 C.E.). These include the Šāyest nē Šāyest (the "Proper and the Improper") and its supplementary texts, both of which are collections of ritual prescriptions based on older episcopal decisions; the Ardā Wīrāz Nāmag, the "Book of the Righteous Wīrāz," which contains an account of a pious Zoroastrian's journey through heaven, limbo, and hell, much like those by the prophet Muḥammad and Dante; and the Pahlavi Rivāyat Accompanying the Dādestān ī Dēnīg. Ritual purity is also discussed in the Pahlavi Dēnkard, "Acts of the Religion," an encyclopedic work composed during the ninth century C.E., and the Pahlavi Rivāyat ī Ēmēd ī Ašawahištān, the "Religious Explanations of Ēmēd, Son of Ašawahišt," which dates from the late ninth or early tenth century C.E. Similarly, the Mēnōg ī Xrad, "[Book of] the Spirit of Wisdom," a catechism in the form of an imaginary dialogue between the Spirit of Wisdom and a sage, and the Pahlavi Rivāyat of Ādurfarnbay and Farnbaysrōš, which contains replies given by two priests to questions posed by the laity during 800 C.E. and 1008 C.E., respectively, preserve important aspects of medieval beliefs on ritual purity. Also important is Dārāb Hormazyār's Rivāyats, known as the Persian Rivāyats, a collection of treatises on matters of religious observance sent by the Zoroastrians in Iran to their coreligionists, the Parsis, in India from 1478 to 1773 C.E.

Purity rituals and doctrines leave few archaeological traces. As a result, the scholar of religious and cultural history is compelled to rely on written records from the past. The detailed references to practices preserved in the writings of Irani and Parsi priests are an invaluable source from which the historical evolution of Zoroastrian beliefs and practices of ritual purity can be elucidated and reconstructed. The data derived from the religious literature must, of course, be correlated, verified, and integrated with modern-day Parsi and Irani beliefs and practices.

In the tenth century c.e. many Zoroastrians, seeking to escape Muslim persecution, migrated from Iran to India and settled in the state of Gujarat by 936 c.e. These immigrants, who came to be termed Parsis, or Persians, formed the community of Indian Zoroastrians. Both the Irani and Parsi Zoroastrian communities dwelt mainly within their own social groups until the late eighteenth century c.e. and preserved several aspects of the purity laws and rites. Exposure to Western ideas, modernization, and secularization in the nineteenth and twentieth centuries has attenuated the practice of many beliefs, rules, and rituals (cf. Choksy 1988). However, numerous regulations on purity and purification are still observed by orthodox Zoroastrian clergy and laity in both Iran and India.

Protection of the Material Creations

The seven material creations of Ahura Mazdā, namely, metal, earth, water, fire, plants, animals, and humans, are regarded as sacred and must be protected from pollution by the impure afflictions of the demons. Each creation is believed to be under the protection of a beneficent immortal. The Lord Wisdom protects human beings; the Good Mind (Av. Vohu Manah; Phl. Wahman) tends the animals; Best Righteousness (Av. Aša Vahišta; Phl. Ardwahišt) safeguards fire; Desirable Dominion (Av. Xšaθra Vairya; Phl. Šahrewar) guards metal; Holy Devotion (Av. Spənta Ārmaiti; Phl. Spendarmad) cares for the earth; Wholeness, or Perfection, (Av. Haurvatāt; Phl. Hordād) tends water; and Immortality (Av. Amərətāt; Phl. Amurdād) nurtures the plants (Bundahišn 3: 7–19). Metal, earth, water, fire, plants, and animals also are homologies of the six states of matter: inorganic hard, inorganic soft, liquid, gaseous, organic hard, and organic soft, respectively (Windfuhr 1976: 299).[8] Each aspect of the world is linked through homologies and alloforms, based on symbols and beliefs, not only to the gods but also to the entire religious cosmos. Protection of the material creations from impurity is, therefore, believed to safeguard the gods and the whole universe. Religious belief thus combines with ritual practice to unify the individual believer with all pure portions of the world that surround him or her.

Metal has to be kept free from rust, tarnish, misuse, and carrion; precious metals should not be given to corrupt individuals (Dēnkard 452, ll. 6–10). Both the Vidēvdāt (7: 73–75) and the Persian Rivāyats (239–241) contain elaborate descriptions of rites for the purification of metals. Metals include stone, crystal, and gems, as these are also considered manifestations of Xšaθra Vairya. According to Zoroastrian theology, there is a hierarchy of metals with regard to their purity and resistance to impurities: gold is the purest and most resistant to pollution, followed by silver, copper, tin, brass, lead, steel, stone, turquoise, ruby, amber and similar substances, earth, wood, and, finally, clay. Zoroastrians believe that a material's susceptibility to pollution increases with its porosity. Here the external boundary posed by the substance determines its vulnerability to defilement.[9] Use of a substance links it to the user and exposes him or her to any pollutants present on or in it (cf. Douglas 1969: 126). Consequently, only ritually clean metals may be utilized in daily life.

The earth, cared for by Spənta Ārmaiti, has to be protected from pollution, and the Vidēvdāt (7: 10–25) prescribes severe punishment by whipping for persons who knowingly defile this creation. According to religious law, the earth must be guarded against noxious creatures, unrighteous people, and demons, and it should be made productive through irrigation and cultivation (Dēnkard 452, ll. 10–16). Earth that has been rendered impure through pollution by carrion has to be left barren and untraversed for one year in order to prevent spread of the impurity (Vidēvdāt 7: 1–9). The Persian Rivāyats mentions numerous acts that must be performed to ensure that land is free of impurities prior to cultivation.[10] Additionally, whenever carrion is spotted on any land, the carrion must be disposed of according to religious law so as to prevent spread of its impurity (Persian Rivāyats 85, ll. 18–19). Practice, however, gradually deviated from ecclesiastic stipulations, and, by the modern period, only land owned by Zoroastrians was cleaned and purified.

Water, protected by the beneficent immortal Haurvatāt, is one of the two most vulnerable and venerated elements in Zoroastrianism and also serves as an object of worship. Water is used by most people and in many religions as the primary purificatory and cleansing agent. Unlike other religions, Zoroastrianism does not regard water as a primary purifying agent. Water is regarded as a secondary purifying agent. It may be used to clean the body only after ablutions have been performed with unconsecrated bull's urine and all impurities have been expunged from the body surface. The use of water to wash away dirt and impurities, or to purify a polluted body, is regarded as a heinous sin, for through such action water is exposed to demonic impurities (Dēnkard 452, ll. 17–21). The Vidēvdāt states that anyone who pollutes water with carrion becomes ritually impure forever (7: 27).[11] Indeed, both carrion and excrement have an equally heinous effect on water (Persian Rivāyats 82, ll. 6–12). The Rivāyats also devotes considerable attention to the purification of defiled waters (86, l. 3–89, l. 5). The Gizistag Abāliš, the "Accursed Abāliš," a ninth-century C.E. Pahlavi text that contains questions and answers on Zoroastrian religious matters from a theological debate supposedly conducted at the court of the ʿAbbāsid Caliph al-Maʾmūn (ruled 813–833 C.E.), mentions that the polluting of water with carrion is equivalent to leading a bull to slaughter by a pack of lions or wolves (2: 2). According to the Zoroastrian laws governing ritual purity, no carrion, excrement, or ritually impure materials should be allowed to come into contact with water.

Water can be used for purification and cleansing only after that which is to be cleaned, be it human, animal, plant, or object, has first been purified with unconsecrated bull's urine. After purification with the urine, dust or earth is often used for a similar purpose, and only thereafter can water be applied.[12] The Ardā Wīrāz Nāmag graphically describes a man's being dragged into deepest hell for polluting water by bathing directly in it without first cleansing himself with unconsecrated bull's urine (58: 4). The fact that elaborate precautions are taken to prevent water from being polluted must always be considered when comparing Zoroastrian purification rituals with those of other faiths, such as Judaism, Christianity, Islam, and Hinduism. Many similarities in intent and usage do exist between Zoroastrian purity rituals and those of the above-mentioned religions. None of those four faiths, however, regards water as vulnerable to pollution when used for purificatory processes; therefore, they base their purity rituals on the cleansing power of water. Zoroastrianism would not consider the use of only water for ablution an act of purification but rather one of deliberate and grave pollution of this sacred element. The Zoroastrian reverence for the purity of the waters was noted by Herodotus in the fifth century B.C.E. when he wrote, "Rivers they chiefly revere; they will neither urinate or spit or wash their hand therein, nor allow anyone else to do so" (1: 138). This reverence is understandable, for water was the source from which much of creation is said to have originated.[13] In addition, water must be protected from pollution because impure water cannot be used for drinking, purifying, or cultivating (Dēnkard 452, ll. 17–21). However, the requirement that unconsecrated bull's urine be applied to the body prior to each contact with water was impractical in daily life. Therefore, ritually clean Zoroastrians were permitted to bathe and wash their clothes, dishes, and other possessions directly in water. This adaptation of religious law to the necessities of life probably occurred at an early date and persists to the present day.

Fire, like water, is considered extremely vulnerable to pollution, is highly venerated, and is used as an object of worship. According to Zoroastrian cosmogony, fire was used by Ahura Mazdā in the creation of human beings and cattle (Bundahišn 1a: 3). Eschatological belief holds that the final renovation of the universe will occur through the medium of this sacred element (Wizīdagīhā ī Zādspram 34: 50). Indeed, fire and water are closely linked, and the Dēnkard states that "all material genesis, maturation, and differentiation occurs from the uniting in due measure of water the female [element], and fire the male [element]" (79, l. 21). Because fire is susceptible to pollution, religious practice dictates that it should always be kept thirty paces away from carrion, fifteen paces from the polluting gaze of menstruating women, and three paces from excrement. Fire should never be polluted by the placing or dropping of materials, other than those that are ritually pure, into it. Hence, only clean, dry, fragrant woods and frankincense are offered to a fire by contemporary Irani and Parsi Zoroastrians. Such Pahlavi texts as the Nīrangistān, however, state that a portion of the fat from a sacrificial animal ought to be offered to the fire (2: 19.8). This offering is also mentioned in the Persian Rivāyats, but it is no longer practiced (264, ll. 6–8).[14]

Pollution of a fire with carrion or excrement was, and still is, considered a grievous sin; the Vidēvdāt dictated that the death penalty be imposed on anyone who deliberately burned carrion over a fire (8: 73–74). The flesh of a ritually sacrificed animal was, however, not regarded as carrion; it could be offered to the sacred fires and consumed by the devotees. Herodotus noticed this reverence for fire and wrote, "Persians hold fire to be a god, and never burn their dead" (3: 16). Similarly, it is a sin to pollute the hearth fire with food while cooking. Both the Avesta (Yasna 9: 11–12) and the Persian Rivāyats (61, l. 18–65, l. 6) mention that a legendary hero named Kərəsāspa was excluded from heaven after his cooking pot accidentally overturned and polluted a fire with its contents. Because of pollution that results from defilement of fire, the Persian Rivāyats instructs Zoroastrians to leave all cooking pots one-third empty to prevent the contents from boiling over and polluting the flames (66, l. 1–67, l. 5). The Pursišnīhā, "Questions," which date from the fifteenth century C.E., also instruct the faithful to ensure that cooking pots do not boil over (20). Similarly, rubbish should not be burned in a fire and must be disposed of in some other manner. Zoroastrians in modern Iran still build a small sealed structure called a *lard* (N.P.), which has a flat roof with a small opening in it through which rubbish is thrown in and then acid poured to destroy the waste (Boyce 1975: 297). Parsis no longer obey this edict, however, and often burn rubbish. Pollution of fire by breath and saliva during religious ceremonies has always been prevented by the mouth and nose mask (Av. *paitidāna-;* Phl. *padām;* N.P. *panām;* P.Gj. *padān*) donned by priests prior to commencing such ceremonies. Additionally, it is believed that a sacred fire should never be extinguished.[15] The sanctity and veneration of fire was depicted in the religious iconography of the Sasanians. Reverses of the silver coinage, or drachmas (Phl. *drahm*), usually bore the image of a fire altar and flames, often tended by two Magi.[16]

Animals and plants can be polluted by evil and rendered ritually impure. For good creatures, many instances of pollution can be avoided through diligent attention to the codes of purity. Some cases of pollution, however, especially those caused by death, which is the most serious affliction cast upon the world by the Evil Spirit, are inevitable, and, therefore, elaborate countermeasures were developed to isolate the source of pollution and restore purity. All living creatures originally belonged to one of two classes in Zoroastrian doctrine: they were either ahuric (beneficent) or daēvic (evil) beings. The basis of this division is seemingly what is useful or agreeable to human beings (Boyce 1975: 298). Ahuric creatures include the dog, hedgehog, cow, goat, sheep, horse, cock, owl, and most plants.[17] Each beneficent plant or animal must be assisted to grow to maturity, and a sin is believed to result if such a creature is slaughtered while in its formative stages (Persian Rivāyats 76, ll. 6–7). Daēvic creatures, however, are regarded as naturally impure and polluting, and to slay them in abundance is considered a positive virtue. Such organisms are referred to as noxious creatures (Av. *xrafstra-;* Phl. *xrafstar*), a term that originally meant "biting or stinging creature" (Bailey 1970: 25–28). This category of creatures includes such insects as the ant, bee, silkworm, and locust, such reptiles as the snake and frog, such rodents as the mouse, such animals as the cat and elephant, and such predatory beasts as the wolf and tiger.[18] This class encompasses creatures that are harmful to people or crops. These animals are thought to pollute the elements with carrion and excrement. For this reason, the slaughter of such creatures is ordered by religious law and is a meritorious act on a par with caring for the good creations (Šāyest nē Šāyest 20: 5; Pahlavi Texts 70, l. 14). The practice of slaying noxious creatures was recorded by Herodotus during the reign of the Achaemenian kings and by Agathias under the Sasanians (Herodotus 1: 140; Agathias 2: 24). In Judaism, too, there is an abomination of reptiles and creeping animals, and Moses is said to have prohibited mice and unclean animals. The

Judaic prohibition was never as detailed or vigorous as that in Zoroastrianism, and contact with such creatures merely made the believer ritually unclean until the evening (Leviticus 11: 4–31). All contact with these unclean creatures is prohibited by Zoroastrian law.[19]

The categories of beneficent and noxious creatures are excellent examples of the manner in which cosmic dualism influenced the categorization of the material world. Those creatures that provided benefit and sustenance to human beings were perceived as aiding the cause of good. By extension, these creatures became good and sacred. Creatures that harmed men, women, children, crops, and livestock were regarded as harming the sacred creations and aiding the cause of evil. Such creatures came to be considered evil, noxious, and profane. However, many Zoroastrians found the products of bees (honey) and silkworms (silk) agreeable and kept cats as pets. Further, elephants were used in the army of the Achaemenian king Darius III at the battle of Arbela and by the Sasanian monarch Xusro II. Thus, in addition to ahuric and daēvic creatures, there evolved a third category of beings, noxious creatures that "Ahura Mazdā alters through omniscience for the advantage of the creatures" (Bundahišn 22: 29). This category included nonindigenous animals, such as the elephant and lion, which were introduced into Iran as the native peoples encountered other civilizations.[20] Hence, religious law was liberalized and this permissiveness granted doctrinal sanction.[21] In time, both the elephant and the lion became symbols of sovereignty.

Human beings, as the foremost of the seven creations, are required to keep themselves spiritually and ritually pure to aid Ahura Mazdā and the other gods in the struggle against evil. The function of each individual is to smite Aŋra Mainyu and his pandemonium and make all evil powerless. In order to combat evil successfully, Zoroastrians have to maintain a constant state of ritual purity. The purity laws and purification rituals were elaborated to ensure the maintenance of purity and to aid the cause of righteousness. Additionally, because they possess powers of reason and action, human beings have been required to be vigilant in their care for the other six creations from the earliest years of the faith. The faithful are instructed "do not sin against water, fire, cattle, [other] beneficent animals, the dog, and [other members of] the canine species, so that the path to heaven and paradise may not be barred [to you]" (Pahlavi Texts 151, ll. 7–9). They must also guard against less potent attacks of evil, such as stench and disease (Dēnkard 482, ll. 9–14).

The rules for protection of the material creations were enforced by the Zoroastrian clergy during the Sasanian period and the early centuries of

Muslim rule in Iran. After the late sixteenth century, however, many of these ordinances gradually fell into disuse. Modern-day Parsi and Irani Zoroastrians adhere only to the general tenets for protecting the material creations from pollution, particularly because Zoroastrians now dwell in multireligious societies in which enforcement of purity laws is usually not possible. In accordance with the general tenets for protection of the material creations, metallic objects are kept rust free if possible, lands and homes are cleaned and any dead matter found on the premises is removed, water is kept free of substances that would pollute it or render it unfit for consumption, and a small quantity of water that has been polluted is usually discarded. Care is taken to ensure that the sacred temple fires and domestic flames are not polluted by human or animal flesh, but food substances do occasionally fall into kitchen fires. Domesticated plants and animals are also cared for and protected.

The Main Causes of Ritual Impurity

As described above, there are numerous material causes for pollution and impurity within the Zoroastrian cosmos. The greatest source of ritual pollution and impurity, however, is believed to arise from the most powerful attack by evil on the good creations: death. Of course, Zoroastrians are not the only religious group who regard death and decay as sources of pollution. Hindus and Buddhists, who share a common but ancient Indo-Iranian heritage with Zoroastrians, also possess similar beliefs (cf. Obeyesekere 1984: III). In Zoroastrian belief there are two types of dead matter: carrion and excrement. When an animal or human being dies, the corpse, or any portion of it, is said to be immediately polluted by the Corpse Demoness (Av. Druxš Nasuš; Phl. Druz ī Nasuš), or demoness of death and decay, who has always been regarded as the main cause of pollution in the material world.[22] Carrion is termed *nasā* (Av. *nasu-, nasav-;* Phl., N.P., and P.Gj. *nasā*), and the Corpse Demoness is the personification of this evil. She is believed to be "of all the demons . . . the most impudent, constantly polluting, and deceptive" (Farziyāt-nāma 10). This symbolic and semantic process of naming natural phenomena as spiritual entities is widespread not only in Zoroastrianism but also in most other religions that either date from ancient times or are primitive. *Nasā* is always in the highest state of ritual impurity unless it has been ritually purified and the demoness driven away. Therefore, it is an abominable sin to bring carrion into contact with any of Ahura Mazdā's creations, especially water or fire (Vidēvdāt 7: 25, 27). The defiling power acquired by the Corpse Demoness upon entering a corpse is directly proportional to the spiritual good standing of the deceased. The corpse of a righteous man is extremely susceptible to impurity, whereas that of an evil man is only slightly susceptible (Vidēvdāt 5: 27–28; Gizistag Abāliš 6: 3). This is because a righteous person who purifies himself or herself through good words, good thoughts, and good deeds is both a pure being and a powerful opponent of evil whose prayers can purify all righteous creations (Vidēvdāt 11: 12). The triumph of the demons, through death, over the body of such a person requires all the forces of evil, and this results in the corpse becoming filled with impurity and producing widespread pollution (Vidēvdāt 5: 28). The demons have little trouble slaying a sinful person whose life and body is constantly filled with evil and impurity. Consequently, very little impurity is present in the corpse of an evil person, which is said to be no more polluting than the "one year old, dried up carcass of a frog" (Vidēvdāt 5: 30). The corpse of a non-Zoroastrian is also less noxious but causes loss of ritual purity if touched (Persian Rivāyats 136, ll. 1–4).

Because the carrion of a human being is extremely impure and polluting, a corpse cannot be buried, burned, or cast into water, as this would pollute the creations of Spənta Ārmaiti, Aša Vahišta, and Haurvatāt, respectively (Vidēvdāt 6: 10–11, 7: 25–27, 49–51).[23] As a result, corpses were exposed to the elements on either a dry desolate peak or ground and, later, within a funerary tower (Av. *daxma-;* Phl. *daxmag;* N.P. *dakhma;* P.Gj. *dokhma*). Although the medieval Zoroastrian community rejected both burial and cremation as polluting the sacred earth and the sacred fire, it appears that burial was a regular part of early Iranian funerary practices. The etymology of the term *daxma-* (Av.), which means "place for exposure of corpses, funerary tower" in attested usage, originally was understood as "grave, tomb" (Hoffman 1965: 238). The origin of the practice of exposing corpses to dogs and birds is unclear, but it is known to have been performed by the pre-Zoroastrian Magi and Persians. Herodotus observed this custom and commented that "the corpses of Persians are not buried before they have been mangled by bird or dog" (1: 140).[24] However, as the rock-hewn tombs at Naqsh-i Rostam and Persepolis demonstrate, the bodies of Achaemenian rulers—unlike those of the Parthian and Sasanian kings—were entombed (cf. Frye 1984*b:* 175–176). These stone tombs would have served as barriers against the spread of impurity from the corpses.

In the attested practice of the late ancient, medieval, and modern periods, religious law required that the corpse be exposed to the gaze of a dog or bird of prey and then be exposed, not buried or cremated, inside funerary towers. The gaze of such a creature was believed to drive away the

Corpse Demoness (Vidēvdāt 7: 3). This ceremony was referred to by the term *sagdīd* (Phl.), "seen by a dog." According to Zoroastrian belief, dogs slay several thousand evil creatures each night (Vidēvdāt 13: 2). This spiritual power to smite demons through pure sight was believed to purify the corpse and protect it from evil. Additionally, several holy utterances (Av. *maϑra-;* Phl. *mānsr*), such as the Srōš Bāj, which includes the Kəm Nā Mazdā prayer, regarded as excellent for the smiting of this demoness, were, and still are, chanted during the funeral ceremony. After *sagdīd* and desiccation, dead matter ceased to be *nasā* and was no longer impure or capable of pollution. Once the body had been exposed, the bones often were collected and placed in an ossuary. The Persian Rivāyats reflects medieval beliefs by reiterating the prescribed funerary practice and condemning variation (79, l. 31; 82, ll. 6–17). During the medieval period, Zoroastrians regarded persons of other faiths who polluted earth, water, or fire through funerary practices as individuals "who are not of good religion and will go to hell" (Pāzand Jāmāspī 7: 2). The numerous funerary towers that dot the Iranian landscape attest to the widespread observance of this practice during the medieval and early modern periods. The nineteenth and twentieth centuries have seen considerable variation in Zoroastrian funerary practices. Exposure of corpses is gradually being phased out in Iran. The funerary tower in Tehran has not been used since 1933, the one in Ray since 1936, and the five towers at Yazd are being eliminated (cf. Fischer 1973: 157–158). Most Irani Zoroastrians now bury their deceased. Parsi Zoroastrians in India and Pakistan do continue the tradition of exposing bodies to vultures in funerary towers, particularly at Bombay and Karachi. However, in Sri Lanka, Australia, England, the United States, and Canada, and even in India and Pakistan, many Zoroastrians follow their Iranian coreligionists' practice of burial. In most cases the body is dressed in white clothes, the funeral rites are performed, a dog is brought into the presence of the corpse and made to gaze upon it, and, finally, it is buried without a coffin. Certain Zoroastrian communities, particularly those in North America, even perform cremations. Burials and cremations are still regarded as causing pollution to earth and fire; yet Zoroastrians often have no option but to conduct such funerary rites, especially in societies that would not tolerate the exposure of corpses.

In addition to carrion, all that issues from the human body as refuse, including skin, saliva, breath, cut nails and hair, blood, semen, the products of menstruation, urine, and feces, are considered dead once expelled or separated from the body. As among the Hindus, the belief in a physical and spiritual boundary between the purity of each human body and pollutants present in the external world is sharply defined. Materials that traverse the boundary of the body lose their protection and are vulnerable to pollution (cf. Douglas 1969: 121). Once they are seized by the Corpse Demoness, these items become ritually impure and capable of pollution. Such matter is termed bodily refuse or excrement (Av. *hixra-;* Phl. *hixr;* N.P. and P.Gj. *hikhra*). Although the Pahlavi Rivāyat Accompanying the Dādestān ī Dēnīg distinguishes between *nasā* and *hixr,* stating that *hixr* is excrement that is not moist, it is clear that in the Pahlavi books *nasā* refers specifically to carrion and *hixr* to both dry and liquid bodily substances after these are detached from the body (55: 3). Originally, however, the distinction between *nasu-* and *hixra-* was less well defined, and the term *hixra-* was used with reference to all polluting matter that issues from corpses (Vidēvdāt 5: 14–16). Ritual impurity caused by excrement is usually less grave than that caused by carrion; an exception to this rule is the effect of excrement on water and fire, where it equals carrion in its polluting power (Persian Rivāyats 82, ll. 6–17).

The presence of *nasā* and *hixr* in the material world constantly exposes Zoroastrians to pollution and the resultant loss of ritual purity. A Zoroastrian who deliberately or accidentally comes into contact with carrion, or in some instances even excrement, loses his or her ritual purity, becomes polluted (Phl. *rēman;* N.P. and P.Gj. *rīman*), and is called a polluted person (Phl. *rēmanīg;* N.P. and P.Gj. *rīmanī*).[25] According to religious law, such persons must be excluded from the religious community until they have regained ritual purity. This segregation, or rite of separation, conforms to the pattern elucidated by van Gennep (1960). It is the preliminal stage of a cycle that eventually reestablishes the devotee's ritual purity and reincorporates him or her into society. Indeed, van Gennep's hypothesis need not be restricted to such rites of passage as initiation, marriage, and childbirth. All Zoroastrian rituals of purification involve rites of passage. The polluted individual proceeds through a temporal, spatial, physical, and spiritual cycle of passage that utilizes ritual purification to expunge impurity and danger from both the devotee and the community.

The Regaining of Ritual Purity

Ritual purity is regained through one of several purification rituals, which are administered to the polluted individual by one or two purifiers (Av. *yaoždāϑrya-;* Phl. *yōjdāhrgar;* N.P. *yozhdāsragar;* P.Gj. *yaozdāthrya*).

One or both of the purifiers must be priests. The purification ritual that is undergone depends on the degree of impurity to which the polluted person was exposed.

Most of the major purification rituals appear to have developed from an ancient process (Boyce 1975: 311–312). This threefold process involved (*a*) the recital of holy utterances in Avestan by both the purifier and the candidate for purification in order to ensure ritual purification through the purificatory power of holy utterances; (*b*) an internal purification of soul and body through the drinking of consecrated bull's urine (Phl. *nērang;* N.P. *nīrang;* P.Gj. *nīrang, nīrangdīn*) to which a pinch of fire ash (Phl. *ādurestar;* P.Gj. *bhasam*) was added; and, finally, (*c*) cleansing of the entire body surface with unconsecrated bull's urine (Av. *gaomaēza-;* Phl. *gōmēz, pādyāb;* D. *pājōw;* P.Gj. *gōmēz*).[26] *Nērang* appears always to have been prepared from the urine of a bull; but *gōmēz* was obtained from a wide range of domesticated livestock (Av. *gav.spənta-;* Phl. *gōspand*), particularly bovines, which were regarded as beneficent animals. By medieval times, the final cleansing with unconsecrated urine was often followed by cleansing with dust (Phl. *xāk;* N.P. and P.Gj. *khāk*) and then water (Av. *āp-;* Phl. and N.P. *āb;* P.Gj. *āw*), a practice continued to the present day. The unconsecrated urine, dust, and water were sprinkled over the candidate's body without contact (Phl. *paywand*) between the purifier, who was in a state of high ritual purity, and the polluted person. It was believed that if contact occurred it would transfer the impurity to the officiating priest. Because this purification was administered from the head or top (Av. *barəšnu-,* "head, top") of the impure individual, the ritual came to be known as the Barašnūm. This purification ritual was carried out in the open during the daylight hours so that the purificatory effect attributed to the sun's rays could aid in the expulsion of the Corpse Demoness.[27] The notion that sunlight purified individuals and objects appears to have been common to the ancient Indo-Iranian tribes, for, in addition to Zoroastrians, Hindus also hold this belief (Gonda 1980: 283).

Three major ceremonies evolved from the basic threefold purificatory ritual: the Barašnūm ī nō šab, which was used to purify Zoroastrians who had been polluted through actual contact with carrion; the Rīman ritual, which was developed by the Parsis for purification from carrion after the Barašnūm ī nō šab had acquired a purely religioritual purificatory function and came to be administered only to priests; and the Nāhn ritual, which was developed for socioritual purificatory purposes. In addition, the Pādyāb ritual, performed daily by all Zoroastrians, initially involved cleansing first with unconsecrated urine and then with water, although now unconsecrated urine is rarely used in this rite. Many variations of the original threefold purification ritual were also developed for simple purification after contact with excrement. The development of purification rituals having specific functions probably occurred due to the evolution in Zoroastrianism of two fairly distinct forms of ritual purity by the late medieval period: religioritual purity, or the state of high ritual purity required solely for the performance of the most sacred liturgical ceremonies, and socioritual purity, or state of ritual purity necessary to perform even the most routine of religious functions. Religioritual purity is required only of priests, but socioritual purity must be maintained at all times by most members of the community. Religioritual purity is usually acquired before entering the priesthood and prior to the performance of such religious rites as tending the sacred fires or consecrating bull's urine in the Nīrang-dīn ceremony. Socioritual purity ensures that every member within the religious community is ritually pure and distinct from all nonmembers. Further, by its reinforcement during such rites of passage as initiation into the faith and community, marriage, and the period after menstruation and childbirth, a basic level of purity is maintained at all times within the community.

The theological linking of the spiritual and material aspects of the universe in the Gāthās forms the basis of every action. All thoughts, words, and deeds can serve to further the cosmic triumph of Ahura Mazdā over Aŋra Mainyu, righteousness over evil. It is believed that only by adhering to the creed of "good thoughts, good words, and good deeds" (Av. *humata-, hūxta-, hvaršta-;* Phl. *humat, hūxt, huwaršt*) can Zoroastrians act in accordance with the will of Ahura Mazdā and the laws of his religion. Additionally, the cosmic and ethical dualism present in the faith provides the basis for the importance of ritual purity in both doctrine and practice. Purity came to be regarded as being embodied by the religion itself, and the purifier who performs the rituals properly is said to delight fire, water, earth, plants, animals, and righteous persons (Vidēvdāt 9: 42). Indeed, it is believed that the soul of such a purifier is rewarded with the bountifulness of paradise (Vidēvdāt 9: 45).

According to Zoroastrian doctrine, every religious ritual serves more than a limited corporeal function; it aids in the final renovation of the entire universe. Therefore, the purification rituals not only cleanse a believer's physical body but also are said to purify the soul, thereby assisting in the vanquishing of evil. As a result, the Pahlavi commentary to the Vidēvdāt emphasizes: "Purity of man [and] purity for the soul is best from birth" (5: 21).[28] Purification is undergone to attain a symbolic religious state of virtue and purity and not merely to achieve physical purity, although this may be an actual result of the rites. Hence, the items used for purification and the rituals themselves have a symbolic role. This role integrates the rituals with the fundamental cosmological and eschatological function of both religion and humanity: the final victory of righteousness over evil.

2 THE BARAŠNŪM Ī NŌ ŠAB RITUAL

It is easier to wash and purify the defilement and pollution that reaches the body than that which reaches the soul.

—ĀDURBĀD Ī ĒMĒDĀN

ĀDURBĀD Ī ĒMĒDĀN, a ninth-century C.E. Zoroastrian high priest, accurately stated the problem confronted by all Zoroastrians: pollution of the body is easier to expunge than that of the soul (Dēnkard 581, ll. 4–6). Yet, unless the soul is purified, physical ablutions are of limited value to human beings and the gods. In order to ensure ritual purity of both the body and the soul, Zoroastrian priests developed the Barašnūm ī nō šab (Phl.), "Purification of the Nine [Days and] Nights." The Barašnūm ī nō šab originated from the basic threefold purificatory process of the early Zoroastrian community. Firmly established as the major purification ritual of the faith prior to the Achaemenian period, it is still performed by Parsi and Irani Zoroastrians. Irani Zoroastrians commonly refer to it as the "Nine Night [Washing]" (D. *Noh Shva*), while Parsis often term it the "Purification of the Nine [Days and] Nights Bath" (P.Gj. Bareshnūm-ī noh shab nāhn) or, simply, the "Bath" (P.Gj. Nāhn).[1] All available evidence indicates that this ritual has remained the most elaborate of Zoroastrian purification rites for much of the faith's history. Due to the presence of extensive pollution, the initial cleansing, or Barašnūm proper, has always been administered in an isolated or sequestered area termed the "site of purification" (Phl. Barašnūm-Gāh; N.P. Barashnum-Gāh; P.Gj. Barsingō). Furthermore, it may only be performed during the day, so that the sun's light can aid in purification.[2]

The earliest references to the Barašnūm are found in the Vidēvdāt and its Pahlavi commentary. Three chapters in the Vidēvdāt describe both the Barašnūm proper and an abbreviated version of it.[3] Thereafter, textual citations of the ritual are frequent, but elaborate descriptions of it remained sparse until the compilation of the Persian Rivāyats in the late medieval period. The authors of the Rivāyats provide descriptions of two distinct forms of the purification: (*a*) the "Ritual" Barašnūm ī nō šab, which was used in both Iran and India to attain religioritual purity for religious purposes and also in India for purification from the Corpse Demoness, and (*b*) the Rīman Barašnūm ī nō šab, which was practiced by Irani Zoroastrians whenever a believer became polluted through actual contact with carrion (Persian Rivāyats 593, l. 1–601, l. 2). The Rivāyats also discusses variations between the Irani and Parsi Ritual Barašnūm ī nō šab, which continues to the present day. Among the Parsis it remains in use solely for religioritual purification purposes: it is undergone by priests to attain the state of ritual purity required for religious ceremonies. The Nāhn rituals are now undergone by Parsis who have had direct contact with carrion. In Iran the Ritual Barašnūm has again been extended to encompass both religioritual and socioritual purification. The Rīman Barašnūm ī nō šab is no longer extant.

The Ancient Ritual

The Barašnūm's original function was purification of Zoroastrians who had been rendered impure through contact with the most noxious pollutant: carrion (Vidēvdāt 8: 35–36, 9: 1–2, 19: 20–21). The degree of contact with carrion determined the complexity of the ritual that had to be undergone to regain purity. After pollution through contact with carrion, and prior to undergoing the Barašnūm ī nō šab, the impure individual was barred from approaching any of the sacred creations (Vidēvdāt 9: 4–5). Only after regaining purity through performance of this ritual could the person "approach fire, water, earth, a beneficent animal, a plant, a righteous man, and a righteous woman" (Vidēvdāt 9: 36). Additionally, this great purification, the most efficacious of all such Zoroastrian rituals, was believed to hasten the soul's journey to heaven, because only if it had been undergone by the person while alive could the gods approach the soul after death.

An elaborate version of the Purification of Nine [Days and] Nights, the Ritual Barašnūm ī nō šab, was reserved for Zoroastrians rendered ritually impure through direct contact with corpses.[4] An individual polluted in this way had to seek out a purifier. The purifier had to be a righteous man who was truthful, versed in recitation of the religious liturgy, and learned in the rites of purification (Vidēvdāt 9: 2). Such an individual was usually a priest who had himself undergone this purification. This priest selected clean, barren, and desolate terrain far from other human beings and animals and cleared an area equal to nine square fathoms, felling any vegetation that was present.[5] This area was required to be at least thirty paces from water, fire, and the barsom twigs used in religious ceremonies and three paces from righteous persons (Vidēvdāt 9: 2).[6] Although Zoroastrians were enjoined not to fell plants unless necessary for use or consumption by human beings or animals, an exception was made for this ritual because impurity had to be isolated from the material creations.

The site of purification, or Barašnūm-Gāh, was laid out in the center of this cleared area as follows (fig. 1): Nine pits (Av. *maya-*) were dug in a straight line.[7] The first six pits were dug at a distance of one pace, or three feet, from each other; the next three pits were also dug at a distance of one pace from each other, but a space of three paces was left between pits six and seven (Vidēvdāt 9: 6–9). Each pit was required to have a depth of two fingers, or 1.5 inches, in summer and four fingers, or 3 inches, in winter. These pits served as the sites of ablution and were receptacles for the ablutionary liquids that washed off the candidate's body. The liquids in these pits—unconsecrated bull's urine (Av. *gaomaēza-*) and water (Av. *āp-*)—became impure after contact with the unclean individual and had to be contained within the pits, without contact with other sacred elements, until evaporation and purification by the sun's rays occurred. Because evaporation was quicker in summer, shallower pits were used. In winter, the pits had to be deeper as evaporation was slower. The direction of these pits is not explicitly stated in the Avestan text, but, since in the Zoroastrian faith south is the direction of heaven and to the north lies hell, the practice was to draw the pits commencing in the north and moving toward the south.[8] Furthermore, the Corpse Demoness was believed to flee toward the north, back to hell, after she was expelled from the candidate. The movement of a candidate toward heaven, and away from hell, as he or she progressively became ritually pure was also in accord with Zoroastrian doctrine, which regards the north as a demonic direction toward which one should never direct prayer or sacrifice. This orientation has been maintained by Irani Zoroastrians to the present day.

Next, the purifier was required to ritually mark off the entire area containing these pits by drawing a furrow (Av. *karša-*) around it using a sharp metallic instrument (Vidēvdāt 9: 10). This furrow was drawn at a distance of three paces in each direction from the pits. Next, twelve furrows were drawn around the pits as follows: (*a*) three furrows were drawn to enclose pits one, two, and three; (*b*) three furrows were drawn around pits one through six; (*c*) three furrows were drawn around all nine pits; and (*d*) three furrows were drawn around pits seven, eight, and nine (Vidēvdāt 9:

South

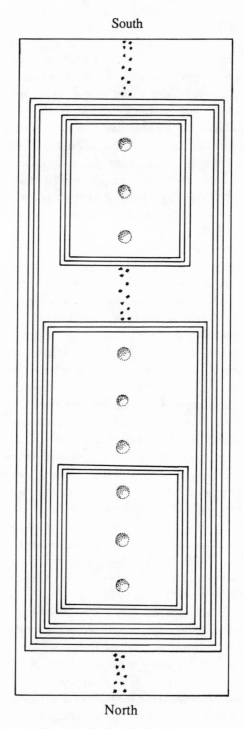

North

Figure 1. Furrows for the Ancient Barašnūm ī nō šab

11). The Pahlavi commentary to the Vidēvdāt adds that the furrows must be drawn starting at the north with recitation of three Ašəm Vohū prayers, "Righteousness [Is] Good"; one Fravarānē, "Confession of Faith"; a Šnū-man, "Dedication," to Sraoša, the god of obedience and prayer, who serves as a messenger; and the Srōš Bāj, a prayer invoking Sraoša (Pahlavi Vidēv-dāt 9: 32). These furrows served to isolate, both physically and spiritually through the power of holy words, the first three pits, in which ablutions with unconsecrated bull's urine were performed, from the next three pits, in which ablutions with unconsecrated urine were repeated, and from the last three pits, in which water was used as the ablutionary liquid. As the candidate proceeded forward from pit to pit, the Corpse Demoness was progressively weakened and, finally, expelled. Because the Corpse Demon-ess and her pollution were believed to be most noxious at the start of a purification ritual, unconsecrated bull's urine was used in the first six sets of ablutions, and pits one to three and four to six were subject to addi-tional isolation through the presence of ten furrows and seven furrows, respectively. By the time a candidate reached pits seven to nine, the Corpse Demoness was believed to have been greatly weakened, and the possibility of her onslaught on the pure creations reduced; therefore, water was used for purification. Once the furrows had been drawn and the pits ritually isolated, hard clods of earth, stones, potsherds, or pieces of wood were placed at regular intervals between (*a*) the north side of the outermost fur-row and the first pit, (*b*) the sixth and seventh pits, and (*c*) the ninth pit and the outermost furrow. Because a candidate stepped on these clods, his or her feet did not touch the ground outside the furrows. This precaution-ary measure further restricted pollution of the environment (Vidēvdāt 9: 11). The maximum length of a site of purification was 54 feet, and its width was 18 feet 8 inches. Each pit was 1.5 inches or 3 inches deep, according to the season of the year, and had a maximum diameter of 8 inches. These pits would have tightly confined the feet of an average person who stood in it, thereby forming a small area within which much of the pollution was neu-tralized and expelled.

There is a curious, inverse parallel between the symmetric, layered, en-closed structure of the ancient Barašnūm-Gāh and the arrangement of li-turgical texts in the Yasna "Sacrifice" ritual (Windfuhr 1984: 147–149; 1987). The innermost pits were surrounded by four sets of furrows that served as barriers to confine impurity. Inversely, the most sacred portion of the Yasna liturgy, the Yasna Haptaŋhāiti (Av.) "Liturgy of the Seven Chapters" (Yasna 35: 1–41: 5), is enclosed during recitation by the Gāthās (Yasna 28: 1–34: 15, 43: 1–53: 9), which are in turn preceded and followed by four *mąϑra* (Av.), "holy utterance(s)" (Yasna 27: 13–15, 54: 1), and these are enclosed by the remainder of the Yasna (1: 1–27: 12, 54: 2–72: 5).[9] The Gāthās, *mąϑra*, and Yasna (1–27, 54–72) form barriers that protect the Yasna Haptaŋhāiti, just as the ritual *karša* enclose the *mayas*.[10]

At the commencement of purification, a candidate advanced to the first pit. The purifier stood outside the furrows and recited, "Praise to Ārmaiti, the propitious" (Av. *nəmasča yā ārmaitiš īžāčā*), whereupon the candidate responded in the same formula (Yasna 49: 10).[11] According to the Vidēvdāt, the Corpse Demoness became weaker at the recitation of each word (9: 13). The purifier then poured a little unconsecrated bull's urine into an iron or lead ladle attached to the end of a stick around which a rope was knotted nine times (Av. *graom nava pixəm*). The purifier sprinkled the urine onto the hands of the candidate, using this stick. The candidate first cleansed his or her hands, for it was believed that "if the hands are not washed one would make the entire body impure" (Vidēvdāt 9: 15).

Once the hands had been purified three times, the urine was sprinkled over the candidate's body, starting with the head and moving downward: forehead, area between the brows, back part of the head, jaw, right ear, left ear, right shoulder, left shoulder, right armpit, left armpit, chest, back, right nipple, left nipple, right side of the ribcage, left side of the ribcage, right hip, left hip, sex organs (for men, first the rear and then the front; vice versa for women), right thigh, left thigh, right knee, left knee, right calf, left calf, right ankle, left ankle, right forefoot, left forefoot, sole of the right foot, and sole of the left foot. The Corpse Demoness was said to move from the body part just sprinkled to another part, which was then sprinkled, and so on (Vidēvdāt 9: 16–24). Finally, the Corpse Demoness was believed to fly to the right big toe. At this stage the candidate was instructed to press his or her heels upon the ground and raise the toes (Vidēvdāt 9: 26). The right toe was sprinkled with unconsecrated bull's urine, at which point the demoness was believed to move onto the left big toe. When this toe was cleansed, the Corpse Demoness fled "to the northern direction in the form of a fly, disgusting, with knees extended, buttocks protruding, [and covered] with unlimited spots like the most horrible noxious creature" (Vidēvdāt 9: 26). Thus, according to Zoroastrian belief, after she had been rendered powerless and innocuous, the demoness was expelled and forced back into hell. Thereafter, the candidate was instructed to recite the Ahunawar prayer, "As [is] the lord," followed by the Kəm Nā Mazdā prayer, "Whom O Mazdā," up to the words "the material worlds of righteousness" (Av. *gaēϑā astvaitiš ašahe*).[12] The entire sequence of ablutions and recitations was repeated by the candidate at each of the second through sixth pits. A dog was presented to the candidate after each ritual ablution (Vidēvdāt 8: 38). This act paralleled the rite of exposing corpses to the gaze of a dog or bird of prey.[13]

Next, the candidate squatted in the space between the furrows separating the sixth and seventh pits. He or she was instructed to purify the body fifteen times with dust and wait there until all the unconsecrated bull's urine on the body had dried (Vidēvdāt 9: 29–30). Thereafter, the candidate advanced to the last three pits, where the priest sprinkled water upon his or her body. Water was sprinkled once at the first pit, twice at the second pit, and thrice at the third pit (Vidēvdāt 9: 31). Finally, the candidate's body was fumigated with sandalwood (Av. *urvāsna-*), benzoin (Av. *vohu.-gaona-*), aloe (Av. *vohu.kərəti-*), and pomegranate (Av. *haδānaēpatā-*). This completed the purification ritual.

Upon completion of the Barašnūm proper, the candidate was required to enter a secluded chamber. He or she could not approach fire, water, earth, plants, animals, and righteous individuals for a period of nine days and nights (Vidēvdāt 9: 33). On the fourth, seventh, and tenth mornings the candidate's body and clothes were purified with unconsecrated bull's urine and water (Vidēvdāt 9: 33–35). Only after the third ablution did the candidate completely regain ritual purity and was then able to return to the Zoroastrian community and approach all the sacred creations (Vidēvdāt 9: 36). The fees that had to be paid to a purifier, which are also stipulated in the Vidēvdāt, depended upon the social status of a candidate. The purifier received one camel in exchange for purifying a district lord, one stallion for purifying a tribal chieftain, a three-year-old ox for purifying the master of a house, a cow for purifying a woman, and one lamb for a young child (Vidēvdāt 9: 37–39). Furthermore, the purifier was required to be proficient in his work and was punished if incompetent, because improper purification permitted the spread of pollution within the community (Vidēvdāt 9: 47–57).[14] A purifier who performed his task well is said to delight the righteous creations, and upon death his soul goes to paradise (Vidēvdāt 9: 42–43).

It has been noted that the Barašnūm has an intriguing assonance with Yasna 53, "The Wedding" (Nyberg 1970: 54–61; Windfuhr 1984: 148 n. 19). The nine stanzas of Yasna 53 parallel the nine *maya* and nine inner *karša* of the Barašnūm-Gāh. They also parallel the nine nights' retreat after the Barašnūm ritual. Furthermore, Yasna 53: 7 mentions the *maga-* (*magahyā*). It is likely that in addition to the double sense of *maga-*, "gift to the bride's father" and "gift to the priest" (Schwartz 1985b: 484–487), directly applicable to the stanza, there is assonance with *maga-* (Gāthic Av.) > *maya*, "pit, hole" (cf. Schwartz 1985*b:* 477). This would explain the phrases in which the faithful ones stand "with thighs on the ground" and "the spirit of the evil [one] will disappear, sinking lower and lower" (Yasna 53: 7), which are otherwise enigmatic. Perhaps Zoroaster was alluding not only to the "gift" but also to purification from evil in his homily to the wedding couple.[15]

An abbreviated form of the Barašnūm arose during the ancient period for purification of votaries who had lost their ritual purity through indirect contact with carrion. This ritual can be termed the Minor Barašnūm ī nō šab. The clergy concluded that the elaborate rite was unwarranted in cases of indirect pollution, probably because it proved to be both time consuming and difficult to administer. During the abbreviated ritual, a candidate for purification entered a set of furrows and, on the instructions of a purifier, recited one hundred Ašəm Vohū prayers and two hundred Ahunawar prayers (Vidēvdāt 19: 22). Next, he or she purified the body four times with unconsecrated bull's urine and twice with water or six times with unconsecrated bull's urine and three times with water. This completed the ritual. Clothes worn by the individual when he or she was polluted were cleansed by exposure to the air for nine days and nights (Vidēvdāt 19: 23). The candidate spent nine days and nights in isolation and was fumigated with fragrant woods on the tenth day (Vidēvdāt 19: 24). After fumigation, the candidate had to recite, "Praise to Ahura Mazdā, praise to the beneficent immortals, [and] praise to all other righteous [beings]" (Vidēvdāt 19: 25). The Pahlavi commentary to the Vidēvdāt compared the fleeing demoness to a scared sheep who had been driven forward (Pahlavi Vidēvdāt 9: 28). The candidate was now ritually pure and could return to the community and engage in devotional acts.

The extant redaction of the Vidēvdāt was compiled during the Parthian period. The Parthians and their predecessors, the Achaemenians, are believed to have been at least nominally Zoroastrian (Stronach 1984: 488; Schwartz 1985*a:* 684–697; Duchesne-Guillemin 1983: 866–868). Hence, it is likely that the Purification of the Nine [Days and] Nights was performed in the manner described in the Vidēvdāt during the entire ancient period of the faith (ca. 1200 B.C.E.–224 C.E.). Toward the end of the Parthian era, attempts to minimize pollution of the environment during the ritual resulted in enlargement of the pits used for purification. According to the practices of at least one priestly school, which followed the edicts of the priest Āfarg, the pits had to be a minimum of one foot deep (Pahlavi Vidēvdāt 9: 32). Often pits large enough to contain the candidate's entire body were dug. Another commentator, Mēdyōmāh, ruled that each part of the body had to be purified three times at each pit. In addition, it was noted that unless all the rites were completed exactly as stipulated the ritual would be void (Pahlavi Vidēvdāt 9: 32).

The Medieval Ritual

The medieval version of the Purification of the Nine [Days and] Nights developed from gradual modifications of the ancient rite after the accession to power of the Sasanian dynasty in 224 C.E. The Sasanians established Zoroastrianism as the state religion of Iran and enforced its propagation (Zaehner 1961: 284–285; Duchesne-Guillemin 1983: 874–896). There is considerable evidence that Zoroastrian beliefs and rituals were widely practiced within the Sasanian empire, and Pahlavi texts that date from the fifth and sixth centuries C.E. contain numerous references to the Barašnūm ī nō šab. Furthermore, detailed descriptions of the ritual from the late medieval period reveal that the Arab conquest of Iran, and subsequent conversion of many Iranians to Islam, had not attenuated the practice of this purification ritual by Zoroastrians. The medieval sources also indicate that major changes occurred in rites of the Nine [Days and] Nights purification. Several of these changes must have arisen prior to migration of the Parsis to India, because they were preserved independently by Parsi and Irani Zoroastrians during the period before extensive communication between the two communities.

Questions on purification by the Barašnūm, present in the Šāyest nē Šāyest (2: 6–8), the Dādestān ī Dēnīg (81: 16), the Rivāyat ī Ēmēd ī Ašawahištān (13: 2–3), and the Handarz ī Xusrō ī Kawādān, "Counsels of Xusrō, the son of Kawād" (l. 4), disclose that the ritual had crystallized into an elaborate ceremony with fixed codes, rites, and functions.[16] Attempts to simplify the ritual were vigorously opposed. Indeed, an edict from Zādspram, the Magus of Sirkan, to simplify the Barašnūm ī nō šab during the ninth century C.E. resulted in the written rebuke in three Nāmagīhā ī Manuščihr, "Epistles of Manuščihr," by Manuščihr, the son of Ĵuwānĵam, who was the high priest of Fars and Kerman and a brother of Zādspram. In these epistles Manuščihr stated: "May the gods protect you who should not refrain from use of the ablution which is the Purification of the Nine [Days and] Nights" (1: 4.1). He also claimed that Ahura Mazdā had established this purification ritual after having said: "For unhappily, Zarathushtra the Spitamid, does the sun shine upon him who has been by the dead, so unhappily does the moon, so unhappily do those stars" (1: 4.3, 2: 3.5).[17] Manuščihr reiterated that a sin occurred when an unclean individual, who had not undergone the Barašnūm, approached water, fire, other sacred creations, and ceremonial objects (3: 11, 20). He concluded that "the custom of [performing] ablutions during the Purification of the Nine [Days and] Nights is approvable and provides salvation" (3: 8). Zādspram had replaced the elaborate ritual with a simple ablution using unconsecrated bull's urine fifteen times and water once (Nāmagīhā ī Manuščihr 3: 1). Manuščihr wrote, in reference to this simplified ablution: "If Zādspram or anyone else ordered its practice, announced, or decreed it in the name of the high priestship, established it as law, propagated it, and gave it authority, my opinion, decision, and action is this: This statement is not proper, the same order is illegal, the same decree is a false teaching, this law is improper, the same promulgation is grievously sinful, and the practice of the same high priestship should not be approved and not acted upon, and whoever has performed it should immediately do penance" (Nāmagīhā ī Manuščihr 3: 17–18).[18] Manuščihr's writings also indicate that the term *pixag šōyišnīh* (Phl.), "ablution with the stick of nine knots," was used during the medieval period as an alternate name for the ritual.

A major change that occurred in the Barašnūm ī nō šab during the early medieval period was the replacement of the nine pits (Phl. *may*) and the place where dust was applied with ten groups of five stones laid on the ground. This change probably occurred because Zoroastrian priests attempted to minimize contamination of the earth through separation of the impure individual from the pure earth through the interphasing of stones.[19] Eleven other groups of three stones were placed between the groups of five stones, so that the candidate could advance from one five-stone set to another without direct contact with the earth during the entire ritual. Another two groups of five stones were placed outside the first furrow, one group on the northern side, where the candidate squatted at the commencement of the ritual, and the second group on the southern side, where the candidate completed the ritual. These stones are still used by both Irani and Parsi Zoroastrians, with the Parsis referring to them as mounts (P.Gj. *pahādyun*). Use of stones as interphases was doctrinally valid, because it paralleled the function of the sky (believed to be made of the hardest stones, such as diamond and rock crystal), which was to trap and isolate the Evil Spirit within the material creation (Bundahišn 1*a*: 6, 4: 12). Indeed, creations under the guardianship of Xšaϑra Vairya, the beneficent immortal in charge of metals, crystal, and stone, are believed to serve in inhibiting spread of pollution to the other creations.

The ritual came to be performed only during months during which the ground was dry, so as to prevent pollutants from seeping through the damp earth and afflicting other pure creations, and plenty of sunlight was available to drive away the Corpse Demoness. As a result, the ritual was usually not administered during winter.[20] Another variation that originated from attempts to prevent spread of impurity was the transfer of three furrows from the seventh, eighth, and ninth groups of five stones to the fourth, fifth, and sixth groups of stones. The additional furrows around these latter stones, on which ablutions were performed using consecrated bull's urine, further restricted escape of the Corpse Demoness who was considered to be fairly potent at this stage of the ritual. Indeed, this new arrangement of furrows exactly replicated the arrangement of furrows around the first three groups of five stones. These changes reinforced separation of impurity from creations that were ritually pure.

Prior to the Arab invasion of Iran, the Barašnūm was conducted on open, desolate ground as stipulated in the Vidēvdāt. After the conquest of Iran, it became necessary to conduct the ritual beyond the gaze of Muslims so as to secure religious sanctity and privacy amid an increasingly large non-Zoroastrian populace. This resulted in the construction of walled enclosures within which the site of purification was laid out. Furrows could be drawn, the candidates purified, and, if necessary, the nine day and night retreat undergone, without contact with non-Zoroastrians, resulting in vitiation of the ritual. These enclosures were roofless in order to permit entrance of the sun's purifying light. In addition, they were round so that there were no corners in which impurities, pollution, and the Corpse Demoness could hide to escape the sun's purifying rays (Boyce 1975: 314). Indeed, the enclosure at Yazd, the Barašnūm-Gāh, was perfectly circular as was the one in the Indian town of Navsari, which was colonized by Parsis in 1142 C.E. (cf. Jackson 1906: 383; Boyce 1975: 314 n. 114). The Persian Rivāyats (595–596) provides evidence for the performance of this ritual within circular walled enclosures during the medieval period.

With the construction of such enclosures, the Vidēvdāt edict that the area in which furrows were drawn should be cleared for nine fathoms had to be abandoned (9: 2). Indeed, these enclosures were usually situated at close proximity to human habitation, often on the outskirts of such towns as Yazd and Navsari. Zoroastrians attempted to create the illusion of a desolate terrain by covering the floor of such enclosures with sand or earth. This sand layer also served as another interphase between impurities and the earth. It was on this surface that the furrows were drawn and the stone mounts placed. These changes must have occurred prior to the separation of the Parsi and Irani Zoroastrian communities as these practices were firmly adhered to by both groups even prior to the reestablishment of fre-

quent contact between the communities. Likewise, the drinking of consecrated bull's urine and the presence of a second purifier must predate separation of the two communities, as these practices are common to both
groups of Zoroastrians. Another major variation that occurred during the
early medieval period was the visual separation of the priest from a polluted woman who underwent the ritual (Persian Rivāyats 601, ll. 2–5).
This practice violated the requirement that pure, healing sight from a purifier (Phl. *pāk yōjdahrgar*), as the officiating priest was called, fall upon the
polluted woman. This sight was believed to be essential for purification.
This change probably occurred for reasons of modesty and to prevent a
man who was not a woman's husband from seeing her naked.

The Persian Rivāyats contains numerous descriptions of the Barašnūm ī
nō šab. Modification of the ritual to include the adding of a second purifier, the drinking of consecrated bull's urine by the candidate, the replac-
ing of pits with stones, the drawing of furrows, and the performing of the
ritual within a walled enclosure are all documented in the Rivāyats (594–
599). Ground plans for the Irani and Parsi arrangement of the furrows for
this purification are also given in the Persian Rivāyats (587, 595) (figs. 2 and
3, respectively).

This purification ritual, as performed by Irani Zoroastrians during the
medieval period, required the presence of two purifiers, both of whom had
to be priests who had undergone the Purification of the Nine [Days and]
Nights, had maintained ritual purity, and had acquired ritual power (Phl.
xūb) through performance of a sacrifice service (Av. Yasna). According to
one priestly tradition, that of Āfarg, priests who sought to administer the
Barašnūm should have performed a Vidēvdāt ceremony dedicated to the
deity (Av. *yazata-;* Phl. *yazad*) Sraoša (Pahlavi Vidēvdāt 9: 32). The chief
purifier took unconsecrated and consecrated bull's urine, consecrated
water, and fire ash to the site where the ritual was to be administered.

Once within the enclosure, both purifiers donned mouth and nose
masks and leggings (P.Gj. *ijār*); performed the Pādyāb-Kusti ritual by
washing their hands, faces, and feet and untying and retying the sacred
girdles; and recited one confessional prayer (Phl. Petīt Pašēmānīh; P.Gj.
Patēt Pashēmānī) for the candidate. Then, they arranged the groups of
stones on the sandy area within the enclosure. Next, the chief purifier picked
up a nine-knotted stick (Phl. *graw kē pixag*), faced the south, and recited
the dedicatory formula, "With satisfaction for Ahura Mazdā [I do this]"
(Av. *xšnaoϑra ahurahe mazdā̊*); one Ašəm Vohū prayer; and five Ahunawar
prayers. At this point, he uttered the priestly formula of permission (Phl.,
N.P., and P.Gj. Dasturī) in a suppressed tone (Phl. *wāz;* N.P. and P.Gj.

bāj). Thereafter, he repeated, "With satisfaction for Ahura Mazdā [I do this]," and said the confessional prayer (Av. Fravarānē) together with an appropriate prayer for each of the five watches (Phl. *gāh*) of the day. Next, the purifier drew a furrow (Phl. *kiš;* N.P. and P.Gj. *kash*), starting from the south, around all the groups of stone mounts while chanting one Ahuna-war prayer. Furrows were then drawn around individual five-stone groups with the chanting of one Ahunawar per furrow. Finally, the purifier completed the *bāj* by reciting the appropriate prayers. After drawing these furrows, the chief purifier poured a few drops of *nīrang* into the vessel that contained *gōmēz*, thereby consecrating it, and added a few drops of consecrated water into a large vessel full of unconsecrated water (Persian Rivāyats 595–596).

The candidate undressed and squatted on the outermost group of stones at the northern end of the furrows. The purifier poured three drops of consecrated bull's urine into a small container and added fire ash to it. The purifier then instructed the candidate to recite the prayer of grace said before meals (Phl. *wāz ī nān xwardan;* N.P. *bāj-i nān khordan;* P.Gj. *jamvānī bāj*).[21] This prayer is the *bāj* of *iϑa* (Yasna 5: 1, 37: 1). After recital of this prayer, the second purifier, or assistant, handed the container with consecrated bull's urine to the candidate. The candidate drank the consecrated urine in three sips and completed the *bāj*. The chief purifier, with the nine-knotted stick in hand, now entered the area within the furrows and advanced to the first group of five stones. He then extended this stick so that the ladle tied to its end rested upon the candidate's head (Persian Rivāyats 596–597). This action symbolized the smiting of the Corpse Demoness, who resided within the candidate's head, by the priest who represented Ahura Mazdā. The purifier was not permitted to touch any of the nine knots on the stick. These knots were believed to prevent the demoness from moving across the stick and polluting the purifier. If direct contact occurred between the purifier and these knots, ritual impurity spread to the purifier and the ritual was vitiated. Although the candidate for purification placed both hands on the ladle, he or she also avoided contact with the knots.

The chief purifier recited the opening portion of the Srōš Bāj, or prayer invoking the messenger deity Sraoša, in order to smite the demoness.[22] He then withdrew the ladle from the candidate's head and, using the nine-knotted stick, handed unconsecrated bull's urine to the candidate. After three ablutions with unconsecrated urine, the candidate covered his or her head with the right hand and underwent the rite of being seen by a dog, *sagdīd*, by touching its head with the left hand. During *sagdīd*, the candi-

South

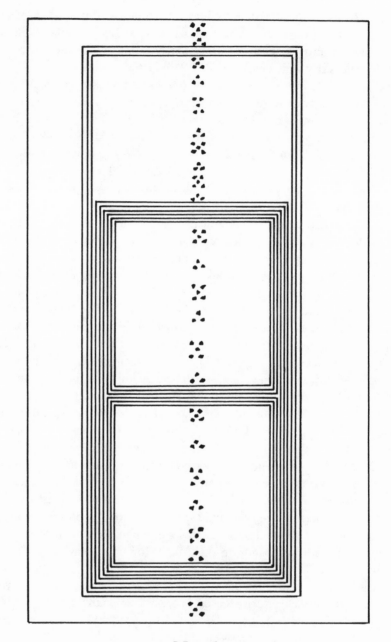

North

Figure 2. Furrows for the Medieval Irani Barašnūm ī nō šab

East

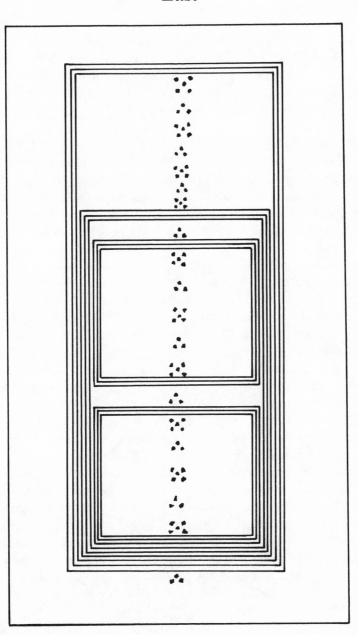

West

Figure 3. Furrows for the Medieval Parsi Barašnūm ī nō šab

date moved southward, naked and in a squatting position, from the first group of five stones, across the intermediate set of three stones, to the second group of five stones. The Kəm Nā Mazdā prayer was recited by both purifier and candidate while moving. Only thereafter was *sagdīd* terminated. This entire process was repeated on the next five groups of five-stone mounts (Persian Rivāyats 597–598).

Purification with dust was undergone, in a similar manner, on the seventh five-stone group. Fifteen handfuls of dust were also sprinkled, by the purifier, over the candidate's head. Water was used once for purification on the eighth five-stone group, twice on the ninth five-stone group, and thrice on the tenth five-stone group (Persian Rivāyats 598–599). The candidate then came out of the furrows at the southern end, washed his or her body three times with water, was seen by a dog, dressed, and draped a sacred girdle over the shoulders. The chief purifier extended the nine-knotted stick, which the candidate grasped, and completed the Srōš Bāj. Next, the candidate repeated after the purifier: "[This symbolizes] the smiting of the Corpse Demoness; the body is pure for the righteous soul" (Pz. *zadan-ī nasuš, pāk-ī tan ašōi ravāne*) and "Pure [is] the priest, righteous [is] the dog" (Pz. *herbad pāk, sag ašō*). Thereafter, the candidate retied the sacred girdle, completing the ritual.

Although purification had been completed, the candidate was required to remain in seclusion for nine days and nights. Instead of fumigation, he or she had to undergo three "Nine [Night] Baths" (N.P. and P.Gj. Noh-Shūy) on the fourth, seventh, and tenth mornings. Each bath was conducted on groups of stones within a set of furrows in order to prevent spread of ritual impurity to the community. The first bath consisted of one ablution with unconsecrated bull's urine and one with water. The second bath consisted of one ablution with unconsecrated urine and two with water. The third bath consisted of one ablution with unconsecrated urine and three with water. The Srōš Bāj had to be recited in order to protect the ritual act (cf. Kreyenbroek 1985: 144–145, 156–157). In this manner, the candidate was gradually purified of any remaining impurity. On the tenth day, after the final Noh-Shūy, the candidate totally regained ritual purity and could reenter the Zoroastrian community and perform acts of devotion to the gods.

The Parsi version of this ritual, used after migration to India, was similar to Irani practice, except that the candidate did not wash himself or herself after emerging from the furrows. Also, the arrangement of stones and furrows was different from that in the Irani Barašnūm, a fact commented on by the writers of the Persian Rivāyats (588) (see fig. 3). This variation persists to the present day. Another major change was introduced by the Parsis in the orientation of the Barašnūm-Gāh itself. As stated earlier, the orientation sanctioned by the religion was from north to south. The Parsi enclosure was, however, oriented from west to east. Thus, the candidate moved toward the rising sun and its purifying rays instead of moving away from hell toward heaven. This change of direction probably occurred at an early date when all the priests were still at the town of Sanjan in Gujarat, India, and before they separated into ecclesiastic groups (P.Gj. *panths*), because the practice remains standard throughout the Parsi community.[23]

The Barašnūm ī nō šab was originally introduced explicitly for purification of Zoroastrians who had become impure through contact with carrion. In this role the ritual persisted for several centuries. Gradually, however, the Barašnūm also came to function as a ceremony that conferred purity upon anyone who underwent it, even if the person had not been polluted. This resulted in variations within the ritual. By the fourteenth century C.E. there was a clear distinction between the Barašnūm ī nō šab as practiced to regain ritual purity lost through contact with carrion, a ritual termed the Rīman Barašnūm ī nō šab, and the ritual used solely for religio-ritual purity. Indeed, it was recorded in the Persian Rivāyats that, whereas the Barašnūm-Gāh for pure persons could be situated near the homes of priests, the ritual for polluted persons had to be located in a desolate place (598, ll. 1–5). In addition, new furrows were to be drawn if a second candidate was of a different category (polluted or clean) from the first person who was purified, but up to five candidates of the same category could use one set of furrows and stones. Furthermore, separate sets of stones were to be maintained for the two categories of candidates (Persian Rivāyats 585, l. 14–586, l. 3). The Rīman Barašnūm ī nō šab (Persian Rivāyats 559, l. 14–601, l. 2) was similar to the usual Ritual Barašnūm ī nō šab of the same period, except for the following:

1. Thirty-two sets of stones were arranged as mounts.
2. The candidate ripped and buried his or her clothes.
3. Petīt Pašēmānīh was recited by the candidate prior to drinking consecrated bull's urine.
4. All purificatory substances were presented to the candidate by both purifiers, who maintained contact with each other via a cloth or sacred girdle to enhance their ritual protection against the Corpse Demoness.
5. Single ablutions were performed with unconsecrated bull's urine on the first twenty-one groups of stones. Fifteen ablutions were performed with dust on the twenty-second group of stones. Water was used once for purification on the twenty-sixth, twenty-seventh, and twenty-eighth

groups of stones. Water was used twice for purification on the twenty-ninth, thirtieth, and thirty-first groups of stones. Finally, the candidate cleansed his or her body three times with water on the thirty-second set of stones.

There is no evidence that the Rīman Barašnūm ī nō šab was ever practiced in India. Its absence indicates that the Irani ritual arose after the Parsi founding fathers had migrated to India in the late tenth century C.E. Parsis used the Ritual Barašnūm ī nō šab for both religioritual and socioritual purification until the Rīman ritual was formulated in the late eighteenth or early nineteenth century, after priests in India ceased to perform the Purification of the Nine [Days and] Nights for polluted laypersons.

The Modern Ritual

The doctrine that every Zoroastrian should undergo at least one Barašnūm during his or her lifetime can be traced to a statement in the Vidēvdāt that the soul of a person so cleansed makes the demons tremble after the individual's death (19: 33). By the early modern period, this doctrine merged with a belief that all persons were tainted by the impurities of birth and mother's milk, which was held to be derived from the mother's blood and, therefore, to be ritually impure (Ṣaddar Nasr 36: 1–2). Hence, it was established that every person should undergo one Purification of the Nine [Days and] Nights by the age of fifteen in order to ensure purity of the body (N.P. and P.Gj. *pāk-i tān*) and protection of the soul after death (Ṣaddar Nasr 36: 3). It was believed that the gods would not approach a soul at the Bridge of the Separator (Av. Činvat̰.pərətav-; Phl. Činwad-puhl) unless it had undergone this purification ritual while incarnate. Such an uncleansed soul was said to stink, and it remained at the bridge until a son or an heir had the ritual performed vicariously in memory of the soul (Ṣaddar Nasr 36: 5–6; Ṣaddar Bondahesh l. 72). Zoroastrians were also required to undergo purification at least once after eight years of marriage, in order to purify the body from possible contamination caused by sexual intercourse. These practices were maintained in both India and Iran into the mid-nineteenth century. In Iran it was even performed in the twentieth century for pious women after menopause (Boyce 1975: 308).

During the eighteenth century, it was enjoined that every candidate for initiation into the clergy had to undergo at least two such purifications, once for purity of the body before the first initiatory ceremony (P.Gj. *nāwar*) and again before the ceremony of second degree of priesthood (P.Gj. *martab, marātib*) was conducted.[24] It also was undergone by a priest after marriage, since his ritual purity was vitiated by the uttering of the marriage vow and possibly by the bleeding due to the rupture of his wife's hymen. Furthermore, this purification became a prerequisite for a priest to engage in such ceremonies as the ritual consecration of bull's urine (Phl., N.P., and P.Gj. Nīrangdīn), which produces the *nīrang* drunk during purification rituals, and the rite of offering sandalwood and frankincense to the sacred fires. Thus, the Ritual Barašnūm ī nō šab became, for the clergy, a means of reestablishing the religioritual purity necessary for religious ceremonies. Because priests usually had no contact with carrion, the Purification of the Nine [Days and] Nights no longer served to purify them from defilement. These specialized uses of the Barašnūm ī nō šab by the priesthood continues today in both Iran and India.

Because contact with non-Zoroastrians caused ritual impurity, Zoroastrians who associated with nonbelievers were required to undergo the nine-night purification. Even in 1875 C.E., a Zoroastrian man and his daughter were refused entry into a fire temple in Bombay until they underwent this purification to regain purity lost through partaking of a meal cooked by a Muslim (Boyce 1979: 193). This was, however, a rare instance in which the practice was enforced at such a late date. Indeed, this rule is no longer obeyed by anyone other than priests, who usually do not eat food prepared by non-Zoroastrians.[25] Converts to Zoroastrianism during the fourteenth to early nineteenth centuries were required to undergo this purification to attain socioritual purity prior to entering the Zoroastrian community (cf. Persian Rivāyats 282, ll. 11–18; 283, ll. 1–2).[26] Conversion to the faith is no longer permitted by the majority of Zoroastrian communities, and even in cases where it occurs in Iran—and recently in the United States—the Barašnūm ī nō šab is no longer required.[27] Zoroastrians in Iran and India who had been polluted through direct contact with carrion continued to undergo the Purification of the Nine [Days and] Nights until the eighteenth century.

During the eighteenth century, administration of this purification ritual to the laity in India gradually ceased, and by the late nineteenth century only priests could undergo it for their own religioritual purity and vicariously for the cleansing of laypersons.[28] This change appears to have begun among priests in Bombay and spread through the entire Parsi community. Indeed, the Bombay Parsi Anjuman in a letter to the Bhagarsat Anjuman of Navsari, dated 1755 C.E., complained that five to seven months had elapsed since priests in Bombay, who owed allegiance to the Bhagaria ecclesiastic group, had performed the ritual for Zoroastrians rendered ritually impure through direct contact with carrion.[29] Reasons for this change are unclear and may be related to a feud between two ecclesiastic leaders in Bombay at that time or to an attrition in the number of priests available for the performance of this ritual. The change is also directly linked to a change, in India, of this ritual's religious function from providing general ritual purity to conferring only religioritual purity for devotional acts by priests. Vicarious purification probably began with the ritual being undergone for the souls of deceased believers. Such practice conflicts with the Zoroastrian doctrine that each individual is responsible for his or her own fate through actions performed while alive. Vicarious performance of rituals had originally been assimilated into the faith from the ancient Indo-Iranian practice of caring for the souls of deceased relatives. Initially, both priests and laypersons served as candidates in vicarious purifications. After the ritual was reserved exclusively for priests, vicarious purification of living individuals was also permitted. Adherents of the Teaching of Joy (P.Gj. Ilm-i Khshnūm), a Parsi Zoroastrian occult movement, still permit laypersons, as well as priests, to directly undergo this purification ritual.

During the nineteenth century, Parsis transformed the Barašnūm-Gāh from a circular enclosure to a rectangular one.[30] This change facilitated location of purification enclosures within compounds, thereby preventing vitiation of the ritual through contact with non-Zoroastrians. In Iran, however, sites for the ritual continue to be circular enclosures (Boyce 1977: 112–113). Furthermore, because such sites are used in Iran to purify individuals polluted through direct contact with carrion, they are not situated near fire temples. As a result, candidates often have to wait within the enclosures until nightfall to ensure that the streets are empty in order to avoid vitiation of the ritual through contact with Muslims (Boyce 1975: 318).

The Barašnūm ī nō šab purification, which is practiced by the Parsi and Irani Zoroastrians during the modern period, directly parallels the medieval Ritual Barašnūm ī nō šab. The ritual, as documented by Modi (1922: 130–134, 138–147), continues today with minor variations. Two priests, both of whom have undergone the Purification of the Nine [Days and] Nights, have maintained ritual purity, and have acquired greater ritual power (P.Gj. *moti khūb*) through a sacrifice service dedicated to Mīnō-Nāwar, the "Spiritual Priest" (also called Nō Nāwar, the "New Priest"), conduct the ritual as the earthly representatives of Ahura Mazdā. These purifiers take consecrated bull's urine, unconsecrated bull's urine, consecrated water, fire ash, and a few pomegranate leaves (P.Gj. *urwarām*) on a metal tray to the site of purification. The following sacred instruments are also necessary: a nine-knotted stick with a ladle attached to one end; two full-bodied, high-necked metal vessels for water; and two shallow

South/East

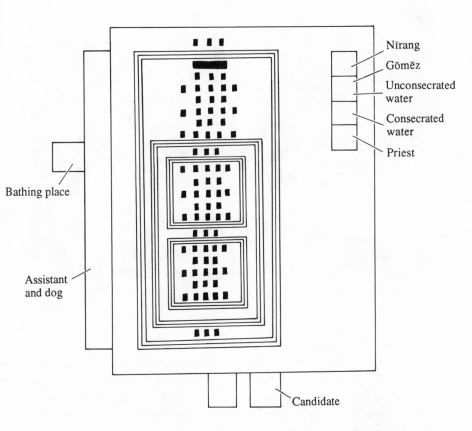

Nīrang

Gōmēz

Unconsecrated water

Consecrated water

Priest

Bathing place

Assistant and dog

Candidate

North/West

Figure 4. Furrows for the Modern Barašnūm ī nō šab

metal bowls for the bull's urine. All these instruments are cleaned, using fire ash and water, prior to the ritual.

Once within the Barašnūm-Gāh, the priests undergo ablutionary baths, don mouth and nose masks and leggings, perform the Pādyāb-Kustī ritual, and purify the sacred instruments.[31] Next, they arrange stone mounts within pure spaces (P.Gj. *pāwī*) created by furrows. Furrows are drawn around the stones while the requisite holy words are recited (figs. 4 and 5).

Today, the stones are simply arranged in rows of alternating three- and five-stone groups. As previously noted, in Iran the stones are arranged along a north-south axis, while in India they are arranged from west to

Figure 5. Priests Preparing the Barašnūm-Gāh

east. Four square, pure spaces are demarcated with furrows for storage of the purificatory substances: consecrated bull's urine, unconsecrated bull's urine, consecrated water, and pomegranate leaves. The fifth purificatory substance, dust or earth, is present within the walled enclosure itself. One priest functions as the chief purifier who will conduct the purification. The second priest acts as an assistant and controls the dog used in the rite of *sagdīd*. Consecrated bull's urine is poured into one of the shallow bowls, and a pinch of fire ash is added to it in order to enhance the purificatory effect. Unconsecrated urine is poured into the other shallow bowl. Both full-bodied metal vessels are filled with water, and the contents of one is consecrated by the sprinkling of a few drops of the consecrated water that the purifier had brought.

The candidate for ritual purification, a Parsi priest or an Irani priest or layperson, bathes in water either at home or at the ritual site and reties the sacred girdle. He or she then enters the walled enclosure and sits cross-legged within a sacred enclosure on the northern (Irani practice) or western (Parsi practice) perimeter of the furrows. The chief purifier makes the candidate recite the prayer of grace and hands him or her a pomegranate leaf on a small cloth in order to prevent connection between the priest, who is in a high state of ritual purity, and the candidate, who is unclean.

Next, the candidate is instructed to drink three sips of consecrated urine contained in the shallow bowl, which is also handed to him or her on a cloth (cf. fig. 9). The pomegranate leaf and consecrated urine are consumed to symbolically purify the candidate's soul. Thereafter, the candidate completes the prayer of grace. The chief purifier returns to his pure space. The candidate now enters another pure space to the left of the previous one and recites the Srōš Bāj. Next, in Parsi practice, he or she states, in suppressed tone: "[I do this] with good thoughts, words, and deeds, [with] good thinking, speaking, and acting, [for] the purity of the body of. . . [name]. . ." (Pz. *humata, hūxta, hvaršta, humanašnī, hugavašnī, hukunašnī . . .* [name] *. . . tan pāk*). These words were introduced into the ritual by the Parsis when vicarious purification was first permitted, and their utterance persists to the present.

The candidate then undresses, enters the ritual enclosure created by the furrows, and squats upon the first group of five stones. On this group of stones, and on each of the next five groups, a Parsi candidate purifies his or her body with three applications of unconsecrated bull's urine. Dust is applied eighteen times on the seventh group of five stones. Unconsecrated water, obtained from the first full-bodied metal vessel, is used to purify the body three times on the eighth group of stones, six times on the ninth group of stones, and nine times on the tenth group of stones (fig. 6). An Irani candidate applies unconsecrated urine once on the first group of stones, twice on the second group of stones, and thrice on the third group of stones (cf. Boyce 1977: 128–130). These applications are repeated on the next three groups of stones. Dust is applied twenty-one times on the seventh group of stones. Purification with water also varies from Parsi practice. Water is used once on the seventh group of stones, twice on the eighth group of stones, thrice on the ninth group of stones, and thrice on the tenth group of stones. Among both Zoroastrian communities, the number of ablutions represent multiples of the Zoroastrian creed: good thoughts, good words, and good deeds. Adherence to this creed is believed to be an important method by which Zoroastrians ensure their spiritual purity. The variation in number of ablutions between the two communities is random and occurred at the beginning of the modern era.

Although unconsecrated urine, dust, and water are still sprinkled over the candidate's body by the chief purifier using the nine-knotted stick, it is performed less exactingly, with the prescribed order of application being neglected.[32] Indeed, these ablutions are now merely symbolic gestures that are performed using only one teaspoonful of substance per application. Finally, the candidate is doused once with consecrated water from the second

Figure 6. Devotee Undergoing the Barašnūm ī nō šab Ritual

full-bodied vessel. This completes the purification, which lasts forty-five to sixty minutes. During these ablutions, both the chief purifier and the candidate recite all the requisite holy words that were used in the medieval version of the ritual.

The rite of being seen by a dog is conducted after each ablution. Among the Parsis, the dog is held by the assistant purifier, and the candidate touches it after each set of ablutions. Irani candidates, however, maintain continuous contact with the dog during the entire ritual via a chain held in the candidate's left hand (cf. Boyce 1977: 128). Another variation present in Iran is a process in which individuals who have been exposed to a single severe pollution perform every ablution using only unconsecrated bull's urine (Boyce 1975: 317 n. 130). This variation derives from a practice of the late medieval period described in the Persian Rivāyats (252, l. 13–255, l. 10).

After purification, the candidate retreats into seclusion for nine days and nights. As in the medieval period, three Nine [Night] Baths are undergone on the fourth, seventh, and tenth mornings within ritually constructed furrows, and the Srōš Bāj is recited on each occasion. Although Irani Zoroastrians use both unconsecrated bull's urine and water for these baths, Parsis have discontinued the use of urine. The number of ablutions with water, however, is the same as in the medieval practice. Because Parsi priests undergo the Purification of the Nine [Days and] Nights to obtain religioritual purity, they perform a Khūb ceremony, which consists of the Yasna and its rites, after ending the retreat. This ceremony endows them with the greater ritual power necessary for all higher liturgical services.

The changes that occurred in the Ritual Barašnūm ī nō šab are summarized in table 1. General summaries of the ancient Minor Barašnūm ī nō šab, the medieval Irani Rīman Barašnūm ī nō šab, and the medieval-modern Noh-Shūy are provided in table 2.

The Magi in both Iran and India regularly undergo the Purification of the Nine [Days and] Nights to maintain and reestablish their ritual purity. The Barašnūm is a requisite precursor, in order to ensure ritual purity, of all higher liturgical ceremonies that a priest can conduct. These ceremonies include the Yasna, "Sacrifice," and the Nīrangdīn, "Consecration of Bull's Urine," in addition to the daily tending of the sacred fires.[33] In Iran the ritual is also occasionally performed on children and adults who suffer only from impurities due to birth and on individuals who have been polluted through contact with carrion (cf. Boyce 1975: 318; 1977: 112). Parsis undergo purification during the dry season, and Iranis during summer. In Iran the ritual is often conducted during the Frawardīgān holidays, the ten days that precede the New Year, on which souls of the departed are invoked. It may also be undergone vicariously in both communities.[34]

No other religion has a purification ritual that corresponds in exact detail to the Zoroastrian Purification of the Nine [Days and] Nights. The closest parallel is found in Hinduism, due to the common heritage of the Indo-Iranian peoples. Among the Hindus there is the twelve-day Dīkṣā purification ritual, which must be undergone before a Brahman can perform the *soma* (Skt.) (Av. *haoma*) pounding ceremony and other high rituals (S. K. Hodivala 1925: 18–19; Gonda 1980: 379, 464). The candidate for purification and initiation has his body sprinkled with water and then smeared with fresh butter by two priests. Next, the priests rub his body

Table 1. Barašnūm ī nō šab Ritual

Purificatory Substances	Consumptions			Ablutions			
	Ancient	Medieval	Modern	Ancient	Medieval	Modern Irani	Modern Parsi
Pomegranate leaf	—	—	1 (Parsi only)	—	—	—	—
Consecrated bull's urine (sips)	—	3	3	—	—	—	—
Unconsecrated bull's urine (purifications of hands)	—	—	—	3	—	—	—
Unconsecrated bull's urine (purifications of body)	—	—	—	6	18	12	18
Dust (handfuls)	—	—	—	15	15	21	18
Water (purifications of body within furrows)	—	—	—	6	6	9	18
Water (purifications of body outside furrows)	—	—	—	—	3 (Irani only)	1	1
Sandalwood, benzoin, aloe, and pomegranate (fumigation)	—	—	—	1	—	—	—

with twenty-one handfuls of *darbha* grass to purify him. The candidate is then led to a ritual precinct where he sits wearing a black antelope's skin over his clothes. He undergoes regular baths during this retreat. After the twelfth day the candidate is pure and may perform all high religious rituals. This twelve-day period is a late elaboration of an original nine day and night sacrifice period consisting of three sacrificial periods of three days each. It thus corresponds to the nine day and night retreat after the Barašnūm ī nō šab. Indeed, in Zoroastrian practice, priests perform the Yasna ritual, including the pounding of *haoma*, on the morning of the tenth day and perform the Vidēvdāt ceremony at midnight on the twelfth day. Behavior during the retreats in the Barašnūm and the Dīkṣā has similarities in

Table 2. *Minor Barašnūm ī nō šab Ritual, Rīman Barašnūm ī nō šab Ritual, and Noh-Shūy Rite*

Minor Barašnūm ī nō šab

Ancient Purificatory Substances	Ablutions
Unconsecrated bull's urine	4 or 6
Water	2 or 3

Rīman Barašnūm ī nō šab

Medieval Purificatory Substances	Consumptions	Ablutions
Consecrated bull's urine	3	—
Unconsecrated bull's urine	—	21
Dust	—	15
Water	—	12

Noh-Shūy

Medieval/Modern Purificatory Substances		Ablutions
Unconsecrated bull's urine	} fourth morning	1
Water		1
Unconsecrated bull's urine	} seventh morning	1
Water		2
Unconsecrated bull's urine	} tenth morning	1
Water		3

its regulation and restrictions, such as the consumption of limited quantities of food. Indeed, other than a difference in some of the purificatory substances, these two rituals have striking correspondences. The Dīkṣā, like the Barašnūm, provides the postulant with access to the deepest zones of sacrality (Eliade 1975: 104).

The ritual impurity to a Brahman caused by carrion or a corpse lasts ten days, especially if the Brahman had touched this pollutant. Ablutions are performed by plunging into water and are followed by a retreat lasting ten days in which all contact with other members of the community is prohibited in order to prevent spread of the impurity. Austere measures, such as the limited intake of food and sleeping on the ground, are practiced during the retreat. The use of water as the primary purificatory liquid is permissible because, as discussed earlier, Hindus do not regard water as being vulnerable to indirect pollution by carrion.

In Jewish religious law, individuals polluted through contact with carrion have to undergo ritual purification using the Water of Separation (Leviticus 11: 25; Numbers 19: 1–12, 17–19). This purificatory ritual is essential because "whosoever toucheth the dead, the body of any man that is dead, and purifieth not himself, defileth the tabernacle of the Lord" (Numbers 19: 13). Furthermore, he or she who does not undergo purification "shall be cut off from Israel" (Numbers 19: 13), and "that soul shall be cut off from my presence: I am the Lord" (Leviticus 22: 3). Preparation of this consecrated liquid is, of course, different from that in Zoroastrianism (Numbers 19: 5–9). But, both religions ascribe purificatory properties to fire ash mixed with consecrated liquids. Similarly, Jews who have undergone this purification must remain isolated from the community, like their Zoroastrian counterparts, and must perform ritual ablutions on the third and seventh days of this retreat (Numbers 19: 11–12, 19; Ezekiel 44: 25–27).

There is considerable evidence of Zoroastrian influence on Judaism during the period of exile in Babylon. This is especially true for the Jewish priestly code and laws of purity, which developed during the postexilic period (Neusner 1977). It is likely that Zoroastrian practices of purity and pollution were assimilated by the Jews. This assimilation resulted in the transformation of the Jewish purity code from means for regulation of cultic practices to laws governing all aspects of daily life (Smith 1971: 100–102; Neusner 1975: 137; Boyce 1982: 190).

Vitiation of the Ritual

Vitiation of the ritual purity conferred by the Barašnūm ī nō šab upon an individual can occur during the ritual and retreat or after the completion of the entire ceremony. In ancient and medieval times, if any of the ablutions were not correctly performed, then the entire ritual was vitiated (Pahlavi Vidēvdāt 9: 32). At the present time, however, ablutions are usually performed less exactingly without the ritual being regarded as vitiated. If, during the ablutions, darkness falls, it rains, or there is any impurity within the pure spaces, furrows, or purificatory liquids, the Barašnūm ritual is vitiated. Rainfall during the ritual proper, or continuous rain for one to two days during the retreat, vitiates the efficacy of the purification because it is believed that the candidate cannot avoid rainwater, which may contain impurities or transfer impurity from the candidate to the pure earth.[35] Similarly, vitiation occurs if a person for whom the ritual is vicariously being undergone dies during the ritual or retreat.

Primitive fears and prohibitions are retained in the maintenance of ritual purity conferred by the Purification of the Nine [Days and] Nights. It should be noted that the term "primitive" refers to an undifferentiated world view in which belief, practice, and fears are based upon the myths and cosmology of a culture. The influences of a secular world view, modern science, and technology are not present in such cultures. Although the world view of the entire modern Zoroastrian community has undergone vast change due to urbanization, modern technology, and secular learning, the rites of purity retain the primitive fears and prohibitions that originated in ancient times. Consequently, the fear of pollution that is believed to result from nocturnal pollution and bleeding still invalidates the purification.[36] After the first Nine [Night] Bath, however, nocturnal pollution and bleeding do not cause loss of the ritual's efficacy. A simple ablution with unconsecrated bull's urine and water ensures continuity of purity, thus negating the need for repetition of the entire ritual. If, however, a candidate is undergoing the ritual to obtain purity and ritual power for the performance of a Nīrangdīn ceremony, in which bull's urine is consecrated, any discharge of body fluids (other than urine) vitiates the entire purification. Likewise, if nocturnal pollution occurs at any time during purification prior to a *nāwar* ceremony, the candidate is deemed unfit for the priesthood, as his act has polluted the world.[37] In Iran, women who commence menstruation prior to the first Nine [Night] Bath lose all purity conferred by the ritual. But, menses after the first bath does not permanently vitiate the ritual; the first bath must merely be repeated for purity to be regained (Boyce 1977: 116). Such flexibility is essential, since the Barašnūm ī nō šab is arduous and most participants are unwilling to recommence the entire ritual.

After the ritual has been completed, the person has to maintain his or her purity with great vigilance. In order to prevent loss of ritual purity conferred by the Purification of the Nine [Days and] Nights, a Zoroastrian has to ensure that he or she has no contact with carrion, eats food produced and cooked by Zoroastrians after saying grace, drinks water that is ritually pure, has no contact with menstruating women, is not burned, and does not bleed or swallow a tooth (cf. Persian Rivāyats 606, l. 3–608, l. 8). No contact with corpse bearers, barbers, bathhouse keepers, and non-Zoroastrians, all of whom are considered ritually unclean, is permitted. Violation of any of these rules vitiates the ritual's efficacy. Hence, priests cut their own hair and usually do not eat food cooked by non-Zoroastrians.

Similarly, the taking of oaths violates ritual purity; it is believed that the need to swear an oath is a slur on a person's character because it implies that the individual may not be speaking the truth (a necessary condition for maintaining purity). In addition, long journeys may require a person to repeat a Barašnūm ī nō šab, because while on such journeys an individual is usually unable to maintain all the practices necessary to ensure ritual purity.

Originally, the falling of the turban or mask resulted in purity being lost. These vestments are regarded as insignia of the priestly office, and their loss symbolizes the deposing of the priest from his office. The Barašnūm ī nō šab must be retaken as part of a reinitiation into his post. But, since it is both time consuming and costly to reinitiate a priest each time such an accident occurs, it is now held that the ritual is vitiated only if these vestments slip off in the presence of a large group of priests or laypersons. Likewise, priests who become involved in activities not befitting their office have to retake the ritual to return to a state of religioritual purity. In 1905 C.E., for example, a quarrel occurred between two priests during a thanksgiving (N.P. and P.Gj. Jashan) ceremony at the Wadi Dār-i Mehr in Navsari. The Bhagarsat Anjuman of Navsari ensured that both priests underwent the Purification of the Nine [Days and] Nights to cleanse their bodies and souls of impurities caused by the quarrel.[38]

Due to numerous problems in maintaining purity after the ritual, most Zoroastrians in Iran retain it only for the required minimum of forty days. Although it is believed to be best to maintain ritual purity for four months and ten days, most persons formally abandon it through the rite of tying it to a tree (Boyce 1977: 137). In this rite, the person who has undergone purification ties a green or white thread to the trunk of a sweet pomegranate tree, fastening it with seven knots while reciting one Ahunawar prayer. Through this act, ritual purity is conferred upon the tree, and the person then eats a dish of unclean broth, made from a sheep's head and feet, to symbolize his or her return to ordinary activity (Boyce 1977: 137–138).[39] This practice is uniquely Iranian, with no parallel among the Parsis. Most Parsi priests endeavor to maintain the efficacy of the Barašnūm ī nō šab for as long as possible.

3 PURIFICATION ON SPECIFIC OCCASIONS

He who has liberated his mind still has to purify himself.
—FRIEDRICH NIETZSCHE

TWO IMPORTANT rituals that arose from the basic three-fold purification are the Nāhn and Rīman rituals. A third ritual, the Pādyāb, existed independently as a smaller unit but appears to have been influenced by the Barašnūm ī nō šab. All three rituals originally involved ablutions with unconsecrated bull's urine, dust, and water but have experienced considerable simplification over time. These rituals are undergone at set times during the day or on specific occasions during each believer's life and maintain both the individual and the community in a constant state of ritual purity. As noted by Friedrich Nietzsche, liberation, or purity of mind, is insufficient. Zoroastrians believe that the body must be regularly purified in order to ensure purity of the mind and soul. Zoroastrians, unlike the ancient Greeks, perceive no distinction between mind and body; the physical body includes the mind, and both must be purified. While evil and impurity exist in the world, even a good mind is said to be unable to fulfill the will of its possessor: "For so long as evil is not annihilated, one whose mind is good cannot perfectly fulfill what one wills" (Škand Gumā-nīg Wizār 8: 56). The Pādyāb, Nāhn, and Rīman rituals are much less arduous than the Barašnūm ī nō šab and can, therefore, be undergone more frequently to purify body, mind, and soul.

The Pādyāb Ritual

The Pādyāb is the simplest purification ritual and is performed several times each day by most members of the faith. The term *pādyāb*, "against water," originally referred to the act of sprinkling *gōmēz*, unconsecrated bull's urine, over the exposed parts of the body, thereby cleansing these areas (Boyce 1975: 296). The use of *gōmēz* as an ablutionary liquid adhered to the requirement of protecting water from impurities. Only after purification with *gōmēz* could water be used. Although Parsis now use water in this purification ritual, Irani Zoroastrians retain the original practice. Indeed, the Parsi interpretation of *pādyāb* as "pure water" is at variance with specific instructions in the Zoroastrian religious literature that unconsecrated bull's urine be used.[1] This ritual ablution was named the Pādyāb after its functional purpose. The Pādyāb forms a part of the Pādyāb-Kustī ceremony, in which the participant first performs the Pādyāb, "Ritual Ablution," and then goes through the Kustī ceremony, which involves the untying and retying of the sacred girdle while reciting select prayers.

In order to perform the Pādyāb-Kustī ceremony, a Zoroastrian must have been properly initiated into the religious community. In ancient times, initiation occurred at the age of fifteen, the ancient Iranian age of majority, when an individual was believed to reach maturity and become responsible for his or her own religious, moral, and communal life (Yašt 8: 13–14; Vidēvdāt 18: 54). According to the Vidēvdāt: "Then the demoness, who is the Lie, replied: 'O Sraoša, righteous and well-formed one, of these males indeed this is the fourth one, a male prostitute, who after his fifteenth year walks forth without either the sacred girdle or undershirt'" (18: 54). This warning, attributed to an evil spirit, underscores the emphasis placed on proper initiation into the faith. During the initiation ceremony, the candidate dons a sacred white undershirt, or vest (Phl. *šabīg;* N.P. *shabī, sudra;* D. *sedra;* P.Gj. *sudra, sudre*), and a sacred girdle (Av. *aiwyåṇhana-;* Pz. *aiwayāhan;* Phl. *kustīg;* N.P. and P.Gj. *kustī*).[2] The term *sedra* (D.), *sudra, sudre* (P.Gj.) was Arabic in origin < *sadri, sudra* (N.P.) "vest, waistcoat," *sadr* (N.P.) "chest," < *sudra* (Ar. sing.) "vest, waistcoat," *sadr* (Ar. sing.), *sudūr* (Ar. pl.) "chest." The term *kustīg* (Phl.), *kustī* (N.P. and P.Gj.) < *kust* (Phl.) "side, waist," probably was a calque on *aiwyåṇhana-* (Av.) < *aiwi* + *yåṇhana-* < *aiwi* + *¹yāh* "to girdle."

The initiation was based on the ancient Indo-Iranian custom of investing male members of society with a sacred girdle as a sign of their membership within that community. A similar practice persists today among Hindus, where all males of the three upper castes, or social classes (Skt. *varṇa-*), are ceremonially invested with a sacred cord at the ceremony of Second Birth (Skt. *upanayana-*), conducted between the ages of eight and twelve (cf. Gonda 1980: 42, 153–154). The sacred cord is knotted by a Hindu priest and worn under the clothes diagonally around the body over the right shoulder and under the left arm. Hindus never untie this cord but simply slip it aside and step out of it when necessary. Boyce suggests that Zoroaster modified this ancient rite, thereby setting his followers apart from their compatriots, in addition to providing them with a recurrent religious exercise (1975: 257–258). However, the pre-Zoroastrian origin of this rite is preserved in the Dādestān ī Dēnīg, where it is stated that the legendary king Yima Xšaēta, or Jamshēd, first introduced the sacred girdle, centuries before the birth of Zoroaster (39: 18–19).[3] Although the exact date of its introduction into Zoroastrianism cannot be determined, this initiation rite has been practiced since the earliest years of the faith. The age of initiation was gradually lowered, with present-day Irani Zoroastrians undergoing it between twelve and fifteen and with Parsi Zoroastrians initiating their offspring at age seven due to the influence of Hinduism. Irani Zoroastrians term the ceremony "Putting on the Sacred Undershirt" (D. Ṣedra Pushun), while Parsis refer to it as the "Newborn [Ceremony]" (P.Gj. Navjote).[4] As in Hinduism, the Zoroastrian initiation symbolizes a spiritual rebirth, or second birth. Indeed, both Hindu and Parsi Zoroastrian terms for this initiation directly refer to the concept of rebirth (cf. Eliade 1975: 104). The Navjote ceremony is regularly performed by Parsis in India, Pakistan, Sri Lanka, Australia, Europe, North America, and elsewhere. Ṣedra Pushun ceremonies continue to be performed on groups of Zoroastrian youths in Iran, even in recent years. Thirty-three Irani Zoroastrians were initiated into the faith at Yazd in 1984, ten individuals from Sistan and Baluchistan in 1985, and twenty-two at Yazd in 1986 (Parsiana 1986: 15). The sacred girdle must be ritually untied and retied every time a Zoroastrian prays or performs Pādyāb-Kustī and must be worn every day during the lifetime of an individual. It is a grievous sin to abstain from wearing the girdle and undershirt, a condition termed "scrambling around naked" (Phl. *wišād dwārišnīh*). According to the Šāyest nē Šāyest: "The sin of scrambling around naked, up to three steps, is a *framān* [for] each step; at the fourth step [it becomes] a *tanāpuhl*" (4: 10).[5]

The Pādyāb must be performed before a Zoroastrian can engage in any religious activity and ensures ritual purity of the believer during these activities. It is enjoined that this ritual be performed early each morning on rising from sleep, prior to the religious act of eating, before ablutions, at the beginning of each of the five watches of the day, and after urination and excretion. In addition, all Zoroastrians must undergo this ablution upon entering the premises of a fire temple, to ensure that every religious act they perform is done so in a state of ritual purity. The Pādyāb-Kustī ritual, because it involves the performance of a purification rite, differs from the simple Kustī ceremony, in which a ritually clean person unties and reties the *kustī* without first performing such ablutions; the simple Kustī ceremony is referred to as "Making New the Sacred Girdle" (N.P. *kustī naw kardan*) or "Tying the Sacred Girdle" (P.Gj. *kustī bastan*). In addition to providing religioritual purity for the performance of such religious functions as praying, approaching the sacred fires, and eating, this ritual also ensures a Zoroastrian's return to a state of socioritual purity after urination, sexual intercourse, and nocturnal pollution.[6]

The ritual has undergone little change, other than the use of water instead of unconsecrated bull's urine by the Parsis, since the medieval period. It takes a few minutes to perform, requires only the participant, and is performed while standing upright (fig. 7). During the daytime, a Zoroastrian faces the sun or fire and at night faces a fire, a lamp, the moon or stars, or any other source of light when performing the ritual; if no light is visible, he or she faces the south, in which direction lies heaven.[7] The north is never faced during purification rituals because it is the direction toward hell. While the ritual is being performed, no other person may cross within three paces in front of the performer; the ritual is vitiated if this occurs (Persian Rivāyats 32, ll. 9–15). The area immediately around the devotee, especially the three paces in front of him or her, is regarded as a pure space that protects the sanctity of the ritual. Violation of this space symbolically parallels the primeval invasion of the material world by the Evil Spirit and invalidates the purification.

The participant faces an appropriate direction, covers his or her head with a prayer cap or scarf, and recites the dedicatory formula, "With satisfaction for Ahura Mazdā [I do this]," and the Ašəm Vohū prayer once. This is the initial part of the framing prayer or speech (O.P. and Av. *vāk-*, Phl. *wāz*, Pz. *vāz*, N.P. and P.Gj. *bāj*) for the ritual.[8] Next, the hands, face, and feet should be washed three times with unconsecrated bull's urine. The order and number of ablutions were formalized by the early medieval period and recorded in several Pahlavi and Persian Zoroastrian texts (Supplementary Texts to Šāyest nē Šāyest 20: 5; Gizistag Abāliš 4: 1–4; Persian Rivāyats 310, l. 19–315, l. 17). First, the hands are washed together with the arms from elbows downward; then, the face from the neck up to the lower part of the chin; next, the crown of the head; and, finally, the feet downward from the knees. Thereafter, the participant wipes dry these body areas with a clean cloth. Upon completing this simple purification ritual, the participant is pure and may proceed to perform the Kustī rite.

In ancient and medieval times, dust was used in ablutions if urine was unavailable (Persian Rivāyats 311, ll. 2–6). Water was not used for the per-

Figure 7. Devotee Performing the Pādyāb Ritual

Table 3. *Pādyāb Ritual*

Purificatory Substances			Ablutions	
Ancient/ Medieval	Modern Irani	Parsi	Ancient/ Medieval	Modern
Unconsecrated bull's urine or water	Unconsecrated bull's urine	Water	3	1

formance of the Pādyāb until unconsecrated bull's urine or dust had first been applied. As mentioned above, this practice is still observed by Irani Zoroastrians, but Parsis presently perform the Pādyāb ablutions with water. Both groups, however, now perform the ritual ablution only once. The changes that occurred over time in the Pādyāb ritual are outlined in table 3.

In performing the Kustī ceremony, the Kəm Nā Mazdā prayer is recited while unwinding the sacred girdle.[9] The participant first unties the square knot behind the waist, then unties the square knot in front, and, finally, unwinds the sacred girdle from the waist. Next, the girdle is folded once at its center, and the central part is held in the left hand, with the two strands of the girdle in the right hand. Consequently, a portion of the double strings is held horizontally between the two hands, and the remainder hangs down vertically (fig. 8).

The participant now commences the Ohrmazd Xwadāy, "Ahura Mazdā [is] the lord," or Kustī Bastan, prayer. The candidate flicks the free ends of the girdle sharply to symbolize the rejection and banishment of Aṇra Mainyu at each reference to him during the prayer. At the words "evil thoughts, evil words, and evil deeds" (Phl. *dušmat, dušhūxt, dušxwaršt*), the fingers are snapped three times to drive away evil with sound.[10] At the words "[good] thoughts, words, and deeds" (Phl. *menišn, gōwišn, kunišn*), the girdle is looped in each hand. When the words "with satisfaction for Ahura Mazdā" are recited, these loops are dropped, and the middle of the girdle is placed across the front of the waist over the undershirt. The girdle is wound twice around the waist with the recitation of the Ašəm Vohū prayer. One square knot is then tied at the front; each of the two parts of this knot is tied while uttering the Ahunawar prayer. The girdle is again wound to the back of the waist, and a final square knot is tied with the recital of one Ašəm Vohū. The closing part of the framing *bāj*, known as the Jasa Mē Avaṇhe Mazdā, "Come to my aid, O Mazdā!" prayer, is then

Figure 8. Devotee Performing the Kustī Ritual

recited. This completes the ceremony of Pādyāb-Kustī; the performer is now ritually pure and may enter a fire temple or engage in other religious tasks.

The efficacy of the Pādyāb-Kustī has to be renewed prior to engaging in each separate religious act and is vitiated by urination, nocturnal pollution, and the glance of a woman in menses who is within thirty paces (Persian Rivāyats 34, ll. 9–12). Originally, the Pādyāb-Kustī was performed by all Zoroastrians. In India and Iran orthodox Zoroastrian women now do not perform Pādyāb-Kustī during menses because they are believed to be "without prayer" (D. and P.Gj. *bī-namāz*). Irani Zoroastrian women also do not wear the sacred girdle and undershirt during menses (Boyce 1977: 100). The origin of this custom is puzzling because the Šāyest nē Šāyest (3: 35) and Persian Rivāyats (208, l. 9) enjoin that the Pādyāb-Kustī and simple Kustī rituals be performed during menses, with the Rivāyats (216, ll. 15–18) stating that Pādyāb-Kustī must be renewed seven times each day. The custom appears to have arisen from the belief that a woman in such a state of ritual impurity could pollute the prayers, the sacred girdle, and the undershirt because her breath, speech, touch, and gaze are believed to spread pollution (Vidēvdāt 16: 2–7; Šāyest nē Šāyest 3: 32; Persian Rivāyats 205, l. 18–222, l. 19). Because this custom of abstaining from performing Pādyāb-Kustī and Kustī Bastan is common to both Irani and Parsi Zoroastrians, it may have originated during the medieval period prior to the separation of the two communities in the tenth century C.E.[11] It is likely that this practice entered Zoroastrianism through contact with Islam, for the Muslims in Iran enforced a similar custom. The belief that sight, touch, breath, and speech can transfer impurity because they form a bond between the performer and the recipient is also present in Muslim and Hindu societies. This idea is an extension of the concept that all forms of communication represent contact and are means of incorporating the one who is contacted into a group (van Gennep 1960: 32–35).

Most Zoroastrians still perform Pādyāb-Kustī each morning and prior to religious rites within the premises of a fire temple. Zoroastrians also perform the ritual each night before sleeping. Modern-day Parsis usually perform the Pādyāb prior to entering their homes after funerals in order to purify themselves from possible contact with the Corpse Demoness. Indeed, this purification is now a simple ritual that confers both socioritual and religioritual purity upon Zoroastrians. As a result, it is still vigorously practiced, even though many other purity rites have fallen into disuse. However, Pādyāb-Kustī before meals, after urination, and at the commencement of each watch of the day is now performed only by priests and extremely orthodox laypersons.

Ritual ablutions similar to the Pādyāb are present in several other faiths. In all these cases, however, water is used as the primary purificatory liquid. Religioritual purity for devotional acts is obtained by Hindus through a ritual bath prior to going to the temple. The sacred water in which Roman Catholics dip their hands upon entering a church probably derives from the Roman "water of lustration" (L. *aqua lustralis*), which was used for ritual ablution. Purity, obtained through washing, was required of Jews before they could approach the altar (Jubilees 21: 16–17). Similar purification had to be undergone after nocturnal pollution (Leviticus 15: 16). In addition, there is the later Pharisaic-Rabbinic requirement that the hands be washed prior to eating (Neusner 1973: 56).

The closest parallels to the Pādyāb, however, are in Islam. Muslim purification rituals are based primarily on the late Qurʾānic passage in the Sūra of "The Table" (Ar. *al-Māʾida*): "O you who believe, when you rise up for prayer, wash your faces, and your hands up to the elbows, and lightly rub your heads, and [wash] your feet up to the ankles. And if you are unclean, purify yourselves. And if you are sick or on a journey, or one of you comes from the toilet, or you have had contact with women, and you can find no water, then go to clean, high ground and rub your faces and hands with it. Allah would not place a burden on you, but He would purify you, and perfect His grace upon you, that you may give thanks" (5: 6). This purification ritual is the Wuḍūʾ or Waḍūʾ (Ar.) (N.P. Vuzuʾ), an ablution of the exposed parts of the body. It is performed either at home or in a mosque before each of the five daily prayers. As among the Zoroastrians, a Wuḍūʾ may be omitted only if the devotee is sure he or she has in no way become polluted since the previous ablution, as when praying is continued from one period of the day to the next without interruption. First, a declaration (Ar. *nīya*) is made that the act is for the purpose of purification. Then, hands, mouth, nostrils, face, and arms from elbows downward are washed three times. Next, the damp right hand is passed over the brow, the beard combed with moist fingers, the ears and the neck cleaned, and the feet washed from ankles downward.[12] The structure of this ablution and the number of washings correspond exactly to the Zoroastrian Pādyāb. The widespread contact between Persians and Arabs in the late sixth and early seventh centuries C.E., due to trade routes from the Yemen that passed through the Ḥijāz to Iran, probably facilitated the transmission of this purification ritual from Zoroastrianism to Islam.[13]

Washing of hands before eating is also required. These ablutions may be performed using dust if water is unavailable; the ritual is then termed the Tayammum (Qurʾān 4: 43, 5: 6).[14]

The Nāhn Rituals

The Nāhn purification rituals are of two types: the Saḍe Nāhn and the Sī-Shūy Nāhn. Zoroastrians adopted the Arabic term *ghusl,* "ablution, washing," for these two minor purifications after the Arab conquest of Iran in the seventh century C.E. (Boyce 1975: 312).[15] The Parsis, after migrating to India from Iran by 936 C.E., adopted the Gujarati word *nāhn,* "ritual bath," to describe the Saḍe and Sī-Shūy (N.P.) rituals and applied the term *ghusl* only to purification from nocturnal pollution.[16] The Saḍe Nāhn, "Simple Ritual Bath," came to encompass the function of the Zoroastrian *ghusl* and was extended to cover purification during rites of passage, such as initiation into the faith and marriage. A more elaborate form of the ritual, the Sī-Shūy (N.P. Sī-Shūr; D. Sī-Shūz; P.Gj. Sī-Shyū), "Thirty Washings," was maintained for ritual pollution of clearly identifiable origin. The religious functions and importance of these two *nāhns* stem from the threefold purification process involving bull's urine, dust, and water. They ensure return of the votary to a state of ritual purity after exposure to conditions that render him or her unclean.

The Saḍe Nāhn

The Saḍe Nāhn ritual is conducted either within the premises of a fire temple or at the candidate's home near a bathing place in which the candidate undergoes the *nāhn* proper. The *nāhn* is administered only during the daylight hours of the morning, afternoon, or evening, with the entire ceremony lasting half an hour. In the Zoroastrian world view, light, a symbol of Ahura Mazdā, helps purify the devotee because it dispels the darkness personified by evil and pollution. The *nāhn* requires the presence of a purifier, a priest who has undergone the Purification of the Nine [Days and] Nights, has maintained ritual purity, and has acquired greater ritual power through performance of a sacrifice service dedicated to Mīnō Nāwar, the "Spiritual Priest."

In this ceremony, as currently practiced by Parsi Zoroastrians in India, the priest takes with him unconsecrated bull's urine, consecrated bull's urine, fire ash, and a few pomegranate leaves on a metal tray to the site where the Saḍe Nāhn will be administered. The following sacred instruments are also necessary: two shallow metal bowls for the consecrated and unconsecrated bull's urine; a full-bodied, high-necked metal vessel for water; and a small vaselike metal container for pouring water. Prior to the ritual, all instruments are cleaned using fire ash and water. The priest dons a mouth and nose mask and leggings and performs the Pādyāb-Kustī ritual by washing his hands, face, and feet with water and untying and retying the sacred girdle. The first short rite performed by the priest during the Nāhn involves purification (Phl. *pāk;* P.Gj. *pāw*) of the high-necked vessel using running water.[17] Once this vessel is purified, water poured into it becomes pure and consecrated. This water is then used to purify the smaller vessel, whose contents function in making pure the two bowls. These two bowls are dried, and consecrated urine is poured into one and a pinch of fire ash is added to it. Unconsecrated urine is poured into the other bowl, which is placed inside the bathing place together with the large vessel filled with consecrated water. A new set of ordinary clothing, consecrated by the sprinkling of a few drops of consecrated water, is also placed in the bathing place for the candidate to wear after his or her purification.

The priest instructs the candidate to perform Pādyāb-Kustī and to recite *iϑa,* the prayer of grace said before meals.[18] After recital of this prayer, the priest places a pomegranate leaf on a small cloth and hands it to the candidate, who then chews the leaf. Next, the candidate is instructed to drink three sips of consecrated urine from the bowl (fig. 9). This bowl is also handed to the candidate on a cloth in order to prevent contact between him and the priest. Before drinking the consecrated urine, a candidate recites in a suppressed tone the dedicatory formula: "I drink this for purity of the body [and] purification of the soul" (Pz. *in xuram pākī-ī tan, yōždasr-ī ruvān rā*). These words symbolize both the religious function of the consecrated urine and the candidate's desire for physical and spiritual purity during his or her life. The holy words are repeated three times, and consecrated urine is sipped on each occasion. Thereafter, because he or she no longer has to consume anything, the candidate completes the *bāj* by reciting the appropriate prayers. Having finished the *bāj,* he or she unties and reties the sacred girdle as is required once a *bāj* has been completed.

Next, the candidate is directed to recite the confessional prayer.[19] Because he or she is undergoing a purification ritual, a candidate has to confess all sins to Ahura Mazdā and repent of them, thereby purifying the soul in addition to the body. If the candidate is unable to recite this lengthy confession from memory, he or she may read it aloud from a Zoroastrian prayer book called the Shorter Avesta (Phl. Xwurdag Abestāg, P.Gj. Khordeh Avesta) or have it recited vicariously by the officiating priest. Vicarious recitation is condoned in the Persian Rivāyats, where it is stated: "If a per-

Figure 9. Devotee Undergoing the Saḍe Nāhn Ritual

son cannot recite the confession daily, then he should ask another person
to perform the confession for him" (36, l. 17). In such a case, while the
priest recites the confessional prayer, the candidate must say the Ahunawar
prayer repeatedly.[20] After this, the candidate enters the bathing place and
recites the short dedicatory prayer formula, "With satisfaction for Ahura
Mazdā [I do this]," and the Ašəm Vohū prayer once each. This short invoca-
tory formula is recited by Zoroastrians at the commencement of most religious actions, and it signifies that a devotee undertakes the action for
Ahura Mazdā. The candidate undresses, removes the sacred white undershirt and girdle worn by all Zoroastrians, places the right hand over his or
her head, and recites the Srōš Bāj, a prayer invoking Sraoša, including the
Fravarānē, "Confession of Faith," and the Kəm Nā Mazdā prayer up to the
words "the material worlds of righteousness."[21] The candidate then applies unconsecrated urine over his or her body from head downward, ritually expelling contamination and impurity from the body. Next, he or she
bathes in consecrated water from the large vessel. Finally, the candidate
dries himself or herself, dons the new set of clothes, including the undershirt and prayer cap, and reties the sacred girdle with recitation of the
Ohrmazd Xwadāy prayer and the Ĵasa Mē Avaṇhe Mazdā prayer, thereby
completing the ritual.

Study of the Saḍe Nāhn as performed over the past century reveals that the ritual has undergone considerable simplification among Parsi Zoroastrians. In the early years of this century, the candidate sat cross-legged on a stone stool during the ritual to reduce contact between himself or herself and the earth.[22] The custom of sitting on a stone stool was connected to the ancient practice of standing within a small pit or squatting on stones, both of which limited contact between the sacred elements and the impure individual, including the impurities present on and in that individual. This method of isolating impurity is still preserved in the Barašnūm ī nō šab and Sī-Shūy Nāhn, but is no longer implemented in the Saḍe Nāhn. The major difference between the Saḍe Nāhn of the nineteenth and early twentieth centuries and that which has been in practice during the past two decades is the simplification of the ritual bath itself. In the earlier practice, the priest handed the candidate unconsecrated urine for application over the body using a nine-knotted stick, instead of placing it within the bathing place. This act was repeated three times. Next, the priest presented dust to the candidate three times for application, and then unconsecrated water three times. Only then was the candidate allowed to dress and complete the Srōš Bāj. This use of unconsecrated urine, dust, and water, along with their order of application, corresponds to the external purificatory process of the original threefold ritual and is still employed in the Barašnūm. The omission of dust during the past few decades is probably because the Saḍe Nāhn had acquired mainly a socioritual function, providing the degree of ritual purity necessary to perform only routine religious functions, and had lost much of its original religioritual purificatory role, providing a state of high ritual purity required for the performance of the most sacred religious ceremonies. Unconsecrated bull's urine and water came to be considered the only essential substances for socioritual purification of the body surface. The use of unconsecrated urine and water in the Saḍe Nāhn parallels the priestly custom of washing the body first with unconsecrated urine each morning prior to bathing in water, a practice that continues today among most clergy and orthodox laity in such towns as Navsari and Surat in India. Similarly, the number of applications was reduced from three, representing the Zoroastrian creed of good thoughts, good words, and good deeds, to one. The changes that occurred in the Saḍe Nāhn ritual are summarized in table 4.

The Saḍe Nāhn is presently performed by Zoroastrians prior to the initiation ceremony, on the day of marriage, and occasionally on holy days, such as the Frawardīgān holidays (the Festival of All Souls) and the festival of Spənta Ārmaiti. As previously mentioned, the Navjote ceremony marks

Table 4. Saḍe Nāhn Ritual

Purificatory Substances	Consumptions	Ablutions Premodern	Modern
Pomegranate leaf	1	—	—
Consecrated bull's urine	3	—	—
Unconsecrated bull's urine	—	3	1
Dust	—	3	—
Consecrated water	—	—	1
Unconsecrated water	—	3	—

the occasion when a child is initiated into the Zoroastrian faith. Every Parsi Zoroastrian initiate has to undergo the Saḍe Nāhn on this occasion to enter the community and religion in a state of purity. Since the Navjote ceremony is the occasion on which a new initiate is first invested with *kustī* and *sudra,* the Saḍe Nāhn on this occasion differs from the general procedure described above insofar as the child initially wears no undershirt and sacred girdle. As a result, on this occasion the Pādyāb consists only of reciting the introductory formula and washing the face and other exposed parts of the body. The Zoroastrian concept of entering both the religion and the community in a state of purity parallels the Brahmanic ceremony of Upanayana (Skt.), in which, as noted earlier, the Hindu boy is invested with the threefold sacred thread and sprinkled three times with water (Stevenson 1971: 30). It also parallels Christian baptism (cf. Eliade 1975: 115–121).[23] The next occasion on which a Zoroastrian is required to undergo the Saḍe Nāhn is on the day of marriage. Both bride and bridegroom must undergo this purification. In ancient Roman society, lustration rites were performed during the marriage ceremony. Hindus also undergo a purificatory bath before marriage (cf. Stevenson 1971: 69–70). Purification by the Saḍe Nāhn during rites of passage represents a liminal stage, after which the devotee is reintegrated into the religious community (cf. van Gennep 1960: 79–82, 104–106, 116–117). The ritual ablutions separate the votary from the profane world and permit his or her incorporation or reintroduction into the pure religious order. Thus, this ritual ensures physical and spiritual purity at a vital point in the devotee's religious life: the moment when he or she is at the spiritual threshold of transcendence. The purification ritual, followed by the initiation ceremony, marks the individual's transcendence and enlistment in the lifelong battle against evil.

The Nāhn may also be undergone on any of the ten days that comprise the Frawardīgān or Muktād holidays, during which souls of the deceased are invoked. It is considered especially meritorious to undergo this purification in memory of a deceased relative during one of the last five days. This practice is still occasionally performed by orthodox Parsi women both during these holidays and on the festival of Spənta Ārmaiti.[24]

The Sī-Shūy Nāhn

In cases where there has been ritual impurity brought about by contact with carrion or bodily refuse, the Sī-Shūy Nāhn is administered. In Iran this purification is now undergone at home, but in India it is usually performed at a desolate spot, such as the premises on which a funerary tower is situated or the site at which the Purification of the Nine [Days and] Nights is conducted. The priest maintains a careful distance from the polluted individual, who is isolated within furrows drawn to confine impurity and prevent its spreading to the priest and the community.[25] The purification site is illustrated in figure 10.

Three furrows are drawn around each enclosure, or pure space, with there being ten such sets of triple furrows arranged from north to south in Irani practice and west to east in Parsi practice.[26] Three groups of stones are arranged linearly within each set of furrows, with three stones per group. Outside each of the first and the last sets of furrows, one similar group of stones is placed. All groups of stones serve as mounts on which the candidate squats while undergoing purification. Stones, being a creation of the beneficent immortal Xšaϑra Vairya, are regarded as impermeable to pollution and serve to isolate the candidate and his or her impurity from the earth. Stone is categorized as a metal and, according to Zoroastrian cosmogony, forms the sky, which encircles the material world, trapping all evil and pollution within it.[27] As in the Saḍe Nāhn, the officiating priest has undergone the Purification of the Nine [Days and] Nights.

The rites of the Sī-Shūy Nāhn are similar to those of the Saḍe Nāhn in all respects except the following: (*a*) the sacred instruments are pure and consecrated (P.Gj. *yashte*);[28] (*b*) Irani Zoroastrians undergo this Nāhn while fasting (Boyce 1977: 111); (*c*) the priest stands outside the furrows and hands the purificatory substances to the candidate using a ladle attached to a nine-knotted stick; (*d*) unconsecrated bull's urine, dust, and water are each applied nine times, followed by a final threefold application of water.

The candidate squats on the first set of stones and drinks the consecrated urine in three prescribed ritual sips after reciting the *bāj* and stating that the action is being performed for purification of the body and the

South/East

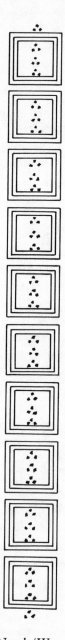

North/West

Figure 10. Furrows for the Sī-Shūy Nāhn Ritual

Table 5. Sī-Shūy Nāhn Ritual

Medieval/Modern Purificatory Substances	Consumptions	Ablutions
Pomegranate leaf (Parsi only)	1	—
Consecrated bull's urine (sips)	3	—
Unconsecrated bull's urine	—	9
Dust	—	9
Water (in spaces 7, 8, 9)	—	9
Water (in space 10)	—	3

soul. In Parsi practice, the candidate chews a pomegranate leaf prior to sipping this liquid. Then, he or she enters the first pure space formed by the furrows. While squatting on the stones in each of the first, second, and third spaces, the candidate purifies his or her body with unconsecrated urine. Dust is applied to the body in the next three pure spaces, and water in the seventh, eighth, and ninth spaces. This completes twenty-seven ablutions. Thereafter, the candidate enters the last set of furrows and performs three final ablutions with water. During these cleansings, the candidate moves, naked and in a squatting position, from north (the direction of hell) toward the south (the direction of heaven) in Irani practice, and from west to east (toward the purifying sun) in Parsi practice. The impurity is diminished by each successive ablution and confined within the furrows (cf. Vidēvdāt 9: 28). The entire ceremony takes half an hour and is conducted during the daylight hours, usually in the open. A general summary of the Sī-Shūy Nāhn ritual is provided in table 5.

This Nāhn is first mentioned in the Persian Rivāyats, which states that it had to be undergone by any Zoroastrian who has been polluted through contact with carrion (88, ll. 2–6). In this case, even after a Sī-Shūy Nāhn had been administered, the person was still fairly polluted and could not approach water or fire until the Barašnūm ī nō šab had been conducted (Persian Rivāyats 135, ll. 1–7). This indicates that the Sī-Shūy Nāhn was not regarded as sufficiently efficacious to completely purify a believer who had been polluted directly by carrion. In ancient and medieval Zoroastrian belief, only the Barašnūm ī nō šab sufficed to purify such an individual. By the late medieval period, however, the Sī-Shūy Nāhn was undergone by corpse bearers (Persian Rivāyats 107, ll. 5–9).[29] Furthermore, this ritual was used in instances when women had been polluted when their impure garments had touched their mouths during menses and when facilities for the Purification of the Nine [Days and] Nights were unavailable after a woman had given birth to a stillborn child (Persian Rivāyats 207, ll. 1–3; 232, l. 18–233, l. 9).

This ritual is still administered to orthodox Irani Zoroastrian women in Yazd after miscarriage (Boyce 1975: 313; 1977: 111). In these cases, actual administration is performed by another woman who has undergone the nine night purification, while the priest stands nearby, out of sight, chanting the requisite prayers. The Sī-Shūy Nāhn is still administered in Iran to corpse bearers. Here, too, the priest stands at a distance reciting the prayers, while the actual administering of the ritual is performed by a layman. This practice prevents loss of the priest's ritual purity due to contact through sight, speech, and breath with the defiled man or woman, who is considered extremely impure. (Here is a religious paradox. The priest's gaze purifies the defiled woman or man. Yet, in seeing, the priest is also seen. Therefore, the defiled person's gaze falls upon the priest and has the potential of polluting the priest.) Irani Zoroastrian men and women occasionally undergo this Nāhn on holy days, such as the annual festival of Spənta Ārmaiti. It was also previously administered to women forty days after accouchement, prior to which time they were not permitted to approach the hearth fire, enter a fire temple, or attend any social functions. In Hinduism there is a similar requirement that mothers undergo a purificatory bath forty days after childbirth. This practice is probably connected, in its basic tenets, to the Zoroastrian Nāhns due to the common Indo-Iranian heritage of the two religions. Muslim women, following Zoroastrian practice, are required to undergo an ablution of the entire body after childbirth.[30] Among Zoroastrians, all persons who had had contact with women who had given birth were also expected to undergo the Nāhn. The ritual is, therefore, a means of purification, enabling the devotee to pass from impurity and separation to eventual reunion with his or her coreligionists. However, by the beginning of the twentieth century, this ritual had been largely replaced by the Saḍe Nāhn, and it is currently administered to extremely orthodox Parsi women on such rare occasions as stillbirth and miscarriage, because in these cases the women are believed to have carried carrion within their bodies.

A major variation that is common to both Irani and Parsi Zoroastrians, which probably occurred prior to the migration of Zoroastrians to India, is the visual separation of the priest from a female candidate. This separation is also the practice when a Barašnūm ī nō šab is administered to a woman, as noted previously, but in both rituals it violates the requirement that pure sight from the officiating priest fall upon the polluted woman.

The gaze of the priest was believed to be essential for purification during the Sī-Shūy Nāhn, just as it is still necessary for consecration in high rituals, because the priest functions as a healer during the purificatory process.[31] As in the Barašnūm ī nō šab, this change probably occurred for reasons of modesty and to prevent a man who was not a woman's husband from gazing upon her naked body. It is doctrinally justified as preventing loss of the priest's ritual purity through indirect contact with pollution.

The Rīman Ritual

The ritual ablutions undergone in the Rīman ceremony directly parallel those of the Barašnūm ī nō šab, and it would be accurate to suggest that the Rīman derives directly from the Purification of the Nine [Days and] Nights. The Barašnūm initially functioned as the major ritual for purification of Zoroastrians who had been exposed to extreme forms of pollution (*rēman, rīman*), especially direct contact with carrion. However, when the Purification of the Nine [Days and] Nights came to serve only a religioritual function, a simplified form of the rite, the Rīman, took its place for the religioritual and socioritual purification of Zoroastrians polluted directly or indirectly by carrion. It is from this association with pollution that the ritual itself gained its name and became an ablution against carrion.

The Rīman ritual is found only among the Parsis and is not practiced by Zoroastrians in Iran. The only references to it date from the eighteenth to twentieth centuries. Its absence from the Avestan, Pahlavi, and Persian texts of the Zoroastrians indicates that it was not practiced in Iran and must have originated after the Parsis migrated to India. The practice of the ritual is without variation among the five Parsi ecclesiastic groups.[32] Since these groups originated in the late thirteenth century C.E., the Rīman ritual may have evolved in the period when all the priests were concentrated in the towns of Sanjan and Navsari in the state of Gujarat. This would date the origins of the Rīman ritual to the late tenth to twelfth centuries C.E. However, evidence from the Persian Rivāyats and Gujarati sources indicates that, until the eighteenth century C.E., both Irani and Parsi Zoroastrians who had been defiled through direct contact with carrion were generally purified by the Ritual Barašnūm ī nō šab or the Rīman Barašnūm ī nō šab ritual.[33] Furthermore, the Gujarati texts from this period do not mention the Rīman ritual. The ritual, therefore, probably evolved only during the eighteenth or early nineteenth century C.E., when priests in India ceased to perform the Purification of the Nine [Days and] Nights for polluted Zoroastrians.

Purification was simplified during the eighteenth and early nineteenth centuries by elimination of the nine day and night retreat. Isolation of the impure individual was, however, strictly maintained through the use of pure spaces formed by the drawing of furrows. The system of furrows was itself simplified, but greater precautions were enacted to prevent contact between the ministering priest and the candidate for purification. Also, instead of two priests, a member of the laity served as the second purifier, and it was he or she who performed all actions involving close approach to the candidate. The use of consecrated bull's urine, unconsecrated urine, dust, and water as purificatory substances was preserved, and the number of applications of the latter three closely parallels that of the Barašnūm. Because the Rīman ritual evolved for the purification of Zoroastrians made impure through contact with the most noxious of all pollutants, carrion, the ceremony is still administered only at sites isolated from the general populace, such as near funerary towers, and never within the confines of a fire temple or a home. Furthermore, like other Zoroastrian purificatory rites, this ritual is administered only during the daylight hours.

The Rīman ritual is of approximately one hour's duration. It must be administered by a priest who has undergone the Purification of the Nine [Days and] Nights, maintained ritual purity, and acquired greater *khūb*, "ritual power." Performance of the Rīman ends the efficacy of a priest's ritual power, and such power must be reacquired before he performs other high rituals. The priest takes consecrated and unconsecrated bull's urine, fire ash, and pomegranate leaves to the purification site. Two shallow metal bowls; a full-bodied, high-necked vessel; a small vaselike metal container; a nine-knotted stick; and two eggshells are also required. These sacred instruments cannot be reused after the ceremony and must be discarded in order to ensure that the pollution does not spread to the rest of the community. The candidate is brought to the site together with a set of new clothes to be worn after purification. At no time is the impure candidate allowed to touch the new clothes or other Zoroastrians.

The nine-knotted stick, with a sharp metal instrument or knife attached to it, is used to draw furrows, which enclose nine adjacent pure spaces (*pāwī*). Seven of these pure spaces must be in a straight line, with the other two perpendicularly to the right of the fourth one (fig. 11). The direction of these enclosures must be oriented such that the candidate's shadow does not fall upon the priest or assistant and the wind does not blow from the candidate toward them. These precautions are believed to prevent even the slightest trace of pollutant being transferred from the candidate to those individuals administering the ritual. Another *pāwī* is drawn some distance

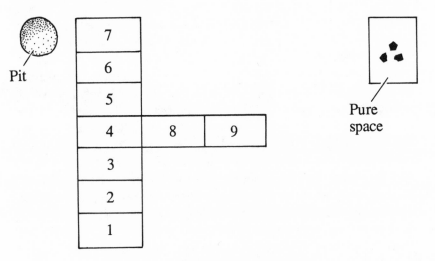

Figure 11. Furrows for the Rīman Ritual

away, and three stone mounts are arranged within it. A circular pit three or four feet deep is also dug. The priest is required to recite one Ahunawar prayer when drawing each furrow, thereby strengthening the enclosures' sanctity with the power of holy utterances. Next, he dons a mouth and nose mask and leggings, performs Pādyāb-Kustī, and purifies the sacred instruments as in the Saḍe Nāhn ritual.

The priest places the consecrated items within the first pure space and then enters this enclosure. The assistant stands a few feet away from the furrows. The candidate undresses and throws his or her clothes into the pit. The assistant instructs the candidate, by gestures, to enter the seventh *pāwī*. The use of gesture reflects the isolation an impure person is subject to and demonstrates the total separation of the pure from the impure. The priest pours consecrated bull's urine (*nīrang*) into one eggshell; places it, together with a few pomegranate leaves, within the ninth enclosure; and returns to the first enclosure. The use of an eggshell is a further precautionary and isolatory measure to avoid even a drinking utensil's coming into contact with the polluted person. The assistant advances to the ninth pure space, picks up the eggshell and pomegranate leaves, and places them within the sixth pure space. He or she then moves away from the furrows. The assistant then gestures to the candidate to enter the sixth *pāwī*, chew the pomegranate leaves, and sip the *nīrang* three times. The candidate follows these instructions, chewing the *urwarām* and drinking the *nīrang* in a manner so as to avoid contact of the lips with the eggshell, which he or she then breaks and tosses into the pit. Orifices of the body are not only points especially vulnerable to pollution (Douglas 1969: 121) but also openings through which pollution emerges from the individual into the environment; therefore, contact between the lips and the eggshell is not permitted. During the Rīman ritual, the candidate drinks *nīrang* while naked, whereas in the Barašnūm ī nō šab this is done while still dressed. Since the candidate is naked, the consecrated urine is drunk without wearing the sacred girdle and undershirt or the taking of *bāj*. He or she is considered so impure as to be unworthy of prayer, and even breath and words that issue from his or her mouth are regarded as a form of pollution.[34] Consequently, the candidate must remain absolutely silent. The drinking of *nīrang* in three prescribed sips represents good thoughts, good words, and good deeds, which are the characteristics of a pure soul and body that the devotee is striving to achieve by internal purification. The candidate then throws a few handfuls of earth into the pit to cover the clothes and eggshells.

The priest takes the second eggshell into his left hand and pours unconsecrated bull's urine (*gōmēz*) into it. He then takes the nine-knotted stick in his right hand and advances to the third space. The candidate enters the sixth pure space. The assistant gestures to the candidate to extend his or her hands, the priest pours the urine from the eggshell into a ladle attached to the end of the nine-knotted stick, and then extends it to the candidate. Because he is separated from the candidate by two enclosures, the priest is safe from any possible pollution. The priest pours the *gōmēz* onto the candidate's right hand while being careful that the ladle does not make contact with the candidate. As in the Barašnūm ī nō šab, the urine is poured quickly, so as to prevent a connection via the stream of liquid, which might pollute the priest. The assistant then instructs the candidate to apply the urine to the body. This short rite of receiving and applying *gōmēz* is repeated fifteen times.[35]

The priest then returns to the first *pāwī*, collects some dust (*xāk*), advances to the third enclosure, and presents this dust to the candidate with the knotted stick for application over the body. This process is the same as that involving unconsecrated urine and must be repeated fifteen times. Next, the priest returns to the first *pāwī*, picks up the small vaselike container full of water, moves to enclosure three, pours a little water into the ladle of the nine-knotted stick, and presents it to the candidate. Once again, the process, as described for *gōmēz* and *xāk*, is undergone fifteen times. It is believed that the Corpse Demoness is progressively weakened during all these ablutions and finally expelled from the body of the polluted individual, causing her to flee toward the north, back to hell. During the ritual, while the Corpse Demoness is still noxious, her escape from the pure spaces to pollute the other creations is prevented by the furrows, which served to trap her within the enclosures in which the candidate stands.

After these ablutions, the candidate returns to the seventh pure space. The priest takes the large metal vessel, which is full of water, places it in the ninth *pāwī*, and then returns to the first enclosure. The assistant advances to the ninth enclosure, picks up the vessel, and gestures to the candidate to enter the *pāwī* that contains the stone mounts. The candidate goes into this enclosure and squats on the three stones. The assistant stands at arm's length from the candidate and pours the water over the candidate's head and body three times. The water is poured in such a manner that it does not sprinkle off the body onto the assistant and transfer the impurity. The candidate then dries himself or herself with a clean towel, dons new clothes, and performs the simple Kustī ceremony, completing the Rīman ritual.

Now the candidate is considered both religioritually and socioritually pure and can reenter the community. The priest places the sacred instruments in the pit, seals the pit by filling it with earth, returns to the fire temple, and ritually purifies himself of any trace of pollution by applying *gōmēz* to the body. He then bathes in water, dries his body, dresses, and reties the sacred girdle. The assistant also purifies himself or herself in a similar manner. If the candidate for purification is male, the priest and a male assistant conduct the entire ritual as described. If the candidate is female, the priest is visually separated from the candidate by a screen, behind which he stands and instructs the female assistant to perform the actual administration of the ritual.

Isolation of the polluted individual is strictly maintained at all times during the Rīman ritual through the arrangement of pure spaces and the regulated movements of the priest, the assistant, and the candidate. The priest and candidate are always separated by at least three enclosures, and no contact is ever established between them. As a result of these elaborate precautions, the priest is not stripped of his ritual purity by direct or indirect contact with impurity and can cleanse himself simply by washing with unconsecrated urine and water. Nor does the priest engage in any form of communication with the impure person: the ritually pure remains separate and aloof from the profane. All interaction occurs only through the intermediary, the assistant, who, although not in a state of high ritual purity, is unpolluted. The assistant symbolizes human beings, who, although alive in a world full of good and evil, assist Ahura Mazdā and the beneficent immortals in the separation and expulsion of evil and impurity from the world. In this sense the Rīman ritual replicates in a ritualized form the

Table 6. Rīman Ritual

Purificatory Substances	Consumptions	Ablutions
Pomegranate leaves	1	—
Consecrated bull's urine (sips)	3	—
Unconsecrated bull's urine	—	15
Dust	—	15
Water (in sixth space)	—	15
Water (in ninth space)	—	3

linear progression of the material world, which is gradually purified by Ahura Mazdā with the assistance of human beings; evil is separated, isolated, rendered powerless, and eventually expelled, and each good creation is then restored to its original purity (see fig. 14).

The rites of purification in the Rīman ritual underwent simplification during the twentieth century.[36] In the early years of this century the candidate buried his or her clothes after undressing, instead of merely casting them into a pit (Modi 1922: 155). An important variation occurred in the structure of the pure space that contains the stone mounts. The process of drawing the furrows for this enclosure was simplified from six concentric furrows to a single square furrow.[37] This simplification reflects the gradual attenuation of orthodox beliefs involving the ritual danger of impurity and the absolute necessity of preventing its spread. This erosion of beliefs about the danger of contamination by carrion is best illustrated by the decline in the use of this ritual during the twentieth century. A general summary of the Rīman ritual is provided in table 6.

Initially, this purification was administered to the following categories of religioritually impure Zoroastrians:

1. Corpse bearers and their families prior to interaction with the rest of the community, marriage, or admission to a fire temple. Before the Rīman ritual was instituted, all corpse bearers had to undergo the Purification of the Nine [Days and] Nights, which was too taxing to be undergone frequently (cf. Persian Rivāyats 599, l. 14–601, l. 2). As a result, corpse bearers and their families were isolated from the rest of the community until the late eighteenth century.

2. Zoroastrians who had become impure through direct contact with carrion.

3. Zoroastrians who had become polluted by swallowing their own teeth, blood, or flesh.

4. Children under the age of eight who had bitten another child and thereby swallowed blood or flesh.

5. Children burned by fire.

6. Mothers who had become impure because their suckling infants fell into fire.

Originally, all these individuals were cleansed through the Purification of the Nine [Days and] Nights. Indeed, even during the last few decades, Irani Zoroastrians have maintained this original practice (Boyce 1977: 112). Parsi priests, however, have rarely administered the Rīman purification during the last decade; if desired, a person of one of the second through the sixth categories may undergo the Saḍe Nāhn or may simply apply unconsecrated bull's urine and water to the body. In addition, individuals of the fifth and sixth categories are now rarely found, and the swallowing of teeth, flesh, or blood is generally regarded by the laity as a natural occurrence. The Rīman ritual is no longer administered for corpse bearers, either. They simply wash their bodies with unconsecrated bull's urine after each funeral, and their families are no longer regarded as polluted. These changes may be attributed to an increasing scarcity of priests to perform such rituals. The decline in the number of candidates for religioritual purification, due to changes in the beliefs on ritual purity resulting from extensive contact with non-Zoroastrians in societies within which Zoroastrians are now a minority, also has contributed to a decline in the practice of this ritual.

PURITY IN DAILY LIFE

Rituals of purity and impurity create unity in experience.
—MARY DOUGLAS

EXTENSION OF purity laws in both belief and practice within the early Zoroastrian community produced the doctrine that all substances that leave or are separated from the human body become ritually polluted. At the moment they become polluted, these materials are regarded as dead matter and become capable of spreading impurity caused by the demons. Thus, all substances leaving the body are considered ritually impure and polluting in varying degrees. Such substances include hair, nails, skin, urine, feces, saliva, breath, blood, semen, and menstrual fluid. As Mary Douglas astutely noted: "We should expect the orifices of the body to symbolise its specially vulnerable points. Matter issuing from them is marginal stuff of the most obvious kind. Spittle, blood, milk, urine, faeces or tears . . . have traversed the boundary of the body" (1969: 121).

In Zoroastrian doctrine, these substances are termed excrement (*hixra-*, *hixr*, and *hikhra*) and are open to grave pollution by the Corpse Demoness. The term *hixra-* is used in the Vidēvdāt with reference to polluting matter issuing from corpses (5: 14, 16). In the Pahlavi and Persian sources, however, *hixr* refers to the "dead matter of the living," that is, bodily refuse (Pahlavi Rivāyat Accompanying the Dādestān ī Dēnīg 55: 3; Persian Rivāyats 82, l. 6–83, l. 17). This indicates that the term was extended during the medieval period to include dead matter produced by both living persons and corpses. Gradually, however, carrion was excluded from the meaning of *hixr*; carrion came to be called *nasā*, and *hixr* came to mean bodily refuse or excrement only. Contact with such excrement renders a Zoroastrian ritually unclean, and minor purification rituals must be undergone to ensure return to a state of purity. Elaborate precautions are required to prevent contamination of the good creations of Ahura Mazdā, and severe punishment after death is said to befall Zoroastrians who pollute the creations with excrement. The Ardā Wīrāz Nāmag graphically describes the sufferings in hell of a woman who polluted fire with hair (34: 1–7). Since food, utensils, clothing, and homes contaminated by excrement can make the believer unclean, elaborate codes exist for determining if a given substance has become polluted and how such pollution may be cleansed. Ritual pollution and impurity caused by *hixr* is usually less grave than that of *nasā*. As mentioned earlier, an exception is the effect of excrement on water and fire, where it equals carrion in its polluting power (Persian Rivāyats 82, ll. 16–17).

It is important to note that hair, nails, and skin are pure as long as they remain part of the body and that semen serves the divinely decreed function of procreation. Even bodily functions reflect the dualism of Zoroastrian doctrine, and daily life is governed by rules to ensure the vanquishing of evil. Therefore, there are rituals for the cutting of hair and the paring of nails; precautions that must be taken to prevent pollution by breath and saliva; ablutions designed to ensure ritual purity after sexual intercourse, nocturnal pollution, and urination; rules for the seclusion of women during menses and rites for purification after menstruation; numerous dietary rules; and methods for purifying articles and homes polluted through contact with impurities or the demise of an occupant. Adherence to the laws and rites that govern purity in daily life creates a common standard of social behavior, or, in Douglas' words, "unity in experience" (1969: 2). The entire community is unified through symbolism, and mundane acts are endowed with religious significance.

The belief that certain bodily substances may render a person ritually impure is widespread. Hindus share many prohibitions and regulations with Zoroastrians. Indeed, all secretions from the body cause defilement among the Hindus (Carstairs 1958: 81). Similarly, among the Jews, "When any man hath a running issue out of his flesh, because of his issue he is unclean," and this impurity can spread to other persons with whom he has contact (Leviticus 15: 2–12). According to the book of Leviticus, ritual purity is regained after a period of seven days, during which both the body and the garments must be purified with running water (15: 13). Like Hinduism, Zoroastrian doctrine holds that all non-Zoroastrians are ritually unclean and that "a non-Zoroastrian is not naturally fit for observing the precautions about carrion" (Persian Rivāyats 85, l. 3). As a result, there were numerous religious stipulations that regulated and limited contact between Zoroastrians and non-Zoroastrians.[1] Although Zoroastrian monarchs in ancient and early medieval Iran had many foreign women among their queens and concubines, including Hindus, Jews, Christians, and pagans, these women were required to accept and practice Zoroastrian purity laws so as to avoid violation of the king's ritual purity. Indeed, the Shāhnāma, "Book of Kings," states that the Sasanian monarch Wahrām V (ruled 421–439 C.E.) entrusted his bride, an Indian princess, to the high priest of the temple of Ādur Gušnāsp for purification prior to her entering his household.[2]

Hair and Nails

Hair and nails, once severed from the body, are believed to be seized by the Corpse Demoness. It is directed that hair (Av. *varəsa-;* Phl. *wars, mōy*) and nails (Av. *srū, srvā-;* Phl. *srū, nāxun*) should not be scattered upon the ground, in order to prevent pollution of the earth. The rituals for proper disposal of hair and nails are based on passages of the Vidēvdāt and probably originated in the rites of the early Zoroastrian community. The deliberate scattering of these two excrements is considered a sinful act through which a person worships the demons and produces noxious creatures, such as lice, "which devour grain in the fields" (Vidēvdāt 17: 1–3). Nails that are improperly disposed of are said to be used by the class of giant demons (Av. Māzainya daēva) as spears, knives, bows, arrows, and slingstones to attack the community (Vidēvdāt 17: 10). Hence, proper fulfillment of ritual practice was perceived as vital for social and cosmic order. Failure to complete the rites exactly as stipulated would have transformed a creative action, the burying of hair and nails, into one that threatened human beings and vegetation (cf. Lincoln 1986: 92).

In ancient times, after hair was cut and nails were pared, they were taken separately to a desolate spot at least ten paces from human beings, twenty paces from fire, thirty paces from water, and fifty paces from the consecrated bundles of barsom (Vidēvdāt 17: 4–9). For the hair, a hole ten finger-breadths deep was dug in hard earth, or twelve-finger-breadths deep in soft earth. The hair was placed in the hole and the short formula, "Then for her, through righteousness, Mazdā shall increase the plants" (Av. *at̰ ahyāi ašā mazdå urvarå vaxšat̰*), was recited (Vidēvdāt 11: 6, 17: 5).[3] Next, three, six, or nine furrows were drawn around the hole with a metal object, such as a knife, and the Ahunawar prayer was chanted a similar number of times. The formulas also functioned as spells for the cleansing of plants. The homology between hair and plants arose from the beliefs that each person is a microcosm and that every element in the body has a counterpart in nature. According to Zoroastrian doctrine, every aspect of the human body returns to nature, from whence it will be garnered at the final renovation of the universe for the creation of the final bodies of all Zoroastrians (Phl. *tan ī pasēn*).[4] The hair-plant homology appears to have been based on their morphological resemblance. Additionally, both hair and plants are characterized by incessant growth: the former on the surface of the body and the latter on the surface of the earth. Nails probably later came to be included in this homology because they also display incessant growth at the extremities of the body. The Avestan passages that refer to the disposal of nails reveal poorer development than those that discuss the disposal of hair. Nor do nails bear close morphological resemblance to plants. As Lincoln has argued, the nexus between nails and plants occurred only due to an extension of the homology between hair and plants to encompass nails (1986: 92, 206 n. 18).

For the disposal of nails, a hole was dug as deep as the first joint of the fifth digit. The nails were placed in this hole, and the short formula, "O Aša and Vohu Manah, that I may be heard before [every] adherent!" (Av. *aša vohū manaṇhā yā sruye parō magaonō*), was recited (Vidēvdāt 17: 7). This formula was theologically understood as "O Aša and Vohu Manah, the nails of the pure [are for you]!"[5] Thereafter, the person drew three, six, or nine furrows around the hole with the recitation of a similar number of Ahunawar prayers. Finally, the following formula was chanted: "O Ašō Zušta, I declare and consecrate these nails to you! May these nails be many spears, knives, bows, eagle-feathered arrows, and slingstones for you against the demons of Māzan" (Vidēvdāt 17: 9). Ašō Zušta, "Friend of Righteousness," is, according to tradition, a theological denomination of the owl. According to Zoroastrian belief, once holy words had been uttered, the nails were ingested by owls and could not be seized by demons.[6] It was believed that nails not consecrated to Ašō Zušta would be seized by demons who utilized them as weapons to attack the material world.

These rituals were elaborated during the Middle Ages. In the case of hair trimmings, the Persian Rivāyats states that the trimmings were placed in a hole with recitation of the Srōš Bāj up to the words "the righteous perceiving [one] should recite" followed by the words "Then for her through righteousness, Mazdā shall increase the plants." Three furrows were drawn around the hole while chanting three Ahunawar prayers, the *bāj* was completed, and one Ahunawar was recited, followed by the Kām Nā Mazdā prayer (Persian Rivāyats 244, ll. 7–11). Thereafter, the believer was required to wash his or her head with unconsecrated urine and water. The Rivāyats also reveals that a divergent custom had arisen in which the hair trimmings were not buried but merely deposited in a desolate spot far from fire or water (244, ll. 12–14). This practice probably resulted from an attempt to prevent any possible pollution to the earth through burial of bodily refuse. A ritualized order for paring nails also arose. First, the nail on the fourth finger, then that on the index finger, followed by the fifth fingernail, the thumbnail, and, lastly, the nail on the middle finger were pared. At each paring, one Ahunawar prayer was recited, and the nail was cut in half and placed on a piece of paper on dry ground with the tapering ends facing north. Next, the Srōš Bāj was uttered. Finally, the nails would be taken to a desolate place and buried according to standard ritual practice (Persian Rivāyats 246, l. 13–247, l. 19).

Many variant forms of these ancient and medieval practices continued into modern times. Among Irani Zoroastrians, hair trimmings and nail parings are gathered separately and placed on scraps of cloth. Furrows are drawn around these scraps with the chanting of the required holy words. Then the cloths are tied up or sewn shut, placed in another cloth, and carried in the left hand to the "place of nails" (N.P. *lard, nākhondān*), which is situated on the outskirts of the village. This structure has no door, only an opening in the flat roof and steps leading up to the opening. The parings and trimmings in the cloth are dropped into the *lard,* where they are isolated from the good creations and periodically dissolved with acid. The devotee proceeds home and purifies the body with water (Boyce 1977: 107–108). Alternatively, the nails and hair are simply placed in a metal vessel, which isolates and confines the pollution, covered with cloth, and emptied into the *lard.* In this case, however, the bearer has to undergo a threefold purification: three stones are set within a pure space marked by a furrow, and ablutions are performed with unconsecrated bull's urine on the first stone, with dust on the second stone, and with water on the third stone (Boyce 1977: 108–109). The vessel is rinsed with unconsecrated bull's urine, scoured with dust, and washed with water. In recent years, however, the threefold purification documented by Boyce has been discontinued by most Irani Zoroastrians. In the late nineteenth and early twentieth centuries, Parsis often kept an old *sudra* and *kustī* for wearing while trimming hair and paring nails. In addition, these tasks were performed while seated on an iron stool or chair so as to isolate the impurity from the environment. The hair and nails were gathered on a cloth and carefully discarded. Thereafter, the person washed the entire body with water to expel any impurity. There is evidence, however, that many devotees were negligent in these practices.[7]

During the last two decades, these rites have gradually been discarded.

Many Parsis and urban Irani Zoroastrians now visit a professional hair-dresser and pare their nails without any ritual precautions. A few orthodox Parsis and rural Irani Zoroastrians still attempt to place hair and nail trimmings in isolated places to minimize pollution to the sacred creations. Many Zoroastrians also continue the practice of bathing the entire body with water immediately after a haircut, although they now justify this in terms of physical hygiene, not demonology.

Local practices among the Muslims of Iran and Iraq reflect many of the Zoroastrian laws of purity relating to hair and nails. Natives of Basra often wrapped nail clippings in cloth and buried them after stating: "O Satan, this is a safe deposit from us as God is our witness." It was also believed that hair trimmings should be buried (Van Ess 1961: 156). These practices reflect an assimilation of Zoroastrian rituals into Islamic practice via converts to Islam in the medieval period. Among the Hindus of India, a cloth is used to catch shorn hair, which is then ritually disposed. Hair that has not been carefully discarded can pollute ritual offerings (Gonda 1980: 290). The similarities between the Zoroastrian and Hindu practices are the results of the common religious and cultural heritage of these two peoples and reflect the rites of the Indo-Europeans prior to their separation in the third and second millenniums B.C.E.

The ritual burial of hair was also practiced by the Romans (Lincoln 1977: 354–355). In Hittite religious law, hair and fingernails, once cut, were said to pollute water and human beings through contact (Pritchard 1969: 207, 209). As shown by Edmund Leach, belief in the religious, magical, and supernatural power of hair is widespread among many different societies (1958). In medieval Spain, for example, there was the practice of tonsuring candidates for the royal throne to prevent them from being perceived as legitimate heirs. This connection between hair and royal legitimacy was also present in Zoroastrian Iran where baldness was seen as an attack by the Evil Spirit upon the individual. Candidates for priesthood and kingship could not be bald at the time of their candidacy as this was a sign of their being afflicted by evil. In Vedic belief the sight of a bald person was regarded as a bad omen (Gonda 1980: 73). Thus, it is clear that, among a multitude of Indo-European cultures, hair was perceived as a sign of life, vitality, divine favor, and good augury.[8]

In one of the earliest anthropological investigations of beliefs and rituals surrounding bodily refuse, James G. Frazer concluded that such substances as hair and nails were disposed of carefully in order to prevent them from being utilized by sorcerers (1955: 267–287). Frazer's observation is not completely applicable to the treatment of hair and fingernails by Zoroastrians. In Zoroastrian belief it is not sorcerers but a class of demons—the giants—who seize this refuse and transform it into weapons with which human beings can be attacked. In addition, as Douglas has demonstrated, from the religious perspective, matter becomes impure and dangerous after traversing the boundary of the body (1969: 121–128). No longer protected by the body, it can be seized by the demons and defiled. Likewise, according to Bruce Lincoln, marginal materials, such as hair and nails, are a part of a cosmic cycle of creation, regeneration, and change (1977: 353–361; 1986: 87–98). Hair, nails, and plants are alternate shapes, or alloforms, of each other, according to Zoroastrian doctrine (Vidēvdāt 11: 6, 17: 5). They consist of the same material that temporarily assumes any one of three different forms. Thus, Lincoln argues that these three alloforms—hair, nails, and plants—are viewed as alternate stages in a process of transmutation (1986: 5, 16–17, 88–92). This process is perceived as perpetuating life and thereby reestablishing the order upon which existence depends. Lincoln (1977: 361) is incorrect, however, in arguing that only his conclusions apply to Indo-European belief and dismissing the observations by Frazer and Douglas. Indeed, the Zoroastrian example reveals that demonology, fear of external and internal boundaries, and myths of cosmic alloforms all combine in the religious perspective to explain the problems of impurity caused by hair and nails. Together they seek to resolve the tension between life and death and extend the promise of immortality.

Breath and Saliva

The emission of breath (Phl. *wād, wēn;* N.P. *bād*) and saliva (Phl. *xayūg;* N.P. *khīv*) is governed by the notion that bodily substances are open to pollution upon leaving the human body. Once outside, such substances can transmit impurity to other Zoroastrians, animals, plants, fire, earth, water, metals, and sacred instruments. Consequently, it has been believed since ancient times that air becomes excrement when exhaled and is capable of polluting all the good creations. Therefore, breath should not make contact with any sacred substances. This aspect of doctrine is hard to practice in everyday tasks but has always been strictly enforced during religious rituals. Every priest dons a mouth and nose mask prior to approaching a sacred fire or engaging in most religious rites. This mask is referred to in the Vidēvdāt, and its use dates at least to the Parthian era. The

Pahlavi commentary to the Vidēvdāt describes the structure of the mask and states that all religious rites should be performed with the "mouth and nose mask [placed] properly over the nose" (18: 1). Blowing at a flame was also believed to pollute fire with breath, and Strabo noted that Persians would never extinguish a fire or lamp in this manner (15: 3.14). These two practices have remained unchanged to the present day among both Irani and Parsi Zoroastrians (fig. 12).

Saliva once outside the body is regarded as excrement, and, as a result, a cup or vessel that has been touched to a person's lips cannot be used by anyone else until it has been cleansed by washing with water. Zoroastrians are also enjoined never to partake of a meal from a common dish as pollution could be transmitted by traces of saliva on the fingertips. Furthermore, no saliva, water, or food should be spat from the mouth onto the ground. To do so is considered a sin for which "the body was forfeit" (*tanāpuhl*) and during the Middle Ages had to be atoned for through the payment of a large fine. Xenophon noted that Cyrus II the Great (ruled 549–530 B.C.E.), founder of the Achaemenian dynasty, "trained his associates not to spit or to wipe the nose in public" (8: 1.42). This classical author also wrote that "it is a breach of decorum for a Persian to spit or to blow his nose or to appear afflicted with flatulence" (1: 2.16). Orthodox Zoroastrians in Iran and India still refrain from spitting, and most of them will not drink from a vessel used by another person or partake from a common dish. Cleansing of a used cup or vessel with water before use by another person is still scrupulously practiced by both priests and orthodox laypersons. Furthermore, many orthodox Zoroastrians prefer to use metal or glass cups and plates instead of clay or ceramic ones because metal and glass, being creations under the protection of the beneficent immortal Xšaϑra Vairya, are regarded as resistant to pollution and defilement.

Sneezing, yawning, and sighing, all of which release saliva and breath into the surroundings, used to be controlled as much as possible. At the turn of the century, Parsis often would say, "May the Evil Spirit be shattered" after sneezing or yawning because they believed that the spasm of breath in these actions was produced by Aŋra Mainyu to defile the world (Seervai and Patel 1899: 219). This practice has now been abandoned by all but elderly orthodox Zoroastrians in the towns of Navsari and Surat. The common Indo-Iranian heritage of the fears that surround breath and saliva are reflected in the Hindu requirement that holy words be uttered to dispel the evil and pollution caused by yawning and sneezing (Gonda 1980: 60, 73).

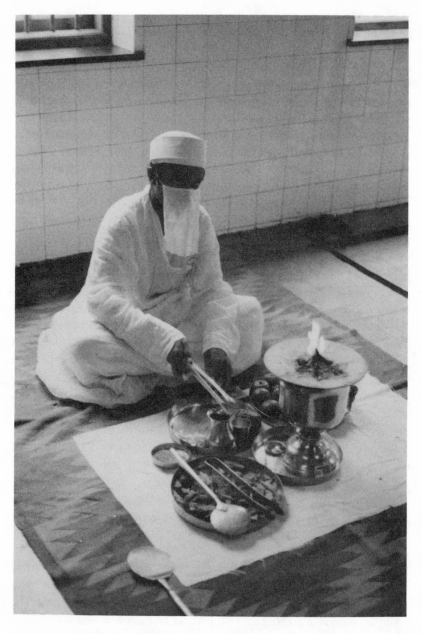

Figure 12. Priest Wearing a Mouth and Nose Mask

Urine and Feces

Zoroastrians are required to perform urination and excretion while squatting, not standing or sitting, as a ritual precaution. This practice dates to the period in which the Vidēvdāt was composed, for in that text a demoness is depicted as saying, "He is the second of my males, who, when urinating, lets it fall upon the upper forepart of his foot" (18: 40). This doctrine was elaborated during the medieval period. According to the Mēnōg ī Xrad, urination while standing is a habit of the demons (2: 39–40). The Šāyest nē Šāyest decrees that a Zoroastrian incurs a *tanāpuhl* sin for performing this deed (10: 5). In the Ardā Wīrāz Nāmag, the righteous Wīrāz is shown sinners being gnawed by noxious creatures in hell for their earthly sin of having urinated while standing (25: 106). Herodotus (1: 133), Xenophon (8: 8.11), and Ammianus Marcellinus (23: 6.79) all noted the precautions taken by Zoroastrians to prevent pollution of the good creations through urination. This ritual precaution was required because both urine and feces are waste products of food, which are liable to pollution by the demons (Bundahišn 28: 16).

The act of urination was safeguarded, and its ritual impurity limited, by ritualizing it and enclosing its performance with a *bāj*. This *bāj* is now termed the Bāj ī Gōmēz Kardan, or Abestāg pad Čamišn (Phl.), "Prayer or Avesta for Urination"; Nask ī pad Čamišn (Phl.), "Portion of the Avesta for Urination"; or Pishāb-nī Bāj (P.Gj.), "Prayer for Urination."[9] The opening part consists of the words "May the Evil [Spirit] be smitten one hundred thousand times" (Pz. *gunāh šekaste sad hazār bār*) and one Ahunawar prayer.[10] After urination, the closing part of this prayer is said at least three paces away from the place where the act was performed. It consists of three Ašəm Vohū prayers; Yasna (35: 2) repeated twice; Yasna (35: 5) repeated three times; four Ahunawar prayers; followed by Yasna (13: 8); the Yeṇhēhātąm, "Whom among the Beings" prayer; another Ašəm Vohū; and the performance of the Pādyāb-Kustī ceremony.[11] The three paces symbolically interpose the Zoroastrian creed of good thoughts, good words, and good deeds between the devotee and the source of impurity. The entire purification ritual, widely practiced by the entire community until the early 1950s, is now performed only by priests who are in a state of religioritual purity. By the late 1950s, all Zoroastrians were still required to purify themselves by washing their hands and performing at least the Pādyāb-Kustī ceremony following urination or excretion.[12] Commonly practiced by Zoroastrians in both India and Iran, and adhered to until the late 1960s by Parsis in Pakistan and Sri Lanka, the performance of this simple purificatory rite has also fallen into general disuse, with only the clergy and a few orthodox laity retaining it.[13]

The same ritual surrounded the act of defecation. In this case, however, dust and water were generally used to purify the individual upon completion of the ritual. As in the case of rites surrounding urination, this custom has been simplified. Zoroastrians now simply wash themselves with water upon finishing the ritual. Human feces can be used as fertilizer only after it has been left in the open from four to six months.[14] The use of feces from non-Zoroastrians as fertilizer was never permitted because they "do not abstain from anything, and every foul thing is mixed in their excrement" (Persian Rivāyats 38, ll. 12–17). Violation of this edict resulted in a sin for which the death penalty applied (Phl. *margarzān*). Even in the case of Zoroastrians, extra caution was enjoined if a person had been ill and passed blood in his or her feces; care was taken to ensure that the polluted feces was not used as fertilizer (Persian Rivāyats 40, ll. 6–9). Zoroastrians in Yazd, Iran, transported their feces for such use during the 1920s.[15] Few Irani or Parsi Zoroastrians still engage in extensive cultivation and now prefer to use cow dung as fertilizer. Cow dung is ritually clean because it derives from a pure animal unless the animals are owned by non-Zoroastrians. It can, therefore, be used without prior purification.

Muslims are similarly required to perform such bodily functions while squatting and to cleanse themselves with water (Qur'ān 4: 43, 5: 6). It is possible that this custom entered Islam from Zoroastrian practice. The use of dust and water for cleansing after urination and defecation is also present among the Hindus and serves a related ritual function (Carstairs 1958: 66–67, 81–82, 115–116).

Sex, Semen, and Nocturnal Pollution

Because all substances leaving the living body were regarded as polluting and ritually impure, the beneficial functions of life that involved emission of bodily substances came to be regulated by religious rules and rituals. Marriage has always been considered a positive virtue because the family unit is considered a part of the divine order of the world and because the begetting of children brings more people into the material world to do battle against the Evil Spirit and his pandemonium.[16] Therefore, sex and procreation became virtuous acts when performed by husband and wife, and semen was viewed as a pure substance in its procreating function. Celibacy was constantly discouraged, and the Vidēvdāt states: "the man who has a wife is superior to him who lives in continence" and "he who has offspring is superior to the childless man" (4: 47). Herodotus noted the practice of this belief and wrote that "every Persian marries many lawful wives, and keeps still more concubines. After valor in battle it is most reckoned as manly merit to show the greatest number of sons" (1: 135–136). Strabo also recorded the same practice (15: 3.17). By the medieval period it was decreed that every man's "second [duty] is to take a wife and to continue the lineage of the world, be diligent in it, and not forsake it" (Čīdag Handarz ī Pōryōtkēšān l. 5).[17] Polygyny persisted during the Middle Ages and was widely practiced by all classes of Zoroastrian society in both Iran and India. By the seventeenth and eighteenth centuries C.E., however, the practice had declined. European travelers to India during the eighteenth century noted that "among them, a man marries only one wife, nor ever takes a second, unless the first happens to be barren" and "[they] marry no more than one woman at the same time" (Niebuhr 1792: 430; Stavorinus 1798: 496). Polygyny is no longer practiced by either Parsi or Irani Zoroastrians.

Similarly, consanguineous marriage (Av. *xvaētvadaϑa*, Phl. *xwēdōdah*) was extolled in the religious literature by the medieval period and became a pillar of the faith. It is mentioned in the Fravarānē, where each devotee still recites: "I pledge myself to the Mazdean religion . . . which upholds consanguineous marriage" (Yasna 12: 9), although this may be a late interpolation. The original meaning of the Avestan word is unclear, but in the medieval period it became the technical term for incestuous matrimony. The Dēnkard (73, ll. 10–11; 448, l. 9–449, l. 12; 626, ll. 19–20), Dādestān ī Dēnīg (18: 1–9), and Rivāyat ī Ēmēd ī Ašawahištān (27: 2–4, 28: 1–2, 29: 5, 30: 1–2) discuss this practice.[18] There were even attempts to sanctify this practice by attributing it to Ahura Mazdā himself:

And Ahura Mazdā practices consanguineous marriage. It is revealed: When Zaraϑuštra sat in front of Ahura Mazdā, and Vohu Manah, Aša Vahišta, Xšaϑra Vairya, Haurvatāt, Amərətāt, and Spənta Ārmaiti were seated around Ahura Mazdā, Spənta Ārmaiti sat in his embrace and her hand lay upon his neck. Zaraϑuštra asked Ahura Mazdā: "Who is this who sits in your embrace and who loves you so much and is so dear to you? You who are Ahura Mazdā do not avert your sight from her, nor does she avert her sight from you. And you who are Ahura Mazdā do not release her from your arms, nor does she release you from her arms." Ahura

Mazdā replied: "This is Spənta Ārmaiti, my daughter, my house-mistress of paradise, and the mother of creation." (Pahlavi Rivāyat Accompanying the Dādestān ī Dēnīg 8: 2—4)[19]

Consanguineous marriage persisted among Zoroastrians in Iran under Muslim rule and among the Parsis in India, until they were convinced by Europeans that the practice should be abandoned. In an attempt to defend the concept of *xvaētvadaϑa*, most modern Parsis deny that con-sanguineous marriage ever occurred and interpret the practice as marriage between first cousins.[20] Nearly one-third of all marriages among both Parsi and Irani Zoroastrians are still between kin.[21]

In the Sasanian empire the dissolution of a marriage could occur at the initiative of either the husband or the wife, but usually both parties had to agree to it. The wife's agreement was not required if she was infertile or guilty of adultery (Mādayān ī Hazār Dādestān 1: 3, ll. 11—14; 1: 4, ll. 1—4). The Achaemenian practice of not divorcing a wife, except on account of adultery, once she had borne children continued under the Parthians and Sasanians and was part of the religious law governing marriage. By the late Sasanian and early Islamic periods, there were four reasons for which a man could divorce his wife: adultery, concealment from him of the fact that she was in menses, practice of sorcery, and sterility (Ṣaddar Bondahesh 33: 8—14).[22] Until the late eighteenth century, Zoroastrian men were permitted to take a second wife if the first was infertile. In 1865 the Parsis adopted the Parsi Marriage and Divorce Act (15 of 1865), accord-ing to which a divorce could be obtained only on account of "lunacy or mental unsoundness, at time of marriage, of which one of the contracting parties did not know; impotency; continual absence of one of the parties for seven years, without being heard of as alive; adultery of the wife; adul-tery, or bigamy with adultery, or adultery with cruelty, or adultery with willful desertion for two years or upwards, or rape or unnatural offense, of the husband" (ll. 27—30).

The grounds for divorce were modified by the Parsi Marriage and Di-vorce Act 3 of 1936 to permit divorce under the following conditions:

(a) that the marriage has not been consummated within one year after its solemnization owing to the wilful refusal of the defendant to consummate it; (b) that the defendant at the time of the mar-riage was of unsound mind and has been habitually so up to the date of the suit; (c) that the defendant was at the time of marriage pregnant by some person other than the plaintiff; (d) that the de-

fendant has since the marriage committed adultery or fornication
or bigamy or rape or an unnatural offence; (e) that the defendant
has since the marriage voluntarily caused grievous hurt to the
plaintiff or has infected the plaintiff with venereal disease or, where
the defendant is the husband, has compelled the wife to submit
herself to prostitution; (f) that the defendant is undergoing a sen-
tence of imprisonment for seven years or more for an offense as
defined in the Indian Penal Code; (g) that the defendant has de-
serted the plaintiff for at least three years; (h) that a decree or order
for judicial separation has been passed against the defendant, or an
order has been passed against the defendant by a Magistrate award-
ing separate maintenance to the plaintiff, and the parties have not
had marital intercourse for three years or more since such decree or
order; (i) that the defendant has failed to comply with a decree for
restitution of conjugal rights for a year or more; and (j) that the
defendant has ceased to be a Parsi." (Sec. 32)

The rules governing marriage and divorce indicate that sexual intercourse with the intent of procreation was always approved of and encouraged by religious doctrine, the clergy, and the community leaders.
However, the emission of semen during intercourse, masturbation, or
nocturnal pollution was thought to result in impurity because the semen is
seized by the Corpse Demoness. As a result, strict rules evolved to regulate
sexual intercourse and prevent the spread of impurity. A husband's con-
sorting with his wife was theoretically limited by religious law to three occasions a month if she was not pregnant (Persian Rivāyats 191, ll. 7–9).
Sexual intercourse between a man and his pregnant wife was forbidden
due to possible harm to the unborn offspring and was not permitted while
the mother suckled a child (Persian Rivāyats 190, ll. 4–9). Due to ritual
pollution that resulted from childbirth, intercourse was also forbidden for
forty days after childbirth (Persian Rivāyats 223, ll. 7–12).

Similarly, because menstruation results in a woman's losing her ritual
purity and becoming capable of spreading impurity to all those who have
contact with her, husband and wife could not have sexual intercourse for
three days after she had performed her postmenstrual ablutions. According to the Vidēvdāt, a man who "ejaculates his semen into a woman who
sees blood [i.e., is in menses], that man who has performed the deed for-
feits his body [i.e., is worthy of death]" (15: 7). The Vidēvdāt claims that
such a man does not act better than if he cooked the corpse of his own son
and offered the child's fat to the fire (16: 17).[23] In the ancient and medieval

periods a man who knowingly had sex with a woman in menses was required to atone for the sin by undergoing up to ninety lashes (Vidēvdāt 16: 13–16). This sin could also be expiated, however, by the paying of a fine, and the actual punishments were probably never inflicted due to their severity.[24] Furthermore, although such copulation was a grievous sin, it was not believed to deserve the death penalty (Rivāyat ī Ēmēd ī Ašawahištān 41: 4). The punishment for failing to expiate this sin was recorded in the Ardā Wīrāz Nāmag, where the soul of such a male sinner had impurity and menstrual discharge pour into his mouth while he cooked and ate his own offspring in hell (22: 1–7). Strict abstinence from sexual intercourse during menses was practiced by the Parsis up to the 1930s and by Irani Zoroastrians even in the 1960s.[25] The attitude of recent generations of Zoroastrians is, however, ambivalent. A few devotees abstain from intercourse during menses and purify themselves after sex, masturbation, or nocturnal pollution, but the majority have ceased to regard these acts as polluting and sinful.

Rituals surrounding sexual intercourse are described in the Persian Rivāyats and Parsi writings in Gujarati. The act of copulation is ritually protected by a prayer. The initial portion of the *bāj* consists of nine Ahunawar prayers, followed by copulation. The closing portion of the *bāj* consists of three Ašǝm Vohūs, two Yasnas (35: 2), one Ahunawar, and a line from the Yasna (13: 8), after which the husband recites a passage from the Vidēvdāt (18: 51–52).[26] Thereafter, both husband and wife must bathe to cleanse themselves of ritual impurity. In the case of a newly married couple, an initial *bāj* of eleven Ahunawars must be repeated (Persian Rivāyats 192, ll. 10–11). To the present day, orthodox priests undergo the Purification of the Nine [Days and] Nights after the marriage night, because, in addition to the impurity caused by the emission of semen, impurity can be caused by the rupture of the hymen and the resulting bleeding. Members of the laity no longer even recall this ritual exercise.

All homosexual behavior was strictly prohibited, and persons who committed sodomy were believed to be demons in both life and death (Vidēvdāt 8: 27, 32). Sodomy was said to be the worst of all possible sins created by the Evil Spirit (Mēnōg ī Xrad 36: 2).[27] Homosexuality was directly attributed to the Evil Spirit, and the sin that resulted from this sexual act became inexpiable (Vidēvdāt 1: 12, 8: 28).[28] The commentary to the Vidēvdāt states that a sodomite could be executed without trial (8: 73–74). Since the medieval period, this ruling has been mitigated, and a sodomite was merely shunned by society because his action was believed to pollute the whole world and to harm the beneficent immortals. If the sinner died unrepentant, no prayers were said for his soul, whose entry to paradise was believed to be denied (Dādestān ī Dēnīg 72: 1–75: 5). As in most religions, homosexuality continues to be regarded by Zoroastrianism as contrary to religious law. However, active ostracism of such individuals no longer occurs.

Nocturnal pollution causes loss of ritual purity because it involves the emission of semen without the purpose of procreation. A demoness, depicted in the Vidēvdāt, claims that "he is the third of my males, who ejaculates semen during his sleep" (18: 46). In order to prevent impregnation of this demoness through nocturnal pollution, the devotee is required to recite the prayers reserved for sexual intercourse. It is believed that, if these prayers are uttered, the demonic offspring will be destroyed in the demoness' womb; if not, they are born and wreak destruction in the material world. It is also recorded in the religious literature that anyone who recites the *bāj* after nocturnal pollution will receive a fifteen-year-old son in heaven (Persian Rivāyats 193, ll. 3–5). Thereafter, a purificatory bath should be undergone using water before any other tasks are performed. In addition, a person affected with nocturnal pollution must recite upon awakening a *bāj* together with the prayer of propitiation (Av. Xšnūmaine; Phl. Šnūman) dedicated to Spənta Ārmaiti, direct the semen at the earth, and then recite Vidēvdāt (18: 51–52).[29] Clothes soiled by semen should be washed first with unconsecrated bull's urine and then with water. Devotees were forbidden from casting semen on the earth. Even today, if nocturnal pollution occurs during the Barašnūm ī nō šab prior to the first Noh-Shūy ablution, the entire ritual is vitiated and must be repeated.[30] If it occurs during the *nāwar* ceremony, when a candidate is initiated into the priesthood, it is held to show that he is unworthy for admission to the clergy.[31]

Many lay Zoroastrians had begun to abandon rigid enforcement of the laws governing purity by the late nineteenth century. As a result, most Parsi and Irani Zoroastrians no longer observe the rules governing sex and nocturnal pollution. The prayers and ablutions required to regain ritual purity after sexual intercourse and nocturnal pollution are currently practiced only by priests and extremely orthodox laity.

Beliefs and practices regulating sex, semen, and nocturnal pollution are not unique to Zoroastrianism. Among the ancient Greeks, the ejaculation of semen resulted in impurity (Hesiod l. 733–734). Jews were required to bathe in water after intercourse, and priests could not touch the holy table prior to purification (Josephus 3: 262–263).[32] Men who had nocturnal pollution were also required to bathe with water (Leviticus 15: 16; Josephus 3: 263). Likewise, clothes soiled by semen had to be washed (Leviticus 15: 17).

Because a mother is ritually unclean after the birth of a child, all sexual contact with her was taboo for forty-one days in the case of a male off-spring and eighty days in the case of a female child (Leviticus 12: 2–5).

Similar religious fears resulted in the Hindus prohibiting sexual inter-course with menstruating women (Carstairs 1958: 117). Hindus believe that sexual intercourse causes pollution, and the Vedic texts enjoin purifica-tion (Gonda 1980: 284). The Sinhalese Buddhists of Sri Lanka, another Indo-European people and the descendants of northern Indian immi-grants, also regard sex as necessary and desirable, yet simultaneously pol-luting (Obeyesekere 1984: 486). Muslims are required to undergo a Ghusl, or ablution of the entire body with water, after sex or nocturnal pollution. According to al-Balādhurī, ritual ablutions were even performed after adultery (1, 491). Intercourse with lactating women (Ar. *ghila*) is permis-sible under Islamic law. Judhama b. Wahb stated: "I was there when the Prophet was with a group saying, 'I was about to prohibit the *ghila*, but I observed the Byzantines and the Persians, and saw them do it, and their children were not harmed.'"[33] This tradition (Ar. *ḥadīth*) may indicate that Zoroastrians did not strictly obey the prohibition of sexual intercourse with women who were suckling offspring. Similarly, Islamic law does not prohibit masturbation, which is regarded as preferable to illegitimate sex-ual intercourse (Musallam 1983: 32–33). Indeed, medieval Muslim jurists viewed the "spilling of semen" as a natural and necessary function of the body. However, a divergence arose between traditional Islamic rulings re-garding masturbation and the edicts of the contemporary Muslim clergy in Iran, according to which masturbation causes pollution.

Blood, Menstruation, and Childbirth

The flow of blood from the body is regarded as an attack by the demons on the perfect creation of Ahura Mazdā. Here primitive beliefs and fears surrounding blood and its power were reinforced by demonology, and elaborate rules evolved to combat the ritual impurity resulting from this dreaded pollution. Blood itself is never impure; but any flow of blood out of the body affects purity because it is a breach of the ideal physical state of human beings, and is vulnerable to pollution from the Corpse Demoness (cf. Boyce 1975: 307). Such beliefs reached their zenith amid the rigid or-thodoxy of the post-Sasanian era between the eighth and eighteenth cen-turies C.E. During the premodern period, all forms of bleeding, including wounds, cuts, sores, burns, and internal injuries, caused pollution and made the believer ritually impure (Rivāyat ī Ēmēd ī Ašawahištān 20: 4–7).

The swallowing of teeth, skin, or blood from the mouth also polluted the believer, who then had to undergo the Purification of the Nine [Days and] Nights (Persian Rivāyats 249, l. 7–250, l. 13). Because blood, once outside the body, is seized by the Corpse Demoness, bloodletting was prohibited, and violators had to undergo purification (Persian Rivāyats 251, ll. 10–17). Pollution resulting from wounds, sores, and other sources of bleeding were atoned for by performing a grace ceremony, which involved consecration of bread, or a praise ceremony (Phl. Niyāyišn; N.P. and P.Gj. Niyāyish) in honor of the gods (Persian Rivāyats 250, l. 15–251, l. 10). In addition, the source of bleeding had to be washed with unconsecrated bull's urine before water could be applied to it.

The belief that menstrual blood is dangerous is widespread among many cultures and religions. As Lévi-Strauss has noted, menstruation is viewed as jeopardizing social order, and, by extension, women are viewed as threatening universal order (1968: 182). In Zoroastrianism, menstruation (Phl. *daštān;* N.P. and P.Gj. *dashtān*) is believed to be a recurrent affliction of bleeding, which results in ritual impurity and pollution. Because blood becomes impure only after it leaves the body, Freud's rejection (1973: 7, 265–283) of the notion that there is a dread of blood that resulted in prohibitions on menstruation is not valid for Zoroastrianism. According to the Vidēvdāt, menses is a blight caused by the Evil Spirit (1: 18–19; 16: 11). The Bundahišn describes the origin of menstruation, stating that it resulted from the Evil Spirit's kissing the head of the Whore Demoness (Av. Jahikā, Jahī; Phl. Jeh; N.P. and P.Gj. Jeh) after she revived him from a three-thousand-year stupor:

> When the Evil Spirit saw that he, himself, and all the demons were powerless on account of the righteous man, he was stupefied. He lay in a stupor for three thousand years. While he was stupefied, the chief demons cackled one by one: "Arise, our father, for we will wage battle in the corporeal world [so] that Ahura Mazdā and the beneficent immortals [will suffer] distress and harm." One by one they related their own evil deeds in detail. But the accursed Evil Spirit was not comforted by this and did not rise from that stupor for fear of the righteous man, until the accursed Whore Demoness came after three thousand years. She cackled: "Arise, our father, for in that battle I will let loose so much affliction upon the righteous man and the toiling bull that, owing to my deeds, they will not be fit to live. I will steal their glory; I will harm the water, earth, fire, and plants; I will harm all the creations that Ahura Mazdā created."

She related those evil deeds in such detail that the Evil Spirit was comforted, arose from that stupor and kissed the Whore's head, [and] the pollution that is called menstruation appeared on the Whore. (4: 1–5)

According to Zoroastrian doctrine, menstruation was created in order to render human beings unfit to engage in battle against evil. The Wizīdagīhā ī Zādspram states that "when the Evil Spirit scuttled into creation, he had the irreligious brood of the Whore Demoness as [his] companion, just as a man has women of good stature. For, indeed, the Whore is a demoness; and he [the Evil Spirit] appointed the Whore Demoness lady of her brood, the chief of all the whore demonesses, the most grievous adversary of the righteous man. And he [the Evil Spirit] joined himself to the Whore Demoness of the evil religion. For the defilement of females he joined himself to her, that she might defile females, and the females, because they were defiled, might defile the males, and cause [the males] to turn away from their proper function" (34: 30–31). The Dēnkard claims that "menstruation, which is from that orifice through the satiety of that demoness, was in the entire body; and from its flow her own stench, corporeal and spiritual, also came forth" (464, ll. 11–13).

Women are created by Ahura Mazdā as opponents of the Whore Demoness. But, because the material world is in a state of mixture of good and evil, all women are afflicted with menstruation. Menses is, therefore, a phenomenon that not only is impure in itself but also renders all women impure (van Gennep 1960: 69). As a result, there arose a tendency to consider women as the polluted allies of the Evil Spirit. Indeed, the Bundahišn contains a passage in which Ahura Mazdā addresses women, saying: "I created you, whose adversary is the Whore species. You were created with a mouth close to your buttocks, and copulation seems to you just as the taste of the sweetest food [is] to the mouth. And you are a helper to me, for man is born from you. But you grieve me, who am Ahura Mazdā. If I had found another garment from which to create man, never would I have created you whose adversary is the whore species" (14a: 1). There is little evidence that this belief represented the general Zoroastrian attitude toward women during the ancient period. Zoroaster himself is presented in the Gāthās pleading: "Whoever, man or woman, will grant me those things which you, Ahura Mazdā, know as best for life—the recompense for truth and the authority of good thought—with [him or her], and all those [individuals] who I bring for your veneration, I shall cross the Bridge of the Separator" (Yasna 46: 10). Furthermore, women were specifically created by Ahura Mazdā to aid him in the battle against corporeal evil.[34] The implied condemnation of sexual intercourse in the Bundahišn is also inconsistent with Zoroastrian practices.

By the early Middle Ages, however, the view of woman as an admixture of good and evil had arisen in Zoroastrian beliefs. Hence, statements attributed to Ādurbād, the son of Māraspand and a high priest during the reign of Shāpūr II (ruled 309–379 C.E.), extol the virtues of modest women while advising men never to place their trust in women or to share secrets with them (Pahlavi Texts 59, ll. 6–7; 62, ll. 3–7, 9–10; 149, ll. 10–12). It appears that with the elaboration of beliefs and practices on ritual purity and pollution, menstruation came to be regarded as a major source of pollution in the material world. Women as the physical source of menstrual pollution became, by extension, inferior, sinful, and evil.[35] Perhaps the influence of Nestorian Christianity on Iranian society during the medieval period reinforced Zoroastrian misogyny. Indeed, the view of woman as an instrument of the devil, both inferior and evil, also developed during the earliest period of the Christian Church, originating in the writings of St. Paul. The ascetic and monastic traditions of Christianity, in both Europe and the Near East, during this period furthered the belief that woman was the supreme temptress (L. *janua diaboli*) (Power 1975: 14–16).

According to Zoroastrian practice during the ancient and medieval periods, at the onset of menses every woman donned garments reserved solely for these occasions. She was then required to withdraw fifteen paces from fire, water, and barsom twigs and three paces from other Zoroastrians; only at these distances did her presence not cause pollution (Vidēvdāt 16: 4; Šāyest nē Šāyest 3: 11).[36] The place in which a woman spent her menses was called the "place for menstruating women" (Phl. *daštānestān,* D. *ganza-i punidun*), usually a small building that had no windows and only a single entrance.[37] During the period of menstruation, a woman's gaze was believed to be capable of pollution as far as her eye could see, and it could pollute sun, moon, sky, earth, water, fire, plants, animals, human beings, and sacred instruments (Ardā Wīrāz Nāmag 72: 4–8; Šāyest nē Šāyest 3: 10; Dēnkard 21, ll. 1–16; Persian Rivāyats 205, l. 18–207, l. 3).[38] The efficacy of every purification ritual was also vitiated by her gaze. As discerned by van Gennep, sight was regarded as a form of contact and could transmit impurity (1960: 32). Similarly, everything she touched, including ash and cow dung, became defiled.

Any Zoroastrian who had contact with a menstruating woman was required to purify himself or herself with unconsecrated bull's urine and water. Sexual intercourse during menses was strictly forbidden. An infant

who had to be suckled could remain with the mother but was required to
undergo ritual ablutions once the woman's menses was over. Likewise, the
approach of such a defiled woman near any of the sacred creations was
believed to render them impure. The Ardā Wīrāz Nāmag describes the fate
of a woman condemned in hell to eat the impurity and filth of men for
approaching fire and water during menses (20: 1–5). During her period, a
woman also could not prepare any food, since everything she touched became polluted; the souls of women who transgressed this rule were said to
suffer punishment in deepest hell (Ardā Wīrāz Nāmag 76: 1–9). Even her
voice was held to be capable of polluting a righteous person. She was required to eat sparingly, and food would be served to her on a metal plate
to limit the spread of impurity. Prior to eating, she had to wash her hands
with unconsecrated urine and don special gloves. Originally, women in
menses were required to wear the sacred girdle and undershirt and to perform the simple Kustī ceremony. However, as previously discussed, orthodox women in menses no longer perform Pādyāb-Kustī or the simple
Kustī ceremony because they are "without prayer."[39]

After the end of menstruation, a woman usually had to pass one more
day in retreat, after which she would recite the Srōš Bāj and purify her
entire body three times with unconsecrated bull's urine and water.[40] The
clothes worn during menses were also washed with unconsecrated urine
and water. It was recommended that she slay many noxious creatures, such
as ants, and recite the Petīt Pašēmānīh for the expiation of her sins. When
menstruation ceased at menopause, a woman was required to have priests
perform a Davāzdah Hamast, or celebration of twelve (to thirty-three)
Vidēvdāt ceremonies devoted to the seven beneficent immortals and the
deities who represent such natural phenomena as water, sun, moon, stars,
and wind (Persian Rivāyats 219, l. 12–220, l. 19).[41]

These practices were preserved by the early Parsi settlers in India and
are reflected in both the Sanskrit slokas of Ākā Adhyāru and the Qeṣṣa-i
Sanjan, "Story of Sanjan," which deal with the Parsi migration to India.[42]
Many of the rules for menses were obeyed by Parsi women during the early
part of the present century. There were no longer separate *daštānestāns*, but
the women would retreat to an isolated room in the home and spend their
menses in solitude (Modi 1922: 174–175). Most families kept an iron bed
and separate bedding for the occasion, and the women wore garments reserved for such periods. The women did not perform any work during this
time, and meals were supplied to them from a distance. Purification after
completing menstruation was enforced, but these baths also usually occurred within the home. By the end of the nineteenth century, however,

the Petīt Pašēmānīh and the Davāzdah Hamast were no longer performed. During the last two decades, as a result of increased secularization, these ritual practices have ceased to be enforced. Most Parsi women now socialize during menses, wear no special clothing, and bathe directly with water. Only a few orthdox elderly women still maintain the practice of staying at home. Some women do keep a separate set of garments to wear only during menstruation. Priests, however, in order to ensure religioritual purity, refrain from all contact with women in menses and strictly obey the prohibition on sexual intercourse during menses. Most Parsi women do not visit fire temples during menstruation, for it is still believed that their presence would defile the sacred fires and vitiate religious rituals.

In Iran during the 1960s, segregation of women during menses was still enforced, but not as vigorously as in the past when the woman had to enter the *ganza-i punidun* (Boyce 1977: 100–107). Special clothing is still occasionally kept for these times, the feet are shod to protect the earth from pollution, and women withdraw to an isolated corner of the home for the first three days of menstruation. These women, however, no longer follow the injunction for silence, and conversation now occurs freely (Boyce 1977: 102). Women in menses still may not prepare any food and must eat simple meals from a metal dish. Such women may leave the house after the third day but should not approach fire or water.

During the seventeenth century, variations of the Barašnūm ī nō šab were adapted for the purification of menstruating women. As a result, threefold ablutions based on the Purification of the Nine [Days and] Nights are usually performed for women on the first, third, and seventh days of menses, although the second ablution can also be performed on the fourth or fifth day. In all cases these ritual ablutions must be performed during the daylight hours, most often in the open behind a screen (Boyce 1977: 103–104). After each such ablution the woman dons a clean set of clothing, and the used clothes are washed in a bowl by a ritually clean woman or girl. Nonsuckling infants are also still kept away from mothers during this time, and such women do not visit fire temples or religious shrines. Although rituals for expiation of the sins that result from menses are no longer performed by Irani Zoroastrians, many orthodox women undergo the Purification of the Nine [Days and] Nights, especially after menopause, to ensure their return to a state of ritual purity (Boyce 1977: 106).

Childbirth also results in ritual impurity to both the mother and the child. The Vidēvdāt states that after childbirth or miscarriage the mother had to remain in seclusion, thirty paces away from fire, water, and barsom twigs, and three paces away from other people for twelve days (5: 45–62, 7: 60–72). This period of confinement was extended in the Middle Ages to forty days (Šāyest nē Šāyest 3: 15; Persian Rivāyats 223, ll. 7–12). Most of the rules for isolation of a menstruating woman were followed during this retreat: she could not contact anything or anyone, for anything she touched became polluted; her meals were served to her from a distance in a metal bowl; and she could not bathe for twenty-one days. Sexual intercourse was also prohibited during this forty-day period (Persian Rivāyats 223, ll. 7–12), although a variant practice enforced this prohibition for four months and ten days (Persian Rivāyats 190, ll. 18–19). All Zoroastrians were thought to be polluted by impurities of birth and their mother's milk, which was believed to derive from blood, and, hence, were required by religious law to undergo at least one Barašnūm ī nō šab to purify their body. It was held that, unless this purification had been undergone, the soul could not enter paradise until his or her son or legal heir had a Barašnūm ī nō šab performed vicariously in memory of the departed soul. During the Middle Ages, each mother was required to wash her body with unconsecrated bull's urine, followed by three washings with water at the end of the forty-day period of impurity. Only after this was she once again ritually pure and fit to reenter the community.

Although the process of birth brings more Zoroastrians into the material world to engage in battle against Aŋra Mainyu and his demons, birth had no place in the perfect world created by Ahura Mazdā prior to the invasion of the world by the Evil Spirit and will be unknown after the final renovation of the universe. Birth thus belongs to the world only in its present state of mixture and can be considered at least partly a result of the demonic forces (Boyce 1975: 308). Indeed, menstruation and childbirth are regulated by the same fears, prohibitions, and ordinances. Zoroastrians, like the ancient Greeks, regard menstruation and childbirth to be processes of a similar nature: "From one aspect the woman who may not be approached is inviolable, holy; from another aspect she is polluted, unclean. . . . And hence in patriarchal society, after woman has lost her control of religion, it is the negative aspect that prevails" (Thompson 1949: 205).

Among the Parsis, the forty-day confinement period was strictly maintained until the early decades of this century unless the woman was ill (Karaka 1884: I, 156–159; Modi 1922: 6). However, the ablutions with urine and water were modified, and women underwent merely a Sī-Shūy Nāhn forty days after accouchement. At present, Parsi women usually do not undergo the forty-day confinement. Furthermore, the Sī-Shūy Nāhn is no longer administered for purification after childbirth; most women simply undergo the Saḍe Nāhn. Even the generally conservative Irani Zoroas-trians are now lax in the enforcement of the rules of purification after childbirth. Most Zoroastrians do, however, keep a lamp or fire burning in the house for three days after childbirth, because of the belief that light dispels the evil forces that lurk in the dark seeking to harm the child.

Miscarriage and stillbirths are graver sources of contamination, because the mother has borne carrion within her womb. Zoroastrian women un-derwent prolonged and rigorous purification during the premodern pe-riod in order to cleanse such extensive ritual impurity. As in the case of women after accouchement, those who miscarried or had stillbirths were required to enter seclusion at a minimum distance of thirty paces from fire and water and three paces from other Zoroastrians (Vidēvdāt 5: 46–49). A woman was not permitted to drink water during the first three days of seclusion unless lack of it threatened her life; instead, she had to consume *nīrang*. The drinking of this liquid was essential for purification of the "fu-nerary tower" that had been created within her body by the dead infant (Vidēvdāt 5: 50–54; Ṣaddar Nasr 77: 1–2; Persian Rivāyats 227, l. 19–233, l. 9). During these three days she was not permitted to consume any meat cooked in water. Cereals and nonjuicy fruits could be eaten, but only if they had not been cooked in water. On the fourth day, she was led to a desolate place where she had to undress and bury her clothes, wash her body with *gōmēz*, and then drink *nīrang*.[43] Thereafter, she was permitted to drink water and eat meat and bread but had to continue her seclusion until the forty-day period was complete.[44] On the day after the period of isolation, the woman had to undergo the Barašnūm ī nō šab ritual, after which she returned to complete ritual purity and could perform all her re-ligious and social duties. Abortion was forbidden because it involved death of a living being.

Zoroastrian practices surrounding menses, childbirth, and miscarriage are rites of both passage and purification. First, the woman is separated from the community to prevent spread of the impurity. Thereafter, she goes through a transitional phase in which purification occurs and social barriers are gradually eliminated. Finally, she is reintegrated into ordinary life. The general outlines of these rites do conform to the scheme outlined by van Gennep (1960: 44), with variations peculiar to the faith itself.

The decline in adherence to the rites of purity surrounding childbirth, miscarriage, and stillbirth during the twentieth century is directly related to an attenuation in fears of the impurity caused by blood and vaginal dis-charges. The rapid urbanization undergone by Zoroastrians in both India and Iran during the past two hundred years has resulted in these prohibitions being considered primitive, antiquated, and unfit for a modern community. Hence, the changing position of Zoroastrian women can be seen in dual terms: on one hand, as an erosion of the ideology that justified isolation and segregation of women in order to maintain purity and, on the other hand, as an attenuation in the means of enforcing laws of purity in modern urbanized societies.

Rituals for purification after menses and childbirth are not unique to Zoroastrianism. Hindu women are still considered unclean, impure, and inferior due to menses and childbirth (cf. Carstairs 1958: 195; van Gennep 1960: 42–43; Stevenson 1971: 11–17). Their touch can contaminate other devotees. A woman in menses is unclean for three days (Gonda 1980: 32). On these three days she should not have any contact with Brahman priests and ritual fires, should not gaze at the sun, moon, and planets, and should not perform routine household activities (Gonda 1980: 78, 88, 157, 309, 402). Purity is regained only after a ritual ablution with water four days after menstruation has ceased (Gonda 1980: 45, 75, 96). The period of seclusion after childbirth lasts forty days, during which a Hindu woman cannot have any contact with her family, the community, the hearth fire, or the cooking utensils (Carstairs 1958: 63, 72–73). All persons who have had contact with such women are also required to undergo ritual ablutions. Similarly, among the Sinhalese Buddhists of Sri Lanka, pollution arising from menstruation and childbirth is held to be capable of defiling the entire family and any religious sites that are visited. Consequently, these women are secluded (Obeyesekere 1984: 15, 386–387, 456).

Among Muslims, menses (Ar. *ḥaiḍ*) is considered a periodic pollution. The Ghusl has to be performed a minimum of three days and a maximum of ten days after the onset of menstruation. The practice was attributed to the prophet Muḥammad, and his youngest wife, ʿĀʾisha, is reported as having said: "A woman asked the prophet as to her bathing after menstruation, so he told [her] how to take a bath" (al-Bukhārī 6: 13). This ablution also has to be performed after childbirth (Ar. *nifās*). Muslim women, like their Zoroastrian counterparts, are exempt from prayer during menses and puerperium. However, in Islamic law there are few other prohibitions against women in menses. The prophet Muḥammad himself is supposed to have commented: "Do everything except sexual intercourse" (at-Tibrīzī 3: 12). In Shīʿīte belief, blood is one of the items that cause ritual uncleanness (Ar. and N.P. *najas*); the other items are feces, urine, and the touch of a nonbeliever. These Shīʿīte beliefs parallel those of the Zoroastrians, and their development in Iran represents a continuation, among the Irani Muslims, of the Zoroastrian beliefs.

Under Jewish religious law, all women in menses had to remain secluded for seven days and then ritually wash their bodies and clothes (Heb. *miqvah*). On the eighth day, each woman would proceed to the temple with two young pigeons or turtledoves as sin and burnt offerings of atonement. Anyone who touched her while she was unclean became polluted and had to wash both body and clothes. Similarly, a man who had sexual intercourse with a menstruating woman became ritually unclean for seven days (Leviticus 15: 19–30). Women were also forbidden from visiting the temple during their monthly period (Neusner 1973: 41). Likewise, bleeding caused by wounds, sores, and cuts also rendered a Jew ritually unclean (Leviticus 15: 2–3). Yet, the stipulations of the Muslim and Jewish communities were never as elaborate as those of the Zoroastrians. The cross-cultural fears that surrounded menses and childbirth reflected a widespread notion that the discharge of blood violated the established physical order. From the religious viewpoint, it also symbolized possible disruption of human social order. As a result, attempts were made through doctrines and ritual prohibitions to control and regulate this danger.

Dietary Rules

Zoroastrian dietary rules have always been based on the beliefs and laws of purity and pollution. As previously discussed, all living beings were divided, by the medieval period, into ahuric, or beneficent, creatures, daēvic, or evil, creatures, and creatures whose evil had been neutralized by Ahura Mazdā for the advantage of all beings.[45] Dietary restrictions were formulated in accordance with the three classes of creatures. The flesh and products of ahuric beings could be consumed, those of daēvic beings were prohibited, and those of some beings from the third category were reluctantly permitted because many Zoroastrians often consumed them.

Every ahuric animal and plant had to be assisted in its growth and could not be damaged, slaughtered, or cut down prior to maturation (Persian Rivāyats 76, ll. 6–7). Only after they were full grown could these creatures be slain for consumption or other uses. Prior to ritual slaughter, beneficent creatures had to be stunned with a log or blunt instrument, and their flesh was to be consumed only by Zoroastrians. Nor could these creatures be tormented or overburdened with labor. The belief that beneficent animals should be protected from harm did, however, result in the practice of vegetarianism by certain Zoroastrians during the medieval period. Traces of such a practice can be inferred from passages in the Pahlavi texts that state that abstaining from consumption of the flesh of animals increases an individual's virtue.[46] This practice is continued to the present day by many Parsis and reinforced by Hindu vegetarianism. According to orthodox Zoroastrian belief, however, all beneficent animals and plants were created for the welfare of human beings. Therefore, the flesh of any such creature except the dog, which has pride of place after human beings among Ahura Mazdā's creations, and the cock, which is the bird of the deity Sraoša and dispels the night by crowing, may be consumed.[47] Little variation has occurred in the consumption of beneficent creatures from medieval to modern times. However, most Zoroastrians no longer ritually slaughter animals but purchase meats from butchers (cf. Boyce 1977: 98). As a result, the stipulation that a creature be stunned prior to slaughter cannot be enforced.

In the ancient and early medieval periods, all daēvic creatures, being noxious, could not be eaten under any circumstances (Dēnkard 446, ll. 20–22). Consumption of noxious creatures instantly rendered a devotee unclean. In time, however, this ritual prohibition underwent attenuation, and present-day Zoroastrians freely consume all foods they desire, including the flesh and products of several noxious creatures. For example, shrimp, crab, and frog legs are consumed by Parsi and Irani Zoroastrians, although all these creatures belong to the daēvic class (cf. Bundahišn 22: 9–10). Indeed, according to the Bundahišn, the crab and frog are two noxious creatures whose physical forms Aŋra Mainyu himself can assume (27: 11).

Consumption of products from the third category of beings, noxious creatures that had been rendered useful by Ahura Mazdā, was also liberalized by the late medieval period. Consequently, there are no prohibitions on laypersons eating the flesh and products of these creatures. The main item from this category consumed by Zoroastrians is honey. However, in both medieval and modern belief, only laypersons may consume honey; priests who do so lose their ritual purity (Persian Rivāyats 268, ll. 4–10).

Personal Property

Maintenance of purity of body and soul involves ensuring that all personal possessions, both immovable and movable, are safe from defilement. If polluted, these possessions must promptly be returned to a state of ritual purity. Personal possessions can be polluted in numerous ways during daily life. Impure objects can, in turn, spread their pollution to the individual. There are elaborate rules for determining whether or not an object has been made unclean and rites for purifying them.

The death of a human being or dog within a house results in carrion from the corpse polluting the house. If the abode was an immovable one, it was cleansed by fumigating and perfuming it with fragrant woods, such as pomegranate, sandalwood, benzoin, or aloe (Vidēvdāt 8: 2). If the abode was a tent, its inhabitants were required to dismantle and fumigate it with the same woods (Vidēvdāt 8: 3). Fumigation of houses to drive away the Corpse Demoness and her allies was continued during the medieval period. It was observed by Muslim writers several centuries after the Arab conquest of Iran. Fire was not brought back into such a dwelling for a period of nine nights in winter and one month in summer to prevent defilement of this sacred creation (Vidēvdāt 5: 42). The medieval Persian Rivāyats vary with respect to this practice. The area of a house in which a person died was occasionally said to be polluted for up to one year, and anyone who entered the area had to wash body and clothes (Persian Rivāyats 124, ll. 10–14; 125, ll. 9–19). More frequently, however, the original prescriptions of the Vidēvdāt were maintained (Persian Rivāyats 138, ll. 1–15). In modern Zoroastrian practice, the area of a house in which a corpse was placed on marble slabs, prior to being taken to a funerary tower, is sprinkled with unconsecrated bull's urine to purify it. This represents a continuation of a practice that arose during the fourteenth century C.E. A small fire is also kept burning in the house to drive away the demons of death. The Zoroastrian practice of cleansing the home after a death has a parallel among the Jews, for the book of Numbers states: "This is the law, when a man dies in a tent: all that come into the tent, and all that is in the tent shall be unclean seven days. . . . And a clean person shall take hyssop, and dip it in the water, and sprinkle it upon the tent, and upon all the vessels, and upon the persons that were there, and upon him that touched a bone, or one slain, or one dead, or a grave" (19: 14–18).

During ancient and medieval times, land defiled by carrion had to remain fallow and untrespassed on for one year (Vidēvdāt 6: 1–2). Violation of this rule resulted in a mortal sin. Carrion discovered on such land could be disposed of only after the rite of *sagdīd* had been performed (Persian Rivāyats 90, ll. 7–10). Carrion spotted on land that belonged to non-Zoroastrians was also to be removed. Since it was possible that Zoroastrians would not be permitted to perform *sagdīd* at such sites, it was permissible to remove the carrion without this rite. Similarly, carrion on a roadway could be moved without *sagdīd* or *paywand* if necessary. Fields had to be examined three times prior to cultivation or irrigation to ensure that no pollution was present (Persian Rivāyats 89, ll. 6–10). When standing water became defiled by a corpse, it usually was regarded as unclean until the pollutant was expunged. Only after the corpse had been removed and one-fifth to one-half of the water had been drawn off could the remaining water be utilized (Vidēvdāt 6: 32; Šāyest nē Šāyest 2: 78). But, according to the Rivāyat ī Ēmēd ī Ašawahištān, water polluted with any form of carrion or excrement could not be used for one year after the pollutant was removed (36: 5). In the case of a river, stream, or irrigation canal, the water was considered polluted for three feet downstream, nine feet upstream, and six feet across from the spot where the carrion lay (Vidēvdāt 6: 40; Šāyest nē Šāyest 2: 77). Removal of the carrion returned flowing water to a state of ritual purity. The carrion could be removed from water only by two Zoroastrians united with *paywand,* each holding one end of the *kustī,* and with the recitation of the Srōš Bāj to drive away the demons.

Fire, too, had to be protected from pollution. If a death occurred near a fire, the fire was carried at least three steps away from the corpse. To place a fire within three steps of a corpse is a grievous sin, and, if the flame reaches the dead body, a mortal sin is incurred (Šāyest nē Šāyest 2: 38–40). The precautions relating to purity of land, water, and fire are still observed in detail by most Zoroastrians. This is especially true when the land, water, or fire is in the possession of a devotee. However, because they no longer have the political authority to enforce their religious stipulations upon other communities, Zoroastrians are compelled to accept, as inevitable, pollution of the environment by nonbelievers.

Bedding that has come into contact with a corpse also becomes unclean. Any bedding directly soiled by blood, semen, urine, or dirt from a corpse used to be ripped and buried to prevent pollution from spreading. The rest of the bedding would be cleansed three times with unconsecrated bull's urine, dust, and water and then exposed to sunlight for six months before it was used (Vidēvdāt 7: 13–15; Šāyest nē Šāyest 2: 95–99). The same practice was used to purify all types of clothing defiled by carrion. In the Persian Rivāyats (136, ll. 7–9), use of dust to clean clothes is not mentioned, indicating that by the fourteenth century c.e. clothes were simply washed in unconsecrated urine and water and then placed in sunlight for a six-month purification. These practices are no longer strictly maintained by most Zoroastrians, who simply wash defiled clothes directly in water and dry them in sunlight for a few hours.

Corn and fodder polluted by carrion could be cleansed, according to the Vidēvdāt (7: 32–35), by sprinkling water on them. By the medieval period more elaborate precautions had been enacted, and the portion of corn or fodder directly in contact with the pollutant had to be discarded (Persian Rivāyats 83, ll. 7–11; 129, ll. 12–17). This practice has been maintained by both Parsi and Irani Zoroastrians. No Zoroastrian consumes any food made ritually unclean through carrion or excrement but promptly discards it. Likewise, all the prepared food in a house where a death occurred was originally considered unclean and had to be discarded. Unprepared foods did not have to be discarded as they returned to a state of purity after nine days in winter and one month in summer (Šāyest nē Šāyest 2: 41). This rule was relaxed by the late medieval period, and only prepared food within three paces of a corpse was held to be unclean (Persian Rivāyats 137, ll. 3–4). In addition, certain foods, such as bread, were said to be ritually clean from all impurities once prepared. Likewise, pollutants that touched a container in which wine or oil was stored did not make the contents unclean. The exception to this rule was clarified butter, which is believed to permeate its container. The stipulations on prepared and unprepared foods are still observed by most Zoroastrians within their own homes. But, since many members of the community now purchase prepared foods from nonbelievers, they are often exposed to ritual pollution through consumption.

Many texts dealing with purity and pollution also contain detailed instructions for the purification of utensils and instruments that have become unclean. Such instruments and utensils are usually cleansed with unconsecrated urine, dust, and water. The number of cleansings each utensil or instrument has to undergo depends on the substance from which it is made. Because the resistance of a substance to pollution is based on the hierarchy of metals, the number of ablutions stipulated varies with the material involved. Gold should be washed once, silver twice, copper, tin, brass, and lead thrice, steel four times, and stone six times with the three purificatory substances. But earth, wood, and clay once polluted are impure forever, and utensils made from these materials have to be discarded if they become unclean. Hindu practice, once again, is similar, and items made of gold, silver, and stone can be purified from defilement, but those of clay and wood cannot. In addition, Zoroastrian law, paralleling Jewish practice (Numbers 19: 15), regards open vessels near a corpse or other forms of carrion as ritually unclean.

Corpse Bearers

Human corpses require special precautions and rituals because they can cause extensive pollution. In order to prevent spread of pollution and attack by the Corpse Demoness, a special class of persons arose whose profession involves transport of corpses to funerary towers. These individuals are termed corpse bearers (Av. *nasu.kaša, iristō.kaša;* Phl., N.P., and P.Gj. *nasā-sālār*). In order to limit their contact with carrion and prevent the impurity from spreading to other members of the community, corpse bearers are required to follow strict rules when disposing of a corpse. It is believed that no one should ever carry a corpse alone; anyone who does so is rendered ritually impure forever by the Corpse Demoness (Vidēvdāt 3: 14). A minimum of two corpse bearers are required for the transportation of a corpse to a funerary tower, and these bearers maintain contact, *paywand,* with each other via a cloth or sacred girdle to enhance their ritual protection against the Corpse Demoness.[48] If contact is broken at any time during the funeral ceremony, the corpse bearers become polluted. Men, women in menses or who have miscarried or had a stillborn child, men and women together, or boys over the age of eight may serve as corpse bearers.[49] If more than two corpse bearers are required to lift the corpse, they should be in multiples of two: four, six, or eight. If at the time of a death only one Zoroastrian is present and available to perform the funeral service, then it is permissible for him or her to act as the sole corpse bearer only if contact is maintained with a dog; if a dog is not available, help must be sought from other Zoroastrians for transport of the corpse to the funerary tower. The Vidēvdāt enjoins that these persons perform their work naked, probably to reduce the spread of impurity via soiled clothing (8: 10), but corpse bearers later donned special clothing to prevent direct contact between their bodies and the corpse, for they had to undergo the Barašnūm ī nō šab if their exposed limbs or body touched the flesh of a corpse (Persian Rivāyats 109, ll. 11–17).

Because the disposal of corpses involved extended contact with carrion, non-Zoroastrians, who are considered naturally unclean, were occasionally employed in medieval Iran as corpse bearers (Persian Rivāyats 144, ll. 8–17). This practice is, however, usually condemned because non-Zoroastrians, since they do not observe the laws of purity, might pollute water and fire by approaching these creations without first purifying themselves in the prescribed manner after the funeral. Indeed, any Zoroastrian who employed a nonbeliever for this purpose was held responsible for any sin committed. Today, corpse bearers must always be Zoroastrians who can properly control the spread of impurity through strict observance of the laws of purity and pollution.

Before a corpse is moved, it must be seen by a dog, as mentioned in chapter 1. The gaze of a dog, *sagdīd,* or bird of prey is held to be purifying as it is believed to drive away the Corpse Demoness and, consequently, reduce the impurity. If the corpse is moved before *sagdīd* is performed, the corpse bearers become unclean and incur a *tanāpuhl* sin (Šāyest nē Šāyest 2: 65–71, 10: 33; Persian Rivāyats 144, l. 19–145, l. 5). Next, the Srōš Bāj, essential for smiting this demoness, is recited to provide the ritual power of holy words. Thereafter, the Dastūrī is recited by the corpse bearers in suppressed tone to obtain permission from Ahura Mazdā, the other deities, important priests of the past, and the present high priest (P.Gj. *dastūr*) to perform the task. The corpse is then carried to the funeral tower in an iron bier because metal, being a creation of the beneficent immortal Xšaϑra Vairya, is less susceptible to impurity than most other substances. Once the corpse is placed within the funerary tower, the Srōš Bāj is completed. If either corpse bearer speaks aloud before the *bāj* is completed, its protective powers are vitiated and both corpse bearers lose their purity. After the funeral, both corpse bearers retreat to a Barašnūm-Gāh near the funerary tower, undress, wash their bodies three times with unconsecrated bull's urine and water, and then don clean clothes. Only after such purification may they return to their homes.[50] The clothing used during funeral services, being soiled through contact with carrion, must be cleansed six times with unconsecrated bull's urine, dust, and water and then exposed to the air for six months (Vidēvdāt 7: 15). These soiled clothes were originally unfit for use by persons other than corpse bearers or women in menses (Vidēvdāt 7: 19). This strict requirement was modified during later centuries, and such clothes were often kept by corpse bearers solely for their professional work (Persian Rivāyats 237, ll. 3–5). This practice is followed to the present day, but the garments are now washed only in water. Corpse bearers presently wear white clothes kept solely for this task. All the required precautions are still taken, except that the corpse bearers no longer wash their entire bodies with unconsecrated urine; instead, only the exposed parts of the body are purified through the Pādyāb ritual followed by the retying of the sacred girdle. Thereafter, they recite the confessional prayer and bathe with water. In premodern times, all Zoroastrian laity present at a funeral were also required to wash their bodies with unconsecrated bull's urine and water. Now, however, only water is used in these ablutions.

Social interaction between corpse bearers and the rest of the Zoroastrian community has varied in extent at different places and times. In India, corpse bearers and their families usually lived apart from the rest of the community, often on the premises in which a funerary tower was situated; this practice has waned during the twentieth century, but many families continue this practice. Because corpse bearers, and through them their families, are constantly exposed to the most serious form of ritual pollution, they tend to be shunned by the rest of the community and live within their own social class. Originally, corpse bearers were not permitted to enter fire temples unless they had undergone the Purification of the Nine [Days and] Nights; this rule has been modified in India and Pakistan, and corpse bearers now need undergo only the Saḍe Nāhn purification prior to entering a fire temple. Corpse bearers also are not welcome on such auspicious occasions as marriages, births, and the ceremony of initiation into the faith. At Zoroastrian villages in Yazd, corpse bearers are now permitted to attend all the annual religious feasts (Phl. and N.P. *gāhānbār;* P.Gj. *gāhāmbār*), although they are served their food apart from the rest of the community; Parsis no longer require such separation (cf. Jackson 1906: 392). Prior to the 1960s, corpse bearers in Iran would often partake of their meals apart from their families. At Navsari, during the early part of the twentieth century, corpse bearers were not permitted to tend the hearth fire, light a lamp, or till the soil lest they pollute these sacred creations.[51] Such restrictions and social ostracism have resulted in many children of corpse bearers shunning the occupation of their fathers and choosing secular employment. As a result there is an increasing scarcity of corpse bearers within both Parsi and Irani Zoroastrian communities. Corpse bearers also generally tend to be underpaid, another factor that has contributed to their diminishing numbers as many seek other forms of employment. Attrition in the number of corpse bearers continues to the present despite the relaxation of social restrictions.

5 PURITY, SYMBOLS, AND ESCHATOLOGY

*Neither a mythology nor a code of ethics constitutes the
inner core of a religion. This is rather to be found in the
ritual, in those symbolical actions which figure forth
the religious message which, in the case of Zoroastrianism
as of Christianity, is the promise of immortality.*
—ROBERT C. ZAEHNER

RITUALS, BELIEFS, and religious doctrines would serve
a limited function unless they possessed and communicated ideas to the
individuals who espoused and performed them. The phenomena of religion and ritual appear to be organized mentally, physically, culturally, and,
ultimately, spiritually around the form of human perception known as
"meaning." Meaning is not, of course, an intangible, for it is usually comprehended in relationship to conventions of culture. In the context of the
cultural parameters of religious belief, meaning becomes a perception of
symbolic images and their interrelationships.[1] Homologies arise from the
symbolic association of objects, natural phenomena, or aspects of nature
and life. Such homologies are usually based on a similarity in meaning or
form and are, in turn, attributed to the common religious origin. Similarly, through symbols that equate them to one another, objects come to
be regarded as alternate forms of each other in a continuous cosmic process whereby one is transformed into the other (cf. Lincoln 1986: 5). Microcosm is viewed, consequently, as an alloform of the macrocosm, matter
as an alloform of spirit, and humanity as a corporeal alloform of the divine.
Because of such alloformic association in meaning, through homology and
analogy, Zoroastrians perceive no disjunction between the tangible activities of rituals and the symbolic meanings of these activities, just as they see
no dichotomy between the material and the spiritual states.[2] As a result of
this cosmic interconnection ultimately based on meaning, the importance
of each Zoroastrian rite lies in a fusion of actions, liturgies, and beliefs
with religious symbols. Indeed, as will be demonstrated, Zoroastrian
sources often indicate the symbolic meanings that underlie ritual practices.
It is the meaning or belief accompanying a ritual, transmitted to the vo-

taries by symbols, rather than the sole quality of the ritual itself, that is important. As Robert C. Zaehner rightly perceived, the Zoroastrian religious system, by means of ritual, provides each adherent with knowledge of the essential conditions by which life must be lived (1976: 119). In other words, the concepts of purity and pollution transmit to votaries the meaning of existence, and the hope for immortality, in the context of religious law. Therefore, it is essential that the analysis and interpretation of Zoroastrian purification rituals be directed at elucidating the meaning of these rituals as expressed through doctrines and symbols.

The theological link between the spiritual and the material aspects of the universe, first recorded in the Gāthās and continuously elaborated thereafter, forms the basis of all actions in the universe. The canon enjoins that every thought, word, and deed must serve to further the triumph of righteousness over evil, Ahura Mazdā over Aṇra Mainyu, in both the material and the spiritual realms. Only by strict adherence to the Zoroastrian creed of "good thoughts, good words, and good deeds" can human beings act in accordance with the will of Ahura Mazdā and the laws of righteousness. According to the religion, all affairs of the body affect the soul, even though the spirit has primacy over the flesh. Therefore, the emphasis of purity laws and purification rituals is not directed solely at the corporeal body but simultaneously at the spirit. This emphasis is best reflected through ecclesiastic advice preserved in the Dēnkard, where it is stated: "In taking care of material things a thousand rituals are nothing. In taking care of spiritual things one ritual is that [essential] thing" (576, l. 22–577, l. 2).[3]

As a result of such beliefs and injunctions, purification rituals are undergone to attain a symbolic religious state of purity and virtue in addition to simple physical cleanliness. The rites not only cleanse the individual's physical body, but, more important, they are thought to also purify the soul. It is purification of the soul, through rituals conducted in the corporeal existence, that is believed to assist in the expulsion of evil and the eventual unification of the devotee with the deities. This notion, whereby the meaning of purity and purification is linked to the need for spiritual and physical salvation, is the vital impetus and organizing power of Zoroastrian religious life. According to the Dēnkard: "Purity is this: separation from the demons" (531, ll. 17–18). Separation from the demons becomes equivalent to detachment from evil and results in the individual's entire person—body and soul—being in union with the creator Ahura Mazdā. This disjunction from evil and reunion with the divine can occur only when a Zoroastrian conforms to all aspects of religious law, including the strict maintenance and regular reestablishment of ritual purity (Dēnkard 544, ll. 1–12). When the ordinances are properly enforced and adhered to and purity rites are correctly practiced, the assault of evil upon the righteous material and spiritual creations of Ahura Mazdā is gradually impeded. It is believed that the progressive diminution of evil will, in turn, lead to the final renovation of the universe and the fulfillment of the promise of immortality. It is for this reason that the Gāthās emphasized: "Purity is best for man from birth" (Yasna 48: 5).[4] Yet, the laws and rites of purity not only connect symbolic meaning to daily life but also actually enact the beliefs. The regular enactment of purification rituals conveys and reinforces these beliefs in the devotees' minds.

As previously mentioned, the beliefs that endow ritual with meaning are transmitted to votaries through the medium of symbols. Ritual functions as a means of communication (Malinowski 1962: 210, 236–237; Tambiah 1979: 119; Turner 1977*b*: 42–43; 1982: 61–88). The manipulation of symbols during ritualized actions and invocations, therefore, is not an empty sequence of events but involves the exploitation of beliefs and ideas fundamental to the participants' common ethos (Lévi-Strauss 1963: 200). The symbols utilize belief to form a matrix of meaning that unifies the candidate with the purifiers, the community, all aspects of the corporeal and the spiritual universe, and the gods themselves. Each ritual collapses past and future into the present by gathering together a world full of meaning and symbolism. A rite of purity thus becomes a threshold of liminality, purification, reintegration, and salvation by symbolically expelling evil from the defiled votary.

Frits Staal has recently argued that ritual is activity governed by rules where only the actions matter, not the thoughts, beliefs, and utterances of the participants or the results of the performance (1979; 1986*a;* 1986*b*). He claims that the rules that govern ritual behavior are totally arbitrary, and the activity as a whole completely meaningless (1979: 9–11, 15–21). Language and ritual appear to be similar because both are regulated by rules, but, unlike language, ritual does not express meaning. Consequently, Staal rejects the notion that the analysis of symbols and semantics is useful in the study of ritual. Additionally, Staal postulates that the study of ritual within the contexts of religion and culture could be valueless because ritual may be independent of these two contexts (1986*b*: 215–218).

A detailed critique of Staal's hypotheses has been presented by Hans Penner (1985). Yet, some aspects of Staal's assertions must be addressed, particularly in relation to Zoroastrian purification rites. Zoroastrian ritual is, indeed, rule-governed activity. The rites must be conducted in accordance with stipulated rules not merely to maintain the rules themselves but also to ensure fulfillment of the goal of purification: expulsion of evil. The expulsion of evil is achieved through the integration of the individual with culture, society, religion, belief, and action, not by ritualized performance alone. If the participants' thoughts, words, and deeds are not those required by the religion, a ritual loses its efficacy. Of course, rules do govern all aspects of the participants' beliefs, utterances, and actions. However, these rules are not arbitrary and meaningless. The rules are based on religious doctrine and direct each ritual toward a religious goal: renovation of the universe. Indeed, the rules—and rituals regulated by rules—are arbitrary only to the extent that religious doctrine may appear meaningless to nonbelievers. For Zoroastrians the rites and rules are specific and meaningful because they are manifestations of the faith.

In addition to the meaning of ritual inherent in religious doctrine, there is also meaning transmitted by performance and utterance. While it is true, as Staal argues, that acts do not possess the equivalent of names, nouns, verbs, and other components of spoken and written language, this does not indicate that ritual actions are not a form of communication. Zoroastrian purification rituals do transmit information about the dualism of good and evil, purity and pollution, and about the conditions under which impurity is expunged, as will be demonstrated in the sections that follow. This information, explicit and implicit, is conveyed by symbols that establish homologies between each human being and the universe.

It is important to understand that the symbols manipulated during Zoroastrian purification rituals do not exist in vacuo. It is society that maintains and transmits the elements of symbolism, and it is society that trains each individual and develops in him or her the knowledge of ritual technique, the appreciation of beliefs and values, and the understanding of symbols. Ritual is addressed primarily to its human participants and observers (Tambiah 1968: 202). Hence, it is essential that the symbolic importance of rituals be elucidated "from the native's point of view" (Geertz 1976). The sacred instruments, purificatory substances, gestures, and utterances become important focal points of symbolic meaning only because the community believes and accepts that they possess such meaning. They mean what the actors say they mean; their value is assigned by the religion and its adherents (cf. Goody 1961: 57). Symbolic objects, gestures, and chants, together with the rituals that unite them, serve as links between the everyday lives of Zoroastrians and the spiritual world, between the mundane and the sacred.

Mary Douglas (1969; 1973), Clifford Geertz (1973*a;* 1973*b;* 1983), Stanley J. Tambiah (1979), and other scholars of social anthropology have been concerned with the extent to which a society's key symbols form a code, a semiotic system that exercises a powerful influence on both the world view and the behavior of those individuals who have internalized this symbolic code. In Zoroastrian society the rules of purity and pollution formed a semiotic system that greatly influenced the lives of most devotees until the mid–twentieth century C.E. As the preceding chapters have demonstrated, erosion of the rigorous implementation of these rules during this century has resulted in the progressive simplification of ritual practices and the symbols transmitted through these practices. The modified rituals serve to confer ritual purity upon believers while not encumbering them with rites now regarded as impractical and overly dogmatic. Within the context of Zoroastrianism's long history, this modification and simplification of rituals should not be regarded as an aberration but rather as an adaptation to changes in the socioeconomic conditions of the faith's adherents. Simplification has not stripped the rituals of essential elements. On the contrary, the process has condensed the essential elements of each action, utterance, and purificatory substance; the key symbols of purity and pollution have been preserved and rendered more poignant. In addition, even simplified rituals, such as the modern Saḍe Nāhn and Pādyāb, remind the entire congregation exactly where each member stands in relation to the religion, community, and cosmos. The symbolism preserved in the modern rituals also sustains belief and orients each votary's spiritual quest toward the fate of both the individual soul and the whole of humanity.

The Symbolism of Purification Rituals

As Victor W. Turner has suggested, ritual provides an important setting for the expression of themes, and ritual symbols transmit these themes (1977*a:* 184–185). Religious themes have multiple expressions, and ritual symbols are multivocal during each ritual. Semantic relationships are established among signs, symbols, and external referents during every Zoroastrian purification ritual. These semantic relationships form a structure within which actions and objects, as perceived by the human senses in ritual contexts, have multiple meanings. The symbols transmitted by the ritual actions and objects unify these multiple meanings through analogy and association in thought and fact. In this manner, the ritualized use of symbolic vehicles communicates elaborate doctrinal stances in condensed forms to the community.

Because Zoroastrian purification rituals are undergone to attain a state of purity, the consecrated items, the sacred instruments, and the entire ceremonies themselves are linked by symbolic relationships to the cosmic battle against evil. As is argued below, each item in a ritual becomes, through semantic interconnection, a fixed point of linkage among the human, animal, vegetable, and mineral kingdoms, which are regarded as a unitary whole. Objects and acts acquire religious value during rites and become real because they participate in a reality that transcends them (Eliade 1974: 3–4). It is this symbolic value and reality that has determined the importance and ensured the survival of Zoroastrian purification rituals through the centuries. It is now necessary, and appropriate given that the rituals themselves have been studied, to elucidate the meanings conveyed by the symbols and homologies that arise in Zoroastrian purity rites. The manner in which semantic relationships are established among signs, symbols, and external referents will also be deduced.

Nīrang, consecrated bull's urine, and *gōmēz*, unconsecrated bull's urine, are regarded as pure substances and not excrement or bodily refuse because they are products of a sacred animal. The religious justification of this notion is based on a myth that beneficent creatures arose from the body of the primordial bull after it was slain by the Evil Spirit. The Zoroastrian legend of the primordial bull is part of the faith's cosmogony and belongs to the Indo-Iranian version of the Indo-European creation myth, which describes the creation of the world from the bodies of a primeval androgynous being and a bovine (Lincoln 1975: 122, 140–141, 144–145). The basic myth is found among the Indic, Greek, Roman, and Germanic peoples.[5] Related versions also occur among the Chinese and Jews (Lincoln 1975: 123–126).[6]

In Zoroastrian cosmogony, the androgynous prototype of humanity, called Mortal Life (Av. Gayō Marətan; Phl. Gayōmard), the primordial bull (Phl. *ēwagdād*), and the first plant were slain by Aŋra Mainyu. This myth was preserved in the Bundahišn, where it is stated: "When it [the bull] died, because it was the source of the plants, fifty-five species of grain and twelve species of medicinal plants grew out of the limbs of the bull from [under] the ground. The light and vitality that were in the semen of the bull were entrusted to the moon. That semen was purified by the light of the moon and prepared into all types. The life-force was created in [the semen], from which a pair of cattle, one male and one female, arose. Then, from each type, two hundred and eighty-two species [of animals] appeared on earth" (6e: 1–4).[7]

The proto-Indo-European sacrifice became, under the influence of Zoroastrian dualism and demonology, an act of murder. However, Zoroastrian cosmogony reworked the myth so that, through the intervention of Ahura Mazdā, the corpse of the primordial bull did not produce carrion and pollution but served as the source of all the beneficent animals and plants. The Evil Spirit's act of destruction had been transformed by Ahura Mazdā into a bountiful sacrifice.[8] Hence, through manipulation of mythology, the murder was condemned while the advantageous results were attributed to Ahura Mazdā (cf. Lincoln 1975: 136). The primordial bull was perceived as having remained unpolluted in both life and death because life arose from its corpse.[9] Zoroastrian doctrine gradually extended this belief to encompass all bovines, who became beneficent animals. Because the primordial bull triumphed over death and evil by producing life, *nīrang* and *gōmēz* came to be regarded as life-giving fluids and essential purificatory substances. It is likely that the purificatory power ascribed to bull's urine derives from a notion of immortality reflected by the transformation of the primordial bull's corpse into plants and cereals. Indeed, as noted in the homology among hair, nails, and plants discussed in chapter 4, plants were endowed with the concept of immortality due to their incessant growth. This notion of immortality was captured and reflected in the beneficent immortal Amərətāt, whose realm encompasses all vegetation and whose name means immortality.

In addition to its link with the immortality of plants, bull's urine was also associated with the notion of immortality reflected in all body organs and fluids, including blood, marrow, and semen. This association of the body with immortality once again leads back to the death of the primordial bull:

Fifth, the Evil Spirit came to the beneficent bull. He struggled against the beneficent bull. As the primordial bull died, fifty-seven species of grain and twelve species of medicinal plants came into being, because it [the bull] possessed the nature and form of plants. They grew from every part of the body in the manner that the details of everything that arose from those bodily parts are revealed in the Dāmdād Nask. Every plant that grew from a part of the body causes the growth of that bodily part. As it is said there [in the Dāmdād Nask]: "The bull scattered its marrow upon the earth. Then, grain grew, together with sesame, vine, and vetch. Because sesame has its origin in the marrow and is itself marrow, it is an increaser of marrow." This too is said: "The vine is from blood. Since wine is itself blood, it has the nature of a plant and is a helper

for the healthy nature of the blood." Likewise it is said: "The species called vetch is from the nose, and that species came to be another name for the nose." (Wizīdagīhā ī Zādspram 3: 42–47)

As noted earlier, the semen of this primordial bull also produced
immortality, for the domesticated livestock was believed to have arisen
from it. Likewise, bull's urine was regarded as a source of immortality
because it is one of the seventeen types of liquid in creation and is the second bodily fluid that derives from beneficent animals. According to Zoroastrian doctrine, the bodily fluids of human beings and beneficent animals
are semen (Phl. *šuhr*), urine (*gōmēz*), saliva (*xayūg*), oil (Phl. *āb andar
pōst*), tears (Phl. *ars*), blood (Phl. *xōn*), fat (Phl. *rōyn ān ī andar*), embry-
onic fluid (Phl. *āb ī andar ham-bundahišnīh*), sweat (Phl. *xwēy*), uterinal
fluid (Phl. *ān ī andar pusyān*), and milk (Phl. *šir*) (Bundahišn 11*b*: 1). All
these fluids were believed to perpetuate life and, by extension, produce
immortality.

The motif of animal sacrifice as a prerequisite for immortality produced
the myth that Yima Xšaēta, or Jamshēd, a king of the legendary Peshda-
dian dynasty, conducted a bull sacrifice and produced meat that conferred
immortality upon its consumers (Yasna 32: 8, 9: 1–4, together with its Pahlavi commentary). Likewise, it is believed that a bull sacrifice will be conducted by Saošyant, the final savior and posthumous son of Zarathushtra, at
the end of time. According to Zoroastrian eschatology, Saošyant will slay a
bull named Haδayąš and prepare the elixir of immortality by combining
the bull's fat—a bodily fluid—with white *haoma* (Skt. *soma-*) (Bundahišn
34: 22). A parallel to these Zoroastrian beliefs of immortality is present
in India, where the dominant Hindu image of bovines is one of long life
and sacrality. The cow is regarded as the granter of life and nutrition
(cf. Gonda 1980: 98–100; Obeyesekere 1984: 100). The five products (Skt.
pañcagavya-) of the cow—milk, butter, curds, dung, and urine—are com-
bined to form a purificatory liquid that removes all impurity from a devotee's body and soul (Hodivala 1925: 139–140; Carstairs 1958: 246). As
in the use of *gōmēz*, Hindus are required to sprinkle *pañcagavya-* upon
themselves and perform ritual ablution with the fluid (Gonda 1980: 47,
114, 185–188). The Hindus also use bull's urine as a medicine because it is
thought to be endowed with curative properties; this belief probably reflects the concept of immortality associated with bovines.

Nirang may be consumed and is believed to purify the soul because it is
a product of the bull that has been consecrated by priests through the ritual power of holy words during the *Nirangdīn* ceremony. Over the ages,

nīrang was gradually invested with magical efficacy. It was thought that "although the body [may] be as black as charcoal, if consecrated bull's urine is given for drinking, then the light of god alights upon the body and it becomes pure and radiant like the sun" (Persian Rivāyats 487, l. 18–488, l. 1). *Gōmēz*, being unconsecrated, cannot purify the soul and, consequently, is not drunk. It is, however, symbolically potent enough to eradicate pollution from the physical body of a person who performs ablutions with it. In Iran it is believed that unconsecrated bull's urine can even withstand the pollution caused through indirect contact with nonbelievers. Therefore, Zoroastrians in Yazd now collect urine from bulls owned by Muslims (Fischer 1973: 61). Urine cannot be collected from humans, dogs, or pigs (Pursišnīhā 9). The use of *nīrang* and *gōmēz* for ritual purification symbolically enlists the assistance of the beneficent immortal Vohu Manah, the "Good Mind," protector of all bulls and cows, in the cosmic struggle against pollution and evil. The homology between Vohu Manah and the bull begins with their common origin as creations of Ahura Mazdā and is reinforced by the role as protector of bovines attributed to this beneficent immortal in the Gāthās and the Bundahišn. In this manner, a microcosmic referent, the bull, is linked to a macrocosmic referent, Vohu Manah, in terms of the deity's active decision to accept bovines under his guardianship (Bundahišn 3: 14).

The addition of *bhasam*, fire ash, to consecrated bull's urine is said to symbolize the presence of fire, Ahura Mazdā's offspring, in the rituals. Once again, fire ash is linked by homology to its source of origin, fire, which is in turn integrated into the macrocosm as the "son of Ahura Mazdā" (Ātaxš Niyāyišn in Zand ī Xwurdag Abestāg l. 5). Cult object, sacred element, and creator deity become alloforms of each other and are, consequently, present in ritual. This symbolic association resulted in fire's being venerated as the "divine purifier" who "takes away impurity" and "grants health and well being" (Yasna 25: 7, 36: 1; Zand ī Xwurdag Abestāg, Ātaxš Niyāyišn l. 1). The glory (Av. *xvarənah-*; Phl. *xwarrah;* N.P. *farr*) said to reside in the sacred fires that are enthroned in Zoroastrian fire temples is also thought to wage battle against the spiritual demons of death and pollution (Wizīdagīhā ī Zādspram 3: 82–83). In addition, Aša Vahišta, "Best Righteousness," another beneficent immortal and the guardian of fire, is enlisted in the struggle against impurity through the use of fire ash. As in the case of bull's urine and Vohu Manah, here, too, a homology was created based upon the characteristics of fire and Aša Vahišta and reinforced by an active choice of the beneficent immortal (Yasna 34: 4, 43: 4, 47: 6; Bundahišn 3: 15).

Aša Vahišta is also symbolized, in a parallel manner, by the rays of the sun, which purify the earth, water, and all candidates who undergo ritual purification (Zand ī Xwurdag Abestāg, Ātaxš Niyāyišn ll. 12–14; Pāzand Jāmāspī 6: 7). Indeed, it is believed that if the sun does not rise, demons will destroy all the seven climes, or zones, of the Zoroastrian world (Zand ī Xwurdag Abestāg, Ātaxš Niyāyišn ll. 12–13).[10] The sun was also regarded as a purifier and protector in ancient Hindu beliefs. It destroyed evil monsters, sorcerers, and witches and drove away disease and death (Rg Veda 6: 71.5, 7: 104.24, 10: 3.4, 37.4).

The *urwarām*, pomegranate leaves, chewed by a candidate for purification, represent the realm of vegetation (Phl. *urwar*). In this case the homology is a direct one, for the pomegranate leaf is a portion of a plant. Not only is there a direct homology, but there is also a symbolic association whereby each leaf represents the entire vegetable kingdom created from the primordial bull's corpse. In this manner, through a sequence of homologies among the pomegranate leaves, the vegetable kingdom, and the primordial bull, the concept of immortality symbolized by both the vegetation and the bull are associated with ritual purification. The devotee who consumes pomegranate leaves incorporates in himself or herself the death-defeating, immortal aspects of bovines and plants. Additionally, as mentioned earlier, all plants are homologies of the beneficent immortal Amərətāt, who personifies immortality. The relationship between the pomegranate leaves and this beneficent immortal was further consolidated by religious statements that claim that Amərətāt chose plants for herself (Bundahišn 3: 19). The pomegranate was also an ancient Near Eastern symbol of fertility and immortality, and this Near Eastern belief would have been assimilated with Amərətāt.

The use of *āb*, water, in the final stages of ritual ablution brings its purificatory effect to the aid of a candidate who is undergoing cleansing. Although highly susceptible to defilement, and therefore restricted to use only after *gōmēz* has been applied, water is viewed as pure, purifying, and health granting (Yasna 68: 10–12, 21). Its use symbolically invokes the support of Haurvatāt, "Wholeness," the beneficent immortal who guards water (Bundahišn 3: 18). Here the homology is based on the notion of completeness, wholeness, and inseparability—literally, the ability to flow together—symbolized by all fluid elements personified by this beneficent immortality. The concept of wholeness personified by Haurvatāt is not limited to physical excellence but includes spiritual perfection.

The two beneficent immortals Haurvatāt and Amərətāt, Wholeness and

Immortality, are closely connected in the Zoroastrian ethos (cf. Yasna 6: 17, 51: 7). Together they uphold righteousness and resist sickness and pestilence (Yasna 63: 1, 71: 17). So important are the concepts personified by these two beneficent immortals that righteousness itself is believed to lead to wholeness and immortality (Yasna 31: 6). Furthermore, immortality of body and soul in the afterlife that will follow the renovation of the universe is created through Haurvatāt and Amərətāt (Yasna 34: 10).

The *xāk,* dust, used in these rites represents the earth with its purificatory and regenerative powers. The homology is based on a direct substantive connection between the dust and the earth. It also symbolically unites the aspirant for purity with Spənta Ārmaiti, "Holy Devotion," a beneficent immortal who "chose the earth" (Bundahišn 3: 17). Like the earth, Spənta Ārmaiti is feminine and life granting: the daughter and wife of Ahura Mazdā and the mother of humanity. According to the Pahlavi Rivāyat Accompanying the Dādestān ī Dēnīg, Ahura Mazdā told Zarathushtra: "This is Spənta Ārmaiti, my daughter, my house-mistress of paradise, and the mother of creation" (8: 4).[11] Together, aspirant and earth goddess toil to overcome evil in matter and to expel impurity. The inclusion of this beneficent immortal in purification rituals achieves yet another link with the animal and vegetable kingdoms, because Spənta Ārmaiti is said to protect and nurture human beings, cattle, and plants in daily life (Yasna 30: 7, 47: 3, 48: 5).

Similarly, Xšaϑra Vairya, "Desirable Dominion," the beneficent immortal who oversees metals, is introduced into purification rites through a homology with ritual objects. The stone mounts and the metal ladle fastened to the end of the nine-knotted stick symbolize this spiritual being by means of a homology in which all stone, crystal, and metal were chosen by, and originated from, this deity (Bundahišn 3: 16). Xšaϑra Vairya is also represented by the pure spaces within which all forms of impurity in and on each devotee are trapped, gradually vanquished, and, finally, banished back to hell. Here the operational analogy is that of ritual space to cosmic sky, both boundaries that confine evil and impurity. The sky, being composed of rock crystal or metal, is regarded as a creation of Xšaϑra Vairya.

The numerous *mąϑra,* "holy utterances," recited during purification rituals are thought by Zoroastrians to be endowed with the power to drive away harm, suffering, pollution, and death (cf. Vidēvdāt 21: 18–23). Each *mąϑra* is believed to be victorious, powerful, and health granting (Yašt 1: 3). Consequently, it was stipulated that holy words should never be taught to nonbelievers and sinners (Pursišnīhā 6). Particularly efficacious is the

Ahunawar prayer, which is said to protect the body from all evil. The Kām Nā Mazdā prayer serves a similar function (Vidēvdāt 11: 3). By symbolically dispersing the demons of impurity and death from the candidate's body and soul, these prayers further the individual's quest for ritual purity. Other holy words, spoken while undergoing ritual purification, unite the devotee with the vegetable kingdom (cf. Vidēvdāt 11: 6, 17: 5) or dedicate actions to Ahura Mazdā and the other gods (cf. Vidēvdāt 17: 7).[12] Recitation of holy words is a central feature of all ritual acts. Avestan, like Arabic, Hebrew, Latin, Pali, and Vedic Sanskrit, is a sacred language; the Zoroastrian canon was orally transmitted, and codified, in this ancient eastern Iranian language. Pahlavi was the language in which the medieval commentaries on the canon were written. A few prayers were also composed in this medieval southwestern Iranian language. Pahlavi was gradually replaced by New Persian and Parsi Gujarati as the languages in which the religious commentaries are formulated. Holy words chanted aloud are meant to be understood by the congregation (cf. Tambiah 1968: 179–180), but, because Avestan and Pahlavi are no longer used by votaries, these utterances are understood only in a general sense by most priests and laypersons.[13]

A few words would be appropriate in regard to the comprehension of holy utterances and, indeed, about the entire relationship between spoken word and performed ritual. Zoroastrian participants in rites have always been influenced by the religion's ecclesiastic tradition that interpreted utterances and practices. Even when the medieval theologians failed to properly comprehend a *mąϑra* (by modern philological standards), they interpreted the liturgy and associated ritual in accordance with medieval Zoroastrian beliefs. Each ritual transmitted nonverbal information, which was utilized, together with the holy words and written sources, to produce a verbal interpretation. This interaction between verbal and performative information, holy words and sacred rites, continued into the modern period. In the nineteenth and twentieth centuries two other powerful influences, philology and the history of religion, came into play in the comprehension of sacred words. Priests and laypersons, believers and nonbelievers, trained as philologists, historians, and scholars of religion now directly understand the *mąϑra*s, elucidate the history of rites, and relate ritual performances to spoken words. As in earlier periods, these individuals disseminate the meaning that they believe is transmitted by the words and acts, and this scholarly literature is read by many Zoroastrians. Consequently, while the actions and holy words of rituals do transmit information and are meaningful, such meaning is not immutable, nor is it always universal. Sacred utterance, ritual action, written doctrine, performer, and observer interact constantly, and, as a result, beliefs and practices undergo change.

The furrows constructed at the commencement of major purification rites preserve an ancient Indo-European tradition: the territorial separating of an area from the outside world (Polomé 1980: 162). They define areas of action within which rules may be established to organize existence in harmony with cosmic order. Usually, furrows create a sanctuary isolated from the profane, distinguished by its own special status and governed by divine law. For example, when Rome was founded, a furrow is said to have been drawn around seven hills, sacralizing space for the city (Dumézil 1969: 31–45, 61–78). Furrows used by the Magi for devotional ceremonies, such as the Yasna, create pure spaces from which all impurity is excluded. Furrows constructed during purification rituals, however, have the opposite function: they entrap impurity within an enclosed space, thereby preventing pollution from spreading. As spatial barriers, these furrows symbolize both exclusion of that which is outside and limitation of that which is inside. They are opened and closed only by the gods and priests, or purifiers. The efficacy of all ritual furrows is reinforced by the recitation of holy words while the furrows are being constructed.

As determined in chapter 2, an important structural parallel exists between the *mą̇ra* and the *karša*. Holy words form barriers that protect the priests and the community from pollution just as the physical furrows do. Indeed, the recitation of holy words during construction of the concentric furrows may be perceived as the creation of multiple barriers, ritual walls composed of both furrows and spells. Here, of course, an inverse homology exists between the purification rituals and the religion itself. The walls of the religion exclude evil; the walls of each purification ritual confine evil and exclude it from the religious community.[14]

The threefold ablutions with unconsecrated bull's urine, dust, and water; the threefold pits; the three-stone mounts; and the triple furrows are believed to represent the Zoroastrian religious creed of good thoughts, good words, and good deeds. They also are symbolically associated in number with the three saviors (Av. *saošyant-*; Phl. *sōšāns*), who will purify the world from evil in the final two millennia of human history.[15] All these threefold doctrinal and ritual arrangements reflect the tripartite cognitive model in terms of which the ancient Iranians, like other Indo-European peoples, viewed the world (Dumézil 1958; Littleton 1982). The five-stone mounts used in the medieval and modern Barašnūm ī nō šab rituals are thought by the Parsis to represent the five Gāthās and the five watches of the day. Irani Zoroastrians, however, believe that these five-stone mounts represent the five evils—deceit, avarice, lust, envy, and anger—which must be symbolically smitten by stamping them under the feet (cf. Boyce 1977: 128).[16]

The officiating purifier, as a priest and a righteous man in the highest state of religioritual purity, is Ahura Mazdā's direct representative on earth. He is the bearer and propagator of religion, the reciter of holy words, and the conductor of rituals necessary for the victory of good over evil. The homology between priest and creator deity is thus founded on a similarity of function: the priest's role on earth duplicates Ahura Mazdā's activities in heaven. Each purifier performs his duties after invoking the authority of Ahura Mazdā; the beneficent immortals; Sraoša, the god of obedience and prayer; the prophet Zarathushtra; exalted priests of bygone eras; and the present high priest of the ecclesiastic group to which the purifier belongs.[17] Symbolically endowed with religious authority from the gods, the prophet, and the renowned Magi of the past, each purifier plays a vital role in the struggle between purity and pollution during ritual purification. The success of every ritual is believed to be dependent on a purifier's ability to perform his religious duties carefully and vigorously. This explains the severe punishments meted out to priests who fail in their duty to carefully conduct every stage of a ritual.[18]

Humanity, the supreme creation of Ahura Mazdā and the means through which the Evil Spirit and his pandemonium will be smitten, is represented by the candidate who undergoes ritual purification.[19] The candidate, like all human beings, is incarnate in a world of mixture (*gumēzišn*) where matter is full of good and evil. He or she strives, through obedience to the laws of purity and performance of purification rituals, to separate (*wizārišn*) the body and soul from evil, impurity, and pollution. Zoroastrian belief links every aspect of the candidate's body to a beneficent immortal. His or her life-force, radiance, consciousness, and intellect belong to Ahura Mazdā, the flesh belongs to Vohu Manah, the veins and fat to Aša Vahišta, the bones to Xšaθra Vairya, the marrow to Spənta Ārmaiti, the blood to Haurvatāt, and the hair to Amərətāt. Because each beneficent immortal is, in turn, united by homology to an aspect of nature, the whole human body functions as an alloform of the entire religious cosmos: "Man's body is the measure of the material world" (Bundahišn 28: 1, 22). The candidate symbolically becomes a microcosmic representation of the universe. The skin is equated to the sky, the flesh to the earth, the bones to the mountains, the veins to the rivers, the blood to the water in the rivers and the seas, the stomach to the oceans, the hair to the plants and the forests, the

vital essences (marrow) to metal, innate wisdom to human beings, learned
knowledge to animals, the eyes to the sun and the moon, the teeth to the
stars, the crown of the head and the brain to the eternal lights of heaven,
the senses to the beneficent immortals and other deities, and the soul to
Ahura Mazdā himself. According to the Bundahišn:

> Every person has [his or her] own height and width; the skin is like
> the sky, the flesh like the earth, the bones like the mountains, the
> veins like the rivers, the blood in the body like the water in the
> seas, the belly like the ocean, the hair like the plants, the places
> where the hair is thick like the forests, the essences of the body like
> metal, innate wisdom like humanity, acquired wisdom like benefi-
> cent animals, heat like fire, the hands and feet like the seven
> [planets] and the twelve [constellations], the stomach—which di-
> gests food—like the clouds and the fire Vazišta, breath drawn in
> and out like the wind, the liver like the Frāxkard sea, which is the
> origin of the summer season, . . . the crown of the head and the
> brain like [the realm of] the endless lights, the head like heaven,
> the two eyes like the moon and the sun, the teeth like the stars, . . .
> the anus like hell underneath the earth [for] the anus is the lowest
> part of the body, the soul like Ahura Mazdā, [and] intelligence,
> memory, perception, thought, knowledge, and understanding like
> the six beneficent immortals. (28: 4)[20]

In this manner, the earth with its living creatures, the celestial spheres, and
heaven with its spiritual beings are all symbolically united in each human
being (fig. 13). Hence, through the body and soul of a devotee who is undergoing purification, the entire universe fights evil and strives to attain
perfection.

In addition to the temporal value and significance associated with purification rites, virtually every symbol found in Zoroastrian beliefs and
practices of purity ultimately bears salvific valence. As will be argued in the
following section, the rituals serve as a means of expressing the devotee's
yearning for the final renovation of the universe and the accompanying immortality of life. By connecting purification rituals to eschatology, symbols reveal the way in which immortality may be obtained. In doing so,
they renew the faith's claims to legitimacy by providing each votary with
the hope of salvation.

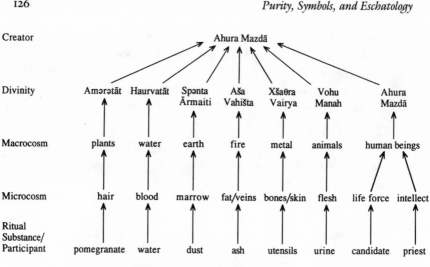

Figure 13. Cosmic Homologies

Ritual Purity and Eschatology

The struggle between good and evil, righteousness and unrighteousness, purity and pollution, life and death, is fundamentally a spiritual conflict. Pollution is an affliction by which Aŋra Mainyu, through impurity in the material world, attacks Ahura Mazdā in the spiritual realm. The attack of evil, through pollution, "is upon an individual's essence, which is the soul, and upon the soul's weapon and garment: the body. . . . Evil strives to annihilate an individual's essence, weapon, and garment, and to defile them. By grievously polluting an individual's essence, weapon, and garment, and by disassociating them [it seeks] to separate and destroy them" (Dēnkard 383, l. 22–384, l. 4). The goal of evil is, thus, nothing less than the total pollution and annihilation of all that is sacred in both matter and spirit. In order to stave off the onslaught of evil and, more important, to actually liberate matter and spirit from the tyranny of evil, every human being is required to direct all actions toward the maintenance of ritual purity and to mount a constant counteroffensive against pollution. The material conflict between purity and pollution is for possession of each individual human soul and, eventually, the entire spiritual world. Hence, as stated in the Dēnkard, Zoroastrians believe that the soul's garment and weapon—the body—must be utilized in combating pollution.

Every Zoroastrian is enjoined, in numerous religious texts, to direct his or her constant vigilance toward the fate of the soul instead of focusing exclusively on the body: "Do not forsake the soul and neglect it for the body's sake" (Pahlavi Texts 153, ll. 2–3; Čīdag Handarz ī Pōryōtkēšān l. 56). The faith seeks to convince its votaries that "the body is mortal, [but] the soul is immortal. Do good deeds, for the soul is [what matters], not the body; the spiritual world is [what matters], not the material world" (Pahlavi Texts 153, ll. 1–2; Čīdag Handarz ī Pōryōtkēšān l. 55). These beliefs emphasize that everlasting joy is found only in heaven and not in the corporeal existence: "Desire rather those things whose fruit is everlasting joy" (Čīdag Handarz ī Pōryōtkēšān l. 57). However, the rewards of heaven are believed to be available only to the souls of Zoroastrians who have upheld righteousness and maintained purity during their lifetimes. Consequently, ritual purity and the function of purification rites become central to the fate of the soul in the afterlife.

The body transmutes into its alloforms after death: flesh and bones become earth and metal, blood becomes water, plants spring from hair, and the life-force forms the wind.[21] Zoroastrians believe that when an individual dies, his or her soul sits near the head of the corpse for three days and nights (Haδōxt Nask 2: 1–6; Yašt 24: 54; Mēnōg ī Xrad 1: 73).[22] During this period, demons prey upon the soul but are kept at bay by a fire that the deceased individual's relatives kindle (Pahlavi Vidēvdāt 19: 29; Bundahišn 30: 4–8). In addition, if the soul belongs to a Zoroastrian who had undergone ritual purification while alive, these demons tremble in its presence: "Then [even] the absolutely evil demon[s] tremble at the scent of his [or her] soul after death, just as a sheep upon which a wolf pounces" (Vidēvdāt 19: 33). Hence, it is clear that ritual purity is believed to provide protection on the three days of transition after death. During this period, the soul of a righteous, pure individual chants the opening section of the Uštavaiti Gāthā, which serves as a song of salvation: "May Ahura Mazdā, who rules at will, grant wishes to him [or her], to whoever has wishes" (Yasna 43: 1). If, however, the soul is that of an unrighteous, impure individual, it recites, in distress, the opening section of the Kima Gāthā: "To what land [can I] flee? Where shall I flee?" (Yasna 46: 1). This verse, directed at Ahura Mazdā, serves as a cry for help (Haδōxt Nask 3: 1–6; Dādestān ī Dēnīg 16: 4). Realizing its impurity, such a soul unsuccessfully attempts to escape the demons who await it (Bundahišn 30: 8; Dādestān ī Dēnīg 16: 4). On the dawn of the fourth day, Sraoša, the god of obedience, approaches the righteous soul; opposes Vīzarəša, the "Demon of Death," Astō Vīδātu, the "Shaker of Bones," and other demons; and leads the soul to the Bridge of the Separator. Here the soul is greeted by its conscience in the form of a beautiful maiden (Av. Daēna; Phl. Dēn) (Haδōxt Nask 2: 7–14; Yašt 24: 55–60; Bundahišn 30: 9–16).[23] Sraoša, however, does not approach the soul of an unrighteous Zoroastrian. Such an impure soul is fettered by the demons and led to the Bridge of the Separator, where it is greeted by its conscience in the form of an ugly hag (Haδōxt Nask 3: 7–14; Bundahišn 30: 17–20; Ardā Wīrāz Nāmag 17: 10–26; Mēnōg ī Xrad 1: 103).

Each soul undergoes individual judgment, presided over by a triad of gods—Miϑra, the god of the Contract; Rašnu, the Judge; and Sraoša—at the Bridge of the Separator. If the soul's good deeds are greater than its evil deeds, the gods intercede on its behalf and save it from the demons. The pure soul is then led across the bridge into paradise by the Daēna and Sraoša (Yašt 24: 61; Vidēvdāt 19: 32; Bundahišn 30: 22–24, 26; Mēnōg ī Xrad 1: 76–100). However, if the soul is unrighteous and polluted, its evil deeds outweigh all the good it did while alive. The impure soul is condemned, bound by the demons, and cast into hell to await the day of universal judgment (Bundahišn 30: 25, 27–31; Mēnōg ī Xrad 1: 104–122). In cases where a soul's good and evil deeds are equal, it is consigned to limbo, or the Place of the Motionless Ones, until the end of time (Bundahišn 30: 32–33).

Purification of the body and purity of the soul are, according to doctrine, prerequisites for access to heaven. Consequently, up to the early eighteenth century it was believed that if the Barašnūm ī nō šab had not been undergone at least once during an individual's lifetime even a righteous soul could not cross the Bridge of the Separator because "the beneficent immortals and [other] gods flee from the stench of that soul, and are not able to make up its account and reckoning. It remains at the Bridge of the Separator, and is unable to cross. It becomes very penitent, but gains no profit thereby" (Ṣaddar Nasr 36: 5–6). As a result of this belief, every devotee underwent the Barašnūm ī nō šab during the ancient, medieval, and early modern periods.[24] This requirement has since been modified, and the Saḍe Nāhn suffices to ensure each soul's ritual purity in life, death, and the afterlife. When necessary, purification can now be undergone vicariously in memory of a deceased Zoroastrian to aid his or her soul in crossing the Bridge of the Separator.

Zoroastrianism originated in an archaic society in which people felt themselves indissolubly connected to the cosmos. This belief, common to many ancient societies, resulted in religions formulating sacred histories to explain the nexus between the individual and the universe (Eliade 1974: xiii–xiv). Zoroastrian sacred history consists of a cosmogonic and cosmologic myth, based on the Indo-Iranian creation beliefs of the earliest votaries, which were elaborated in the medieval period and preserved in the Bundahišn. This sacred history is divided into two periods (Choksy 1986a: 239–240). Prior to the first period was eternity, when Ahura Mazdā and Aŋra Mainyu were separate from each other. The first period was that of creation, and it lasted six thousand years. The initial three thousand years of this period were marked by the first encounter between Ahura Mazdā and Aŋra Mainyu, the genesis of beneficent and malevolent spiritual beings by the Lord Wisdom and the Evil Spirit, respectively, and an offer of peaceful coexistence in purity and righteousness, which was rejected by the Evil Spirit. After Aŋra Mainyu had spurned Ahura Mazdā's overture, he was temporarily defeated by the Lord Wisdom, who chanted the Ahunawar prayer. On hearing these holy words, the Evil Spirit collapsed, stupefied, back into the darkness. The next three thousand years passed while Aŋra Mainyu lay in a stupor, and Ahura Mazdā transformed the spiritual creations into corporeal ones.

This was followed by the current period of mixture between good and evil, which will also last six thousand years. Aŋra Mainyu was aroused from his stupor by the Whore Demoness, invaded the world, polluted it, and—as mentioned earlier—slew Gayō Marətan, the primordial bull, and the first plant. Humanity arose from the semen of the prototype of humanity, animals and some plants from the body and semen of the first bull, and other plants from the seed of the initial plant. Human history passed by with the rise and fall of legendary dynasties until the prophet Zarathushtra was born in the religious year 8970. Thirty years later, Zarathushtra received revelation from Ahura Mazdā and preached the Lord Wisdom's faith. According to this sacred history, the era of Zarathushtra was followed by those of the Achaemenians, Parthians, and Sasanians. Thereafter, the Arabs conquered Iran and were succeeded by the Turkic invaders. These conquests, and the reduction of Zoroastrianism to the status of a minor religious community, were incorporated into the faith's history and explained in terms of a steady increase in evil and pollution, which heralds the advent of the final days (Bundahišn 33: 20–26). The custom of burying the dead practiced by these invaders is lamented as defiling the sacred earth, thereby increasing evil and enfeebling the Zoroastrian faith (Bundahišn 33: 22–23). Political strife, personal calamity, and pollution of both body and soul are all viewed as originating from the Evil Spirit. Hence, as strife and calamity increase in the final days, so will impurity, until finally: "In that basest time carrion and excrement will become so widespread that [whenever] a person strides [forth] he will be walking on impurity" (Zand ī Wahman Yašt 4: 28).

The present years of evil, pollution, and suffering will, in Zoroastrian belief, be followed by two millennia during which three saviors, Uxšyaṱ-ərəta, Uxšyatnəmah, and Astvaṱərəta, or Saošyant, will be born, one every thousand years, to purify the world. Finally, in the year 11,973, Saošyant will resurrect the dead. This resurrection, performed by Saošyant, will be commanded by Ahura Mazdā. When each person's final body (*tan ī pasēn*) is created at the end of time: "I [Ahura Mazdā] shall demand the bones from the spirit of the earth, the blood from the water, the hair from the plants, and the life-force from the wind, even as they received them at the primal creation" (Bundahišn 34: 5). Another Pahlavi source echoes this theme: "Ahura Mazdā asks for the bones from the earth, the blood from the water, the hair from the plants, and the life-force from the wind. He mixes them, one with the other, and creates the form that each [individual] has" (Pahlavi Rivāyat Accompanying the Dādestān ī Dēnīg 48: 55).

After all, as another Middle Iranian source argues, since Ahura Mazdā created the creatures in perfection at the beginning of time, he can restore them to life, purity, and wholeness at the end of time. This argument was attributed by Zādspram, the ninth-century c.e. Zoroastrian priest who dwelt in Sirkan, to the creator deity himself: "Ahura Mazdā said: 'I was able to create those creations when they were not [in existence], and now that they have existed, and are dismembered, it is easier to restore them'" (Wizīdagīhā ī Zādspram 34: 6).

Once again, the influence of microcosmic-macrocosmic comparisons is apparent. The period of the final days is perceived as an act that reverses not only death and impurity but also the cosmogony itself. The three creations—human being, animal, and plant—from whom the cosmos was made at the beginning of time are now re-created from the cosmos. As Lincoln has observed, the bodies of Gayō Maratan, the primordial bull, and the first plant were transformed at death in order to produce the cosmos, and when the cosmos is transformed at the end of time the bodies of all humans, animals, and plants are re-created from it (1986: 128). This final reversal of the eschaton reinforces the need for purity and purification at all times past, present, and future. For, if human beings or any other sacred creations are polluted and impure, the cosmos becomes polluted when the creations are transmuted into their alloforms, and, consequently, an impure cosmos could not produce final purity at the final resurrection.

Thereafter, Ahura Mazdā will descend to earth with the other deities, and the final savior will separate the righteous individuals from the evil ones. Each sinner, having already suffered in hell after death, will be purified of his or her transgressions and impurities by means of an ordeal involving molten metal. The legendary bull Haδayąš will be slain, and its fat mixed with the mythical white *haoma* to produce the elixir that will grant immortality of body and soul to all human beings who consume it. Ahura Mazdā, the beneficent immortals, and the minor deities will then annihilate all the demons and noxious creatures. Aŋra Mainyu himself will be rendered innocuous and forced to scuttle out of creation back to hell. Finally, hell will be sealed shut with molten metal, safeguarding the spiritual and corporeal worlds from evil, impurity, and pollution forever: "The Evil Spirit and [the demon of] Lust, their weapons shattered, will be made powerless by the Gāthic incantation, and they will scuttle out into the darkness and gloom through that passage in the sky by which they [had] penetrated [the world]. . . . molten metal will flow into hell, and all the stench and pollution that was in hell will be burned by that molten metal and become pure. The passage through which the Evil Spirit penetrated will be sealed by that molten metal" (Bundahišn 34: 30–31).

Once the separation of evil from good has been accomplished, Ahura Mazdā will renovate, or "Make Excellent," (*frašō.kərəti-, frašagird*) the universe in the year 12,000: "Then the renovation will take place in the world; [and,] as it desired, the corporeal world [will become] immortal forever and eternally" (Bundahišn 34: 32).[25] Human history will then end, eternity will recommence in absolute purity and perfection, and humanity will dwell in happiness upon a refurbished earth.[26] Thus, according to the Zoroastrian world view, human history is actually a twelve-thousand-year linear progression of sacred history. This period of finite time (Phl. *zamān ī kanāragōmand*), or the "Time of the Long Dominion" (Phl. *zamān ī dagrand xwadāy, zurwān ī dagrand xwadāy*), is bounded at its commencement and conclusion by infinite time (Phl. *zamān ī akanārag, zurwān ī akanārag*), which functions in accordance with the will of Ahura Mazdā.[27] The Zoroastrian system, in which the duration of the material world is limited to twelve thousand years and where cosmogony and eschatology are interchangeable, reveals an attempt by the Magi to incorporate ancient Indo-Iranian beliefs on infinity and the cyclicity of time into the faith's cosmic dualism. Good and evil, purity and pollution, could not be permitted to cycle infinitely but had to be transposed into a linear system the cyclicity of which lay in the nexus between primal creation and final renovation.

The material world is not merely the arena in which human beings combat evil. Orthodox Zoroastrian commentaries regard it as the trap into which the Evil Spirit was lured. Once trapped in matter, Aŋra Mainyu is gradually vanquished by the gods and votaries acting in unison. The Škand Gumānīg Wizār describes this belief by comparing the Lord Wisdom to a wise gardener who protects his garden, which is paradise:

> Ahura Mazdā is like the owner of a garden or a wise gardener whose garden destructive animals and birds seek to ruin. . . . The wise gardener, to save himself trouble and to exclude those destructive creatures, devises means like gins, snares, and bird-traps by which to capture them. When the creature sees the trap and attempts to escape, it is ensnared inside it. . . . The strength and power which the creature has within its body are neutralized by its own struggles . . . since its strength is insufficient, its power to resist diminishes and it is vanquished. Then, the wise gardener . . . drives the creature out of the snare. The creature retains its essence, but is powerless. The gardener [then] returns his snare and gin undamaged to his storehouse where he refurbishes it. Similarly, the creator Ahura Mazdā . . . is like a gardener who safeguards his garden from that which is harmful to it. That destructive creature who [seeks to] ruin the garden is the accursed Aŋra Mainyu who disrupts and attacks creation. The good snare is the sky within which the righteous creatures are guests, and the Evil Spirit and his miscreants are entrapped. The gin and trap which prevent the destructive creature from fulfilling its desire are the time established for the battle. . . . Only the creator can bring about the salvation of his creation from eternal adversity and reconstitute its proper progress, just as the wise owner of the garden [refurbishes] his gin and snare. (4: 63–80)[28]

The sphere of the sky serves as the fortification of the cosmic snare within which Aŋra Mainyu was trapped. The Wizīdagīhā ī Zādspram dramatically recounts this event: "When the Evil Spirit came within the sky, the Spirit of the Sky, [who], like a gallant warrior clad in armour, maintains the sky, said to the Evil Spirit with a loud voice and harsh shout: 'Now that you have entered, I will not let you exit until Ahura Mazdā builds another stronger fortress.' . . . The immortal souls of the righteous warriors were stationed around that fortress, riding horses and bearing spears in hand like hair upon the head, as prison wardens who watch the prison from outside. . . . The Evil Spirit struggled to return to his own abode of darkness, but found no passageway" (3: 1–4).[29]

After having entered the space surrounded by the sky, Aŋra Mainyu could not escape, for Ahura Mazdā had ensured that the sky was inviolable and unpollutable (Ṣaddar Bondahesh 75: 1). The sky (Phl. *asmān*) cannot be polluted because it is believed to be composed of the hardest stone, rock crystal, or metal (Yasna 30: 5; Dādestān ī Dēnīg 90: 2; Bundahišn 3: 16).[30]

The vault of the sky is thought to enclose the earth, planets, stars, moon, and sun. The Mēnōg ī Xrad preserves a belief that the vault of the sky resembles the shell of an egg: "The sky, earth, waters, and everything else are inside the egg-shaped [vault] that is like the egg of the birds. The sky above the earth and below the earth, like an egg, is established by the work of the creator Ahura Mazdā; and the earth is in the center of the sky, like the yolk in the center of the egg" (44: 8–10).[31]

In Zoroastrian cosmology, the firmament (Av. *ϑwāša-;* Phl. *spihr*) is equivalent to the space contained within the vault or sphere of the sky (Dēnkard 207, l. 1–7; Bundahišn 2: 2, 3: 6–7, 4: 23; Wizīdagīhā ī Zādspram 30: 1).[32] Likewise, space is identical to place and time. Place, space, and time are linked through the firmament in a single entity with the sky and serve as a boundary that confines evil. Furthermore, space, time, and religion are said to be Ahura Mazdā's coworkers in the struggle against the Evil Spirit (Bundahišn 1: 2, 12, 2: 2, 11). Together they endeavor to smite Aŋra Mainyu, who has been bounded and trapped in space, time, and matter. The contest between Ahura Mazdā and Aŋra Mainyu, good and evil, purity and pollution, is thus conducted in limited space and time. In this manner, Zoroastrian cosmology and eschatology attempt to reassure the congregation that the problems of evil and suffering are limited to a finite period of time, after which there will be no impurity, pollution, suffering, and evil.

The Wizīdagīhā ī Zādspram contains an important analogy that compares the form of human beings to the firmament: "The likeness of people [is] as the revolving firmament of the sky" (30: 1). Zaehner comprehended the equation of microcosmic individual to macrocosmic universe visible in this passage (1972: 112). Yet, the text does not merely propose such an equation alone. More important, the firmament with all its contents is equated to the entire human body with its parts. In such an analogy, each person has a physical boundary—the skin—with inner and outer surfaces just as the firmament has a boundary—the sphere—with an inside and an outside. The sphere of the sky was penetrated by death and impurity when the Evil Spirit invaded the material world, and, likewise, the skin is penetrated by pollution when the Corpse Demoness attacks the body. This complex interrelation between human body and universe, human life and cosmic myth, is preserved mainly in Zoroastrian sources that date from the medieval period, namely, the texts written in Pahlavi.[33] The increased cosmological speculation of the Magi evidenced by these texts may explain why consumption of consecrated bull's urine was introduced into medieval purification rituals: the inside of the body, where the mortal soul (Phl. *ruwān*) resides, has to be purified in order to ensure that the entire body is pure. Thus, the interior of the firmament and the inside of the human body both serve as spaces within which evil is combated. Once confined in these spaces, the Corpse Demoness is vanquished in real, or human, time, while the Evil Spirit is neutralized during mythic, or cosmic, time.[34]

Zoroastrians must think good thoughts, speak good words, perform good deeds, and purify their bodies and souls in order to assist Ahura Mazdā during the finite period of cosmic time. Each devotee is offered heaven after death and salvation at the end of time as a reward for his or her righteous and pious endeavors (Čīdag Handarz ī Pōryōtkēšān ll. 22, 39). Hence, life on earth becomes a necessary precursor to the life of the spirit in heaven after death. The soul's afterlife is itself only a prologue to the final resurrection at which the soul and body are reunited, purified, and made immortal (cf. Zaehner 1961: 278–279). Consequently, Zoroastrians believe that all human actions must be directed at obtaining final salvation, which will occur only if the gods, men, women, animals, plants, and other sacred creations unite in maintaining ritual purity and combating all forms of impurity, disorder, and evil.

Lévi-Strauss has argued that the functionalist thesis advocated by Durkheim, Malinowski, and other scholars is invalid and that there is no direct causal link by which myth overtly justifies the patterning of rites (1963: 206–231).[35] Lévi-Strauss also concluded that among certain peoples, such as the Pawnee American Indians, there are no myths underlying rituals as a whole, and when foundation myths do exist they generally relate to details of the rituals that appear secondary or supernumerary (1987: 204). It is not the present study's aim to establish or reject Lévi-Strauss' claim that there is no universal charter relationship between myth and ritual. However, it is imperative to realize that Lévi-Strauss' conclusions are valid for Zoroastrian purification rituals only insofar as the underlying mythology, cosmogony, cosmology, beliefs, and symbolism are not explicitly stated each time a rite is performed. Furthermore, as Eliade noted for religious practices in general, each and every Zoroastrian ritual has a divine model (1974: 21–27). A single cosmic archetype provides the beliefs, justification, purpose, and importance of every Zoroastrian purification rite. In addition, various aspects of every purification ritual have their own celestial connections, and each feature of the cosmos has a ritual expression. Tambiah (1979: 120) has observed that cosmological considerations are central to religious rituals in numerous societies; Zoroastrians form one such society.

As described earlier, all features of Zoroastrian purification rituals are symbolically connected to nature and the gods. The celestial bonds and parallels are then united by a single foundational belief or myth that utilizes doctrines, laws of purity and pollution, and ritual practices of purification to provide votaries with a symbolic means of ensuring final salvation. This foundational belief is that of the final renovation of the universe, and the divine model for the rituals is the faith's linear sacred history. Eschatological belief and ritual purification reciprocally complete each other, and, in doing so, reassert humanity's role in the universe.[36]

Ahura Mazdā, the beneficent immortals, the seven sacred creations, and numerous other aspects of the religious universe are symbolically present and involved in Zoroastrian purification rituals just as they are at the final renovation of the universe. They engage in combat, during the rituals, with the Corpse Demoness, who is the manifestation of death and pollution inflicted by Aŋra Mainyu upon the material and spiritual worlds. This ritualized battle is conducted in finite time, the duration of the ceremony, and within limited space, the pure spaces enclosed by the furrows and the body of the devotee. Evil and pollution are confined within the finite space and time of a ritual, are vanquished by prayers, substances, and actions that represent the gods and sacred creations, are cast out of the world, and are driven back into hell. The devotee undergoing the ritual is purified, symbolically refurbished, and granted immortality because his or her body and soul have been freed of evil, harm, suffering, pollution, and death. Therefore, it is accurate to conclude that Zoroastrian purification rituals are patterned on the cosmic archetype provided by sacred history: the invasion of the profane into the sacred, the entrapment of the invader in material space and time, the neutralization of evil and impurity, and the final expulsion of the Evil Spirit from creation forever. This represents, in microcosm, an enactment of macrocosmic renovation at the end of time. Metaphors of eschatology are symbolically connected via ritual to corporeal life and manipulated to create order, temporary perfection, and the hope of eventual transcendence. The ritual cycle is hence viewed as an intrinsic part of the cosmic events that are initiated and regulated by Ahura Mazdā. Inside the confines of the human body and the ritual furrows, as within the arch of the sky, evil is vanquished, matter utilized to enhance spiritual purity, and

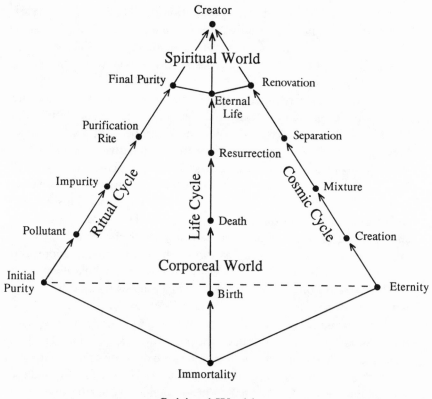

Figure 14. Ritual, Life, and Cosmic Cycles

spiritual salvation assured. In this manner, the life of each Zoroastrian is related to the events of the cosmos through a ritual cycle. The interconnection of ritual, life, and cosmic cycles is illustrated in figure 14.

The foundational myth of the renovation of the universe and the salvation of all human beings, when coupled with its ritual expression during purity rites, functions as a sophisticated religious theory based on homologies, analogies, alloforms, and symbols that establish a direct relationship between the individual and the universe. Each person is viewed as the microcosmic image of the universe, and the universe as the macrocosmic projection of the individual. The isomorphism between the divine macrocosm and the human microcosm together with the enactment of universal eschatology through the beliefs and practices of purification provide a symbolic culmination of the human quest as envisaged by Zoroastrianism.

These rituals remind the congregation that suffering and death are never final: they are, according to religious ethos, always followed by purification and resurrection; every defeat by evil is neutralized, counteracted, and transcended by final victory (cf. Eliade 1974: 101).

The specific pattern described by the purification rituals is timeless; it explains the past and present, as well as the future, providing the rituals with their operational value (Lévi-Strauss 1963: 209). The terror of history and the sufferings of individuals are rationalized in religious terms, and beliefs and practices—of which purity is an important aspect—are provided to aid the believer in life and eventual death. This hope of purity and immortality is an attempt to ensure faith rather than despair at the human condition. Consequently, despite the ambivalence toward evil and death expressed by some modern Zoroastrians (cf. Dhalla 1938) and claims that the religion is simply a code of ethics (cf. Modi 1962), most followers have retained the faith's core beliefs (cf. Axelrod 1974; Irani 1980) and continue to practice simplified versions of the purification rites. They also still regard their raison d'être as the combating of Aŋra Mainyu and absolve Ahura Mazdā of all evil (cf. Mistree 1982).

The Zoroastrian beliefs and practices of purity and pollution are integrated into the religion and presented as a unified part of the planned and purposeful handiwork of the supreme deity and creator of the universe: Ahura Mazdā. These beliefs and practices connect the material and spiritual worlds, making the entire universe a holy singularity whose purity must be strictly maintained at all times to ensure triumph over evil. For this reason Ahura Mazdā was described in a Middle Iranian catechism as advising the prophet Zarathushtra that "in that material world of mine, I who am Ahura Mazdā [preside] over the righteous man, Vohu Manah over cattle, Aša Vahišta over fire, Xšaθra Vairya over metal, Spənta Ārmaiti over the earth and virtuous women, Haurvatāt over the waters, and Amərətāt over the plants. Whoever teaches care for these seven [creations] does well and pleases [us]. Therefore, his [or her] soul will never arrive at kinship with Aŋra Mainyu and the demons. If an individual has cared for them [i.e., the creations], then he [or she] has cared for the seven beneficent immortals, and this he [or she] must preach to all persons" (Supplementary Texts to Šāyest nē Šāyest 15: 5–6).[37]

APPENDIX: PRAYERS FOR PURIFICATION

Ahunawar (Ahuna Vairya) (Av.)

As [is] the lord, so should the judge be chosen in accordance with righteousness. Establish the power of actions that result from a life lived with good purpose for Mazdā and the lord who was made shepherd for the poor.[1]

Ašəm Vohū (Av.)

Righteousness [is] good, it is best. According to [our] wish it is, according to our wish it shall be. Righteousness belongs to Aša Vahišta.[2]

Dastūrī (Pz.)

[We do this] with the religious authority of the creator Ahura Mazdā, with the religious authority of the beneficent immortals, with the religious authority of righteous Sraoša, with the religious authority of Zarathushtra the Spitamid, with the religious authority of Ādurbād, son of Māraspand, [and] with the religious authority of the [present] high priest . . . [name]. . . .[3]

Fravarānē (Av.)

I profess myself a Mazdean, a follower of Zarathushtra, opposing the demons, accepting the doctrine of Ahura, one who praises the beneficent immortals, who worships the beneficent immortals. I accredit all good things, those that are indeed the best, to Ahura Mazdā the good [being], [who is] rich with treasures; to the righteous, rich, [and] glorious [one], whose is the cow, whose is righteousness, whose is the light; may his blessed worlds be filled with light.

I choose for myself Spənta Ārmaiti the good. Let her be mine. I renounce theft, raiding of cattle, harm, and destruction of Mazdean abodes.

I shall grant movement and lodging at will to those [individuals] who are worthy, those who are upon this earth with [their] cattle. With reverence for righteousness [and] upraised offerings, I declare: henceforth, through caring for body or life, I shall not bring harm or destruction upon Mazdean abodes.

I forsake the company of the accursed demons, the impious, lawless, evil doing, the most demonic of beings, the foulest of beings, the least good of beings, the company of demons, and the followers of demons, of sorcerers and the followers of sorcerers, of those who cause harm to any beings by thoughts, words, deeds, or manifest signs. Truly, I forsake the company of all this as belonging to the demon, as [being] contemptuous.

Even as Ahura Mazdā taught Zarathushtra at each instance, at each deliberation, at each encounter at which Mazdā and Zarathushtra conversed.

Even as Zarathushtra forsook the company of demons at each instance, at each deliberation, at each encounter at which Mazdā and Zarathushtra conversed, so I forsake, as a Mazdean and follower of Zarathushtra, the company of demons, just as Zarathushtra [himself] forsook it.

In [accordance with] the choice of the waters, the choice of the plants, the choice of the beneficent cow, the choice of Ahura Mazdā who created the cow, who [created] the righteous man, by the choice of Zarathushtra, the choice of Kavi Vištāspa, the choice of Frašaoštra and Jāmāspa, the choice of each of the saviors [who] bring about renovation, in [accordance with] that choice and doctrine I am a Mazdean.

I profess myself a Mazdean, a follower of Zarathushtra, having pledged myself to, and acknowledged, the faith. I pledge myself to the thought [that is] well thought; I pledge myself to the word [that is] well spoken; I pledge myself to the deed [that is] well performed.

I pledge myself to the Mazdean religion, which casts off attacks, which causes weapons to be laid down, which upholds consanguineous marriage, which is just, which is the greatest of all [the religions] that are and will be, the best, the finest, which is Ahuric [and] Zoroastrian. I accredit all good things to Ahura Mazdā. This is the confession [of faith] of the Mazdean religion.[4]

Jasa Mē Avaṇhe Mazdā (Av.)

Come to my aid, O Mazdā!
Come to my aid, O Mazdā!
Come to my aid, O Mazdā!

I profess myself a Mazdean, a follower of Zarathushtra, having pledged myself to, and acknowledged, the faith. I pledge myself to the thought [that is] well thought; I pledge myself to the word [that is] well spoken; I pledge myself to the deed [that is] well performed.

I pledge myself to the Mazdean Religion, which casts off attacks, which causes weapons to be laid down, which upholds consanguineous marriage, which is just, which is the greatest of all [the religions] that are and will be, the best, the finest, which is Ahuric [and] Zoroastrian. I accredit all good things to Ahura Mazdā. This is the confession [of faith] of the Mazdean religion.

(Recite the Ašəm Vohū once.)

Kəm Nā Mazdā (Av.)

Whom, O Mazdā, have you appointed protector for one such as me, if the Evil One should dare to harm me? Whom other than [your] fire and [good] mind by whose actions, O Lord, righteousness is nourished. Proclaim this teaching for my conscience. Who shall be victorious to protect, in accordance with your teaching, those who are the offspring in my house? [As] world-healer, promise us a judge. Then let obedience come to him with good mind, O Mazdā, to him whosoever you wish. Protect us from the fiend, O Mazdā and Spənta Ārmaiti! Perish, O demonic lie! Perish, O demonic offspring! Perish, O demonic miscreation! Perish, O demonic begotten-being! Perish, O lie! Crawl away, O lie! Disappear, O lie! In the north you shall perish. You shall not destroy the material worlds of righteousness. Reverence [with] which is devotion and religious zeal.

(Recite the Ašəm Vohū once.)

Ohrmazd Xwadāy or Kustī Bastan (Phl. and Av.)

Ahura Mazdā [is] the lord! He keeps Aŋra Mainyu away, he holds him back. May Aŋra Mainyu be smitten and shattered, [together] with the demons, lies, sorcerers, sinners, hostile rulers, hostile priests, tyrants, evildoers, heretics, sinners, enemies, and deceivers. May they be smitten and shattered! May evil rulers be kept away! May enemies be defeated! May enemies be kept away! Ahura Mazdā [is] the lord! I am penitent for all sins. I repent for all bad thoughts, bad words, [and] bad deeds that I thought, spoke, [and] did in the material world, which arose [from me], which originated [from me]. I am contrite, Ahura Mazdā, for those sins of thought, word, [and] deed, of body [and] soul, corporeal [and] spiritual. I repent [for them]. I am penitent [for them] with three words. With satisfaction for Ahura Mazdā [and] scorn for Aŋra Mainyu [I do this]! [May there be] the complete fulfillment of what is most excellent according to [Ahura Mazdā's] will! I praise righteousness!

Petīt Pašēmānīh (Phl.)

The text and translation of this long confessional prayer are provided by Dhabhar (1927: 54–61; 1963: 100–122) and, therefore, are omitted from this Appendix.

Srōš Bāj (Av. and Pz.)

(Opening section:)

With satisfaction for Ahura Mazdā [I do this].

(Recite the Ašəm Vohū once.)

In the name of God. May the bountiful power and glory of Ahura Mazdā the lord increase. May it reach Sraoša the righteous, the strong, the command incarnate, who has a hard weapon, a mighty weapon, the commander of the creations of Ahura Mazdā. I expiate [and] repent of all sins. I expiate every evil thought, evil word, [and] evil deed [that] I have thought, said, [and] done, [which] occurred through me, [or] has originated from me in the corporeal world. I expiate with three pronouncements—[being] penitent and repentant in mind—those evil thoughts, evil words, [and] evil deeds of the body [and] the soul, of the corporeal world [and] the spiritual world.

(Recite the Ahunawar five times.)

(Recite the Ašəm Vohū three times.)

I profess myself a Mazdean, a follower of Zarathushtra, opposing the demons, accepting the doctrine of Ahura.

(Recite a Gāh for the appropriate watch of the day.)

Propitiation to Sraoša accompanied by Aši, the valiant, incorporated with the holy word, the strong-weaponed, the follower of Ahura, for worship, adoration, propitiation, and praise. "As [is] the lord [chosen]" the priest should recite to me; "So should the judge be chosen in accordance with righteousness" the righteous perceiving [one] should recite.

We worship Sraoša, accompanied by Aši, handsome, victorious, world promoting, righteous, the judge of righteousness.

The Ahunawar protects the body. (Repeat this phrase three times.)

(Recite the Ahunawar once.)

(Recite the Kəm Nā Mazdā once, up to ". . . the material worlds of righteousness.")

(Closing section:)

(Recite the last line of the Kəm Nā Mazdā, "Reverence [with] which is devotion and religious zeal," three times.)

(Recite the Ašəm Vohū once.)

(Recite the Ahunawar twice.)

I praise the worship, adoration, strength, and vigor of Sraoša, accompanied by Aši, the valiant, incorporated with the holy word, the strong-weaponed, the follower of Ahura.

(Recite the Ašəm Vohū once.)

Wealth and glory to him. Health of body to him. Firmness of body to him. Victoriousness of body to him. Possession of riches bringing much fortune to him. Successful progeny to him. Lengthy long-life to him. The best existence of the righteous to him, the radiant, with all happiness.

Thus may it come about as I wish.

(Recite the Ašəm Vohū once.)

A thousand remedies, ten thousand remedies. (Repeat this passage three times.)

(Recite the Ašəm Vohū once.)

Come to my aid, O Mazdā! (Recite this phrase three times.)

To Ama [the god Might], well built, handsome, victorious, created by Ahura, [and] to conquering Uparatāt [the goddess Superiority], [and] to Rāman [the god of Peace] of good pastures, [and to] Vayu [the Wind] of superior activity, superior to the other creatures, to that [portion] of you, Vayu, which belongs to Spənta

Mainyu, to autonomous Θwāša [the Firmament], to boundless Zurvan [Time], to Zurvan of the long dominion.[5]

(Recite the Ašəm Vohū once.)

I do righteousness for the love of my soul, for the reward of virtue, and [for] the redemption of sin. May all the virtue of all the good ones of the seven climes of the earth reach the width of the earth, the length of the rivers, [and] the height of the sun in their primal form. Be righteous [and] live long.

Thus may it come about as I wish.

(Recite the Ašəm Vohū once.)[6]

Yeṇhēhātąm (Av.)

We worship all those male and female beings whom Ahura Mazdā knows are best for worship according to righteousness.

NOTES

Preface

1. In this work, Near East refers to Iran, Iraq, the Gulf states, Saudi Arabia, Syria, Jordan, Israel, and Lebanon.

Introduction. Analysis of Beliefs and Practices

1. For a detailed discussion of the problems involved in elucidating the past, see Harvey (1966: 68–101). Harvey's conclusions are valid not only for historians but also for anthropologists and scholars of comparative religion.

2. For a concise survey of the history of the Zoroastrians, see Boyce (1979). Zaehner provides a general description of their religious beliefs (1961).

3. The access to these rituals, extended to Boyce by Irani Zoroastrians, reflects a gradual decline, during the last twenty-five years, in the belief that the presence of non-Zoroastrians vitiates religious ceremonies. There is little evidence for the presence of nonbelievers at Zoroastrian rites prior to this time.

4. Edward G. Browne noted the presence of a Zoroastrian theological college (Ar. *madrasa*) for priests in Iran during 1887 and 1888 (1893: 409). Priests were trained at several *madrasa*s in India during the nineteenth century C.E. (Karaka 1884: 2, 235–237). Priests continued to be trained in Iran until the late 1950s. By the 1960s, however, Irani Zoroastrians had to journey to Bombay, India, to be initiated into the priesthood (cf. Boyce 1977: 28). Most Zoroastrian Magi are now trained at the Athornan Boarding Madressa located in Dadar on the outskirts of Bombay, India. This institution is one of two colleges at which priests are still actively trained. Another *madrasa*, the M. F. Cama Athornan Institute located at Andheri in Bombay, has been recently reopened. Additionally, a few priests are privately trained in India, Pakistan, and Iran.

5. For the proposal that religion is a culturally constituted defense against the sociological problems raised by death and evil, see Geertz (1966: 19–24).

6. Ronald L. Grimes (1982: 21–31) provides a detailed, important discussion of the questions and problems that arise in the definition and study of rituals.

7. According to Geertz: "For the overwhelming majority of the religious in any population, however, engagement in some form of ritualized traffic with sacred symbols is the major mechanism by means of which they come not only to encounter a world view but actually to adopt it, to internalize it as part of their personality" (1971: 100).

8. See Ellis (1965: 263) for a detailed description of taboo in Polynesian society.

9. See Evans-Pritchard (1965), Geertz (1976), Leach (1968), and Turner (1967) for evaluations of anthropological approaches to the study of religion, ritual, and problems of interpretation.

10. Lévy-Bruhl's (1926) approach to the analysis of beliefs and practices clearly anticipated the formulations of Boas (1940).

1. Laws of Purity and Pollution

1. Neither the date nor the location of Zarathushtra's ministry has been firmly established. Many scholars, such as Ernest Herzfeld (1947), Walter B. Henning (1951), and Robert C. Zaehner (1961), believed that the prophet lived in western Iran during the sixth century B.C.E. More recent studies, based on linguistic similarities between the Avesta and the Ṛg Veda and on the social structure of society as portrayed in the Gāthās, have led Mary Boyce (1975; 1982), T. Burrow (1973), A. Shapur Shahbazi (1977), and Gherardo Gnoli (1980) to locate the prophet in northeastern Iran or northern Central Asia during the twelfth to eleventh centuries B.C.E. However, Helmut Humbach has demonstrated that Khwarazm, in northern Central Asia, which has been regarded as the region in which Zoroaster dwelt, was probably not the prophet's homeland (1985: 327–334). The site(s) of Zoroaster's birth and ministry remain unknown. For a detailed discussion on Zoroaster's priestly training, see Boyce (1970: 22–36).

2. Personal communication from Professor Gernot L. Windfuhr.

3. The Dēnkard states that "pain and misery come into the material world from the ailment and disease of the demons" (541, ll. 11–12).

4. See Choksy (1986a: 239–240) for a description of the Zoroastrian scheme of cosmic history and humanity's role in it.

5. See Zaehner (1961: 161–165), Gershevitch (1964: 17–38), Frye (1984a: 67, 81, 121), and Schwartz (1985a: 696–697) for discussions of the problems involving the ascent of the Magi. Schwartz (1985b: 484–485) analyses the term *magu-*.

6. See the Rivāyat ī Ēmēd ī Ašawahištān (42: 2–7, 19: 5–7) and the Persian Rivāyats (271, ll. 6–13), respectively. See also Choksy (1987b: 24–25).

7. For an analysis of the Vidēvdāt's significance, see Benveniste (1970).

8. Bailey (1971: 88–89, 104–105) discusses the associations among the states of matter, elements, and corporeal creations.

9. The arrangement of this list was clearly influenced by the economic importance of commodities, with the most valuable metals heading the list.

10. See the Persian Rivāyats (84, l. 13–85, l. 18) for a detailed list of these precautions.

11. See also the Ardā Wīrāz Nāmag (38: 1–7).

12. The Dēnkard mentions that unconsecrated bull's urine must be used to purify the hands prior to the use of water, especially after contact with blood, semen, carrion, or excrement (468, ll. 6–11).

13. According to the Bundahišn (1a: 3) and the Wizīdagīhā ī Zādspram (34: 50), all creations except human beings and animals arose from water.

14. In India, pressure from Hindus gradually compelled the Parsis to abandon the sacrifice of large animals. The same occurred in Iran under Muslim rule. But, according to Dastur Dr. Firoze M. Kotwal, the ritual sacrifice of small animals, such as goats, continued at Parsi settlements, such as Navsari, until the late nineteenth century (personal communication).

15. During the Sasanian era, however, regnal fires were regularly extinguished after a ruler's demise.

16. Numerous examples of these coins are reproduced in Göbl (1971).

17. For a list of the beneficent creatures, see the Bundahišn (13: 1–36).

18. For a list of the noxious creatures, see the Bundahišn (22: 8–28) and the Persian Rivāyats (272, ll. 7–12). The term *xrafstra-* is first used in the Avesta (Yasna 28: 5, 34: 5).

19. Zoroastrians who violate this edict lose their ritual purity; see the Dēnkard (446, ll. 20–22).

20. See Tafazzoli (1975: 395–398) for an account of the elephant as a demonic creature and a symbol of royalty.

21. The Mēnōg ī Xrad (16: 64–65) and the Persian Rivāyats (268, ll. 4–8) state that silk should be avoided if possible.

22. The Vidēvdāt (3: 14, 7: 2–4, 8: 35–72) and the Dādestān ī Dēnīg (16: 7) describe this demoness.

23. The burial of a corpse is said to displease the earth, and exhumation of it rejoices the earth, as does the demolishing of tombs (Vidēvdāt 3: 12–13, 7: 50–52). Similarly, cremation is believed to be a product of the Evil Spirit aimed at polluting fire (Vidēvdāt 1: 17). Sins that result from placing a corpse in water are listed in the Vidēvdāt (7: 25–27, 49–51).

24. See also Plutarch (18: 5).

25. Two other terms were also used for polluted persons: *hamrīd*, "one who is directly defiled by carrion," and *patrīd*, "one who is indirectly defiled by carrion"; see the Vidēvdāt (19: 20–22).

26. The Vidēvdāt (5: 51) refers to the mixture of consecrated bull's urine and fire ash. The recitation of holy utterances and the ablutions with unconsecrated bull's urine are also mentioned in the Pahlavi Vidēvdāt (19: 22).

27. The purificatory effect of sunlight is described in the Zand ī Xwurdag Abestāg (Xwaršēd Niyāyišn ll. 12–14). See Dhabhar (1963: 34–36) for a translation of this passage.

28. This line is a misunderstanding of a passage from the Avesta (Yasna 48: 5), but the sense in which compilers of the Vidēvdāt understood it reveals the importance acquired by ritual purity.

2. The Baraśnūm Ī Nō Šab Ritual

1. See Boyce (1975: 314; 1977: 111).
2. See chapter 1 regarding sunlight.
3. Chapters 8, 9, and 19 of the Vidēvdāt.
4. If, however, the corpses had been exposed to the gaze of a dog or bird of prey, the capacity for pollution was far less, and the polluted individual could be purified simply by cleansing his or her body with unconsecrated bull's urine and water (Vidēvdāt 8: 36).
5. Since one fathom measures six feet, the area was equal to 2,916 square feet.
6. The original barsom (Av. *barəsma-;* Phl. *barsom;* P.Gj. *barsam*) was a species of grass. By the medieval period, twigs had been substituted for the grass. For the past two centuries, Parsis have used metal rods instead of twigs. The original bundles of grass were several feet long, but the rods are presently only nine inches long and one-eighth inch in diameter; see Boyce (1982: 38–39).
7. On the Younger Avestan term *maya,* see Schwartz (1985*b:* 477).
8. Evidence that the pits were arranged from north to south is provided by the Pahlavi commentary based on the edict of Āfarg (Pahlavi Vidēvdāt 9: 32).
9. A description of the Yasna ritual is provided by Modi (1922: 266–329). A videotape with commentary of the Yasna is available through Audio-Visual Services of Colorado State University, Fort Collins, Colorado 80523. The ceremony continues to be performed as Modi described it.
10. This system of barriers, or walls, may derive from a belief that the religion itself is protected by seven walls. This belief is preserved in the Dēnkard: "The religion has seven walls. The outermost one was said by them to be holy utterance and exegesis" (519, ll. 5–6).
11. The passage should read: "And praise, devotion, and religious zeal." However, the Pahlavi commentary translates it as: "Praise to Spənta Ārmaiti, the propitious" (Phl. *niyāyišn spendarmad ī abzōnīg*). This reveals that the words were used in reference to the earth goddess, who receives the purificatory liquids after these have cleansed the candidate.
12. According to the Vidēvdāt (9: 27), these holy utterances are both victory granting and curing.
13. See chapter 1.
14. Punishment for malpractice theoretically included execution.
15. I am grateful to Professor Gernot L. Windfuhr for his advice on this passage.
16. These texts also indicate that anyone who touched a corpse had to undergo purification before performing any devotional acts.
17. This is a quote from the Vidēvdāt (9: 41).
18. See also the Nāmagīhā ī Manuščihr (1: 4.4–7).

19. See Boyce (1975: 314 and n. 17).

20. Irani Zoroastrians maintain this practice. In India, Parsis do not conduct the ritual during the rainy seasons for similar reasons.

21. See Boyce and Kotwal (1971*a*: 63; 1971*b*: 303, 305–306) for the text, translation, and commentary of this prayer of grace.

22. Kreyenbroek (1985: 143–163) examines the role of Sraoša in ritual observances.

23. Additionally, in 1746 C.E. a disagreement over the religious calendar caused the Parsi community to divide into the traditionalists (P.Gj. Shenshai, Rasimi) and the ancient ones (P.Gj. Kadmi). The Kadmis rejected many Parsi variations in ritual and adopted Irani practices. Hence, Kadmi priests readopted the original orientation of the ritual furrows and stones and now arrange these from north to south.

24. The *nāwar* and *martab* initiations are described by Modi (1922: 197–209).

25. Personal communication from Dastur Dr. Firoze M. Kotwal.

26. There is evidence in the writings of Zoroastrians that conversion to the faith did occur in both Iran and India, although not on a large scale (Persian Rivāyats 281, ll. 1–2; 282, l. 18). Karaka noted the conversion of Hindus in India during the nineteenth century (1884: 1, 168–169). Browne was told by Zoroastrians in Yazd that the Muslim wives of votaries were often sent to Bombay for conversion to Zoroastrianism (1893: 416–417). The prohibition on conversion arose in the late nineteenth and early twentieth centuries.

27. There are individual communities, both Parsi and Irani, notably those in Iran and the United States, that permit conversion. For example, an American named Joseph H. Peterson was converted in 1983 at the Zoroastrian temple in New Rochelle, New York. Peterson had the support of Zoroastrian priests in Chicago and the agreement of the Zoroastrian Association of Greater New York, which permitted its facilities to be used for his conversion ceremony. These conversions occur because some priests sanction them and have the support of portions of the lay community. Most priests and laypersons, however, do not regard the conversions as valid.

28. Karaka noted the occasional performance of this ritual upon members of the laity during the 1880s (1884: 2, 237–238). Modi states: "Up to about fifty years ago it was not rare to see persons, both male and female, themselves going through the ceremony. . . . But, now-a-days the priests are paid to take *Barashnūms* on behalf of other persons" (1924: 16 n. 2).

29. This letter was reprinted in a Parsi newspaper, the *Navsari Prakash,* October 12, 1924, pp. 4–5.

30. Note the rectangular walls of the Barsingō at the Wadi Dār-i Mihr in Navsari, visible in figure 5.

31. Kotwal and Boyd (1977: 23–24) describe the purification of sacred instruments.

32. See Boyce (1975: 315).

33. For reference to the Yasna ceremony, see note 9. Modi (1922: 446) describes

the Parsi version of the Nīrangdīn ceremony, and Boyce (1977: 93 and n. 1) mentions the Irani version.

34. In India the fee for having a priest undergo it vicariously is 600 to 800 rupees. There is no fixed fee in Iran.

35. This is because a candidate has to leave the room in which the retreat is conducted to perform the Noh-Shūy ablutions and bodily functions.

36. This practice arose during the medieval period; see the Pahlavi Rivāyat of Ādurfarnbay and Farnbaysrōš (35: 1–2) and the Persian Rivāyats (606, l. 3–608, l. 8).

37. Senior priests usually watch the candidate at all times during the retreat in order to prevent nocturnal pollution from occurring. The dearth of new initiates into the priesthood makes it vital that potential applicants not be disqualified by this ritual technicality.

38. Personal communication from Dastur Dr. Firoze M. Kotwal.

39. Although sheep are believed to be ritually pure animals, their heads and feet become unclean once separated from the body and are usually not consumed.

3. Purification on Specific Occasions

1. See the Persian Rivāyats (310, l. 19–315, l. 17). The term *pādyāb,* "against water," refers to the interposing of bull's urine between the pollutants and the water.

2. The *ṣudra* is a white undershirt that has a small pouch at the chest, which symbolically receives all good deeds performed by the devotee. The *kustī* is a single cord of six interwoven strands, each strand of twelve white woolen threads. Hence, the sacred girdle consists of seventy-two threads. The six strands are braided together at each end of the girdle to form three tassels, which contain twenty-four threads each.

The sacred girdle's symbolism was elaborated over the centuries. The six strands are equated to the six religious feasts, the twelve white threads to the twelve months, the twenty-four threads of the tassels to the chapters of the Visparad, "All the Chiefs"—which consists of an extended Yasna and Vidēvdāt—and the seventy-two threads of the entire girdle to the chapters of the Yasna. Tying the *kustī* around the waist is believed to separate the head and heart from evil, and the will of the mind from the passions of the loins. The Pahlavi Čīm ī Kustīg, "Reasons for the Sacred Girdle," states: "And the place of all beauty, light and wisdom is the higher part, the head [, which], like paradise, [is] the place of lights . . . and that lower half, the place of darkness and desolation, is like hell . . . the reason for wearing the sacred girdle is to show the two sides" (42–47). See also Browne (1893: 404) for similar Irani Zoroastrian beliefs during the years 1887 and 1888.

3. The Wizīdagīhā ī Zādspram mentions that Zarathushtra donned a sacred girdle, which was obtained from his father, Pourušaspa, upon reaching the age of maturity (20: 1–2).

4. The Parsi initiation is described by Modi (1922: 190–196), and the Irani version by Boyce (1977: 238–240).

5. A *framān* is a minor degree of sin. A *tanāpuhl* sin, however, disables the soul

from safely crossing the Bridge of the Separator after death; its expiation cost three hundred staters.

6. After nocturnal pollution, however, the Pādyāb is usually performed over the entire body.

7. These instructions, first codified in the Persian Rivāyats (32, ll. 9–15), are now taught to every new initiate.

8. Boyce and Kotwal (1971*a:* 58) describe this *bāj* and reproduce the texts.

9. During the simple Kustī ceremony, however, this prayer is omitted.

10. Similarly, a bell is rung three times in fire temples during offerings to the sacred fires in the Bōy ceremony (Modi 1922: 233–239). Sounds produced in prayer and ritual are thought to be powerful weapons against the forces of evil.

11. See Boyce (1977: 100).

12. See Schacht (1913) and Burton (1988).

13. See Morony (1984: 445).

14. See Wensinck (1913).

15. It should be noted that in Islamic practice the *ghusl* is an ablution performed after more serious defilement, including sexual intercourse and nocturnal pollution.

16. The term *nāhn* is a contraction of *snān-* (Skt.), "ablution, bath," from the root *sna-*, which has the cognate form *snā-* (Av.), "to bathe, to wash."

17. See Kotwal and Boyd (1977: 23–24) for a detailed description of this process.

18. For this *bāj*, see Boyce and Kotwal (1971*a:* 63; 1971*b:* 303). See also ch. 2 n. 21.

19. The word *petīt*, "penance, repentance," is a contracted form of Av. *paitita*, "expiation," from the base *paiti.ay-*.

20. The Ahunawar may be recited in place of any other prayer because it is regarded as the most potent of Zoroastrian holy utterances.

21. Zoroastrians are enjoined never to recite any prayer bareheaded, hence the necessity of covering the head with the right palm.

22. Modi (1922: 96–99) describes the ritual as performed in the 1920s.

23. Purification of the initiate occurs in all three religious traditions. However, unlike Hinduism and Christianity, Zoroastrianism does not regard water as a primary purifying agent because this liquid is extremely vulnerable to pollution, as noted earlier. According to Zoroastrian doctrine, water can be used for purificatory purposes only after unconsecrated urine has first been applied to expel all impurities from the surface of the body; see chapter 1.

24. Frawardīgān is the festival dedicated to the immortal souls of human beings. It is celebrated during the last five days of the twelfth month and the following five days. The goddess Spənta Ārmaiti is the protector of women. To honor her, Parsi women undergo the Saḍe Nāhn during her festival. Zoroastrian women in Iran often undergo the Sī-Shūy Nāhn on this occasion. See also Boyce (1975: 313).

25. This arrangement is given in Persian Rivāyats (600).

26. Boyce (1977: 111) states that in Yazd, Iran, this ritual is now administered using furrows drawn for the Barašnūm ī nō šab.

27. See chapter 1 for the Zoroastrian hierarchy of metals with regard to their

purity and resistance to impurities. The use of stone mounts in the Sī-Shūy Nāhn satisfies both ritual and economic considerations. See also the Vidēvdāt (7: 73–75) and the Persian Rivāyats (239, ll. 8–10). For a discussion of the nature and function of the sky, see chapter 5.

28. This process is described by Kotwal and Boyd (1977: 23).

29. It was not possible for corpse bearers to undergo the Purification of the Nine [Days and] Nights after each funeral. Hence, the purificatory effect of the Sī-Shūy Nāhn was deemed sufficient to prevent the spread of pollution through the usual activities of this social group. However, corpse bearers had to undergo the nine night purification prior to entering a fire temple. During the last decade, neither purification has been regularly undergone by Zoroastrian corpse bearers in India because the laws governing ritual purity and pollution have gradually lost favor with an increasingly secular Parsi community; see chapter 4.

30. The period of uncleanness lasts for forty days according to Sunni law and ten days according to Shī'īte law. For a description of the *Ghusl* see Bousquet (1960).

31. See chapter 2.

32. The five ecclesiastic groups are the Sanjanas at the town of Sanjan, the Bhagarias serving Navsari, the Godavras at Anklesar, the Bharuchas at Broach, and the Khambattas of Cambay.

33. See chapter 2.

34. This parallels the situation of women in menses; see chapter 4.

35. The number fifteen is believed to represent a fivefold multiplication of good thoughts, good words, and good deeds.

36. The Rīman ritual, as practiced during the first twenty years of the present century, is described by Modi (1922: 154–157).

37. Compare the modern enclosure (fig. 11) with that described by Modi (1922: 154–155).

4. Purity in Daily Life

1. See chapter 1.

2. For this passage, see the Shāhnāma (7: 138–139).

3. This formula is based on the Yasna (48: 6). The line was probably chosen because it refers to plants, which arise from human hair; see Bundahišn (28: 4, 34: 5).

4. Bundahišn (28: 4, 34: 5). See also chapter 5.

5. This formula is based on the Yasna (33: 7), with a play upon the word *sruyē*, "I may be heard," and the dual form of *sruya-*, "nails of both hands," together with an inaccurate apprehension of *maɣaonō*- as "pure." See also Darmesteter (1895: 191).

6. This belief was recorded in the Vidēvdāt (17: 10), the Bundahišn (24: 28), and the Šāyest nē Šāyest (12: 6).

7. For example, Seervai and Patel (1899: 219) complain: "After shaving his head a Parsi should bathe before touching anything. . . . In practice, though they know they are laid down in their religion, Parsis neglect many of these rules . . . when the

nails or hair are cut, texts should be said over them and they should be buried four inches underground. Temple priests are careful to observe this practice."

8. Lincoln (1986: 87–98) provides an interesting study of the interconnection between plants, hair, and baldness. He also examines the widespread practice of tonsuring members of Indo-European societies.

9. See the Šāyest nĕ Šāyest (3: 9, 10: 5). For a translation of this prayer, see Dhabhar (1963: 3–5).

10. The Vaeϑā Nask (ll. 112–113) gives a parallel opening formula: "The Evil Spirit, the lie, shall be smitten."

11. See the Vaeϑā Nask (ll. 111–116) and Boyce and Kotwal (1971*b*: 311).

12. This was originally stipulated in the Šāyest nē Šāyest (10: 5).

13. Parsis in Pakistan and Sri Lanka even performed the Pādyāb-Kustī in public places, such as markets.

14. See the Pahlavi Rivāyat of Ādurfarnbay and Farnbaysrōš (26) and the Persian Rivāyats (38, l. 12–40, l. 9).

15. Modi (1932: 139 n. 1) wrote that he witnessed this practice at Yazd in 1925.

16. The Parsi marriage ceremony is documented and discussed by Modi (1922: 17–46).

17. See also the Čīdag Handarz ī Pōryōtkēšān (l. 50).

18. References to consanguineous marriage in the Dēnkard were deleted by the editor of the standard version (Madan 1911) but are now available in a facsimile edition (Dresden 1966).

19. See also Zaehner (1972: 151–153).

20. Frye (1985: 445–455) provides a careful analysis and evaluation of problems of the term *xvaētvadaϑa* and a summary of the Iranian evidence for the practice of incest. The relevance of Roman tax records from Egypt, which demonstrate the practice of consanguineous marriage in a classical population, to the Zoroastrian practice is also evaluated in the article. As Frye demonstrates, there is no evidence for the widespread practice of consanguineous marriage among Zoroastrians prior to Sasanian and early Islamic times.

21. See Fischer (1978: 211 and n. 19).

22. Fischer (1978: 200 n. 23) is thus incorrect in concluding that divorce was a twentieth-century innovation among Zoroastrians and that apostasy was the only recognized grounds for divorce prior to the modern period.

23. The Pahlavi commentary to this passage notes: "Not that the two deeds are equal, but that neither is good." This indicates that copulation with a menstruating woman is a *tanāpuhl* sin and can be atoned for through the payment of a fine. However, the burning of a corpse is a sin for which there is no atonement.

24. According to the Ardā Wīrāz Nāmag (22: 7), it is a sin of fifteen and a half *tanāpuhls,* which equaled 4,650 staters.

25. Isolation of women in menses enforced this abstinence; see Modi (1922: 174–175) and Boyce (1977: 100–102).

26. The Persian Rivāyats (191, ll. 12–19) provides a detailed description of this rite.

27. This belief is still widely prevalent among Zoroastrians.

28. See the Persian Rivāyats (311, l. 19–315, l. 3) for the legend on the Evil Spirit's homosexuality.

29. Compare the Persian Rivāyats (193, l. 11–195, l. 2), which describes the ritual and rewards for practicing it.

30. See chapter 2.

31. Personal communication from Dastur Dr. Firoze M. Kotwal.

32. See also Neusner (1973: 46).

33. Compare Musallam (1983: 15–16).

34. Zaehner's hypothesis that "the 'Whore' is the First Woman just as Gayō-mart is the First Man" (1976: 43) is, therefore, incorrect, as is Riencourt's elaboration (1983: 83–84) of Zaehner's conclusions.

35. Boyce (1975: 308 and n. 83) recognized the ambiguity in women's status but claimed that it did not represent the "general or standard Zoroastrian attitude."

36. The Persian Rivāyats (207, l. 3–209, l. 18) directs that a distance of thirty paces be maintained from fire, water, and barsom twigs. This reveals that the precautions against pollution had become even more elaborate between the fourteenth and eighteenth centuries.

37. See Boyce (1977: 100) for a description of the Irani seclusion chambers.

38. This parallels the effect of the Whore Demoness, whose gaze withers plants, water, earth, good thoughts, good words, and good deeds, and the strength and the righteousness of devotees (Vidēvdāt 18: 61–65).

39. See chapter 3 for a discussion of this omission of the rituals.

40. These ablutions are based on the Vidēvdāt (16: 12). See also the Rivāyat ī Ēmēd ī Ašawahištān (34: 2–7) and the Persian Rivāyats (207, l. 3–209, l. 18).

41. This action is believed to have the value of atoning for 100,000 death-deserving sins.

42. For translations, see Schmidt (1960) and Hodivala (1920: 94–117), respectively. There is very little evidence that either account is based on historical events.

43. According to the Vidēvdāt, a Purification of the Nine [Days and] Nights was conducted (5: 54). By the period in which the Persian Rivāyats was composed, a simple ablution with unconsecrated bull's urine sufficed (229, l. 10–232, l. 6).

44. The Vidēvdāt states that seclusion continued for nine days after the first ablution (5: 52–56). Medieval sources, however, give the period of seclusion as forty days. It appears that this period was lengthened to safeguard the community from any possible pollution (Ṣaddar Nasr 77: 4; Persian Rivāyats 228, l. 5–233, l. 9).

45. See chapter 1.

46. A passage in the Dēnkard states: "Be vegetarians, you men, so that you may live long. Keep away from the flesh of beneficent animals, for the reckoning is great. Ahura Mazdā, the lord, created plants in great number for assisting beneficent animals" (533, l. 21–534, l. 2). The Pahlavi Texts advise people to "refrain

strictly from consuming the flesh of cattle and [other] beneficent animals, lest strict reckoning be upon you in this world and the next" (145, ll. 14–16).

47. On the dog, see the Vidēvdāt (13: 1–56) and the Bundahišn (24: 50–51). On the cock, "who foreshadows the coming of dawn" and protects the house from demons, see the Vidēvdāt (18: 14–15) and the Bundahišn (24: 48–49).

48. This practice is based on edicts in the Persian Rivāyats (107, l. 14–108, l. 17; 144, ll. 8–17). Parsis now use a piece of cotton cloth or tape, while Irani Zoroastrians still use an old sacred girdle. See also Boyce (1977: 151).

49. This stipulation of eligible persons is found in the Šāyest nē Šāyest (2: 8) and the Persian Rivāyats (115, l. 11–116, l. 1; 117, ll. 1–10).

50. The Irani rites for the dead are garnered in Boyce (1977: 148–163). The Parsi rites continue in the manner described by Modi (1922: 52–75).

51. Personal communication from Dastur Dr. Firoze M. Kotwal.

5. Purity, Symbols, and Eschatology

1. Roy Wagner (1986: 5–11) deciphers the role of "meaning" in cultural life.

2. The uniqueness of Zoroastrians' notions on spirit and matter and the influence of these notions on eschatological beliefs are carefully examined by Shaked (1971).

3. See also the Yasna (48: 5) and the Vidēvdāt (5: 21).

4. This phrase is echoed in the Vidēvdāt (5: 21) and the Nāmagīhā ī Manuščihr (1: 2.8).

5. Lincoln (1975) has convincingly demonstrated that this myth is definitely proto-Indo-European in origin and not a myth found throughout the world whenever societies reach the tuber-cultivation stage of the palaeoplanters (Jensen 1963) or a manifestation of the universal structure of the human mind (Neumann 1954).

6. The closest parallels to the Zoroastrian myth are found in the Vedic legends of Puruṣa (R̥g Veda 10: 90) and Yama (R̥g Veda 10: 13.4).

7. See also the Bundahišn (4: 20–21, 4a: 1–6).

8. The role of sacrifice and death in the origin of plants and food is widespread among a range of Indo-European cultures; see Lincoln (1986: 65–86).

9. Details of an ancient sacrifice that produced cereals are also present in Mithraic reliefs of the "tauroctone." When the god Mithras (Av. Miϑra; Skt. Mitra) conducted the bull sacrifice, useful herbs and plants sprang from the body of the moribund bovine. Initially thought to reflect Zoroastrian theology (Cumont 1956: 21, 39, 132–137), these reliefs are now known to preserve ancient Iranian sacrificial ideology, which was modified under Greco-Roman iconographic influences (Christensen 1917: 101; Hinnells 1974: 242–260; 1975: 304–309; Roll 1977: 53–68). The cult of Mithras probably originated as the result of contact between Roman troops and Iranians in the Crimea and in the Danubian region and was then transferred in its attested Greco-Roman form to Syria and Italy (Beskow 1978: 7–18).

10. The Vidēvdāt preserves a belief that demons thrive and carrion becomes more noxious after the sun has set (7: 58).

11. See chapter 4 and note 19.

12. Numerous examples of such prayers are found in chapters 2, 3, and 4.

13. The same is true for many groups of Hindus and Muslims in India and Sri Lanka. The Sinhalese Buddhist laity of Sri Lanka also fail to understand the chants of monks (cf. Tambiah 1968: 179). A similar situation persisted within Roman Catholic communities around the world prior to the Vatican's sanctioning use of vernacular languages in place of Latin in 1965.

14. See chapter 2 and note 10.

15. On the role of the three saviors, see the Bundahišn (33: 29, 32, 34: 3–33). See also Choksy (1986a: 240).

16. Parallels may be drawn to some of the seven mortal sins of Christianity: pride, covetousness, lust, envy, gluttony, anger, and sloth.

17. This is done by reciting the Dastūrī, which names the deities and individuals; see Appendix.

18. Chapter 2 contains a discussion of these punishments.

19. The close relationship between Ahura Mazdā and human beings is discussed in the Bundahišn (3: 12).

20. An excellent study of the nature of humanity is found in Bailey (1971: 78–119). Numerous other homologies and alloforms between microcosmic humans and macrocosmic referents are found in the Pahlavi passages cited by Bailey. Humanity's microcosmic reflection of the macrocosmos was also examined by Molé (1963: 406–411, 418–420). For a discussion on the notion of the senses as preserved in the Pahlavi books, see Bailey (1971: 102). Indic legends of the body as microcosm are analyzed by Wayman (1982: 172–190).

21. The ancient Indo-European speculation on the nature of bodily parts thus yielded an understanding of the cosmos. Numerous cultures were heirs to this world view, based on mythic physiology and mythic cosmology. Even Shakespeare proclaimed it in *The Tempest* (1: 2):

> Full fathom five thy father lies;
> Of his bones are coral made;
> Those are pearls that were his teeth;
> Nothing of him that doth fade,
> But doth suffer a sea-change
> Into something rich and strange
> Sea-nymphs hourly ring his knell.

(Noted by Lincoln 1986: 216 n. 21)

22. For a detailed description of Zoroastrian belief in the afterlife of the soul, see Pavry (1929), who provides translations of the relevant primary sources.

23. According to the Mēnōg ī Xrad, the Daēna approaches the soul only after judgment (1: 74, 81–90).

24. See chapter 2.

25. On the term *frašō.kərəti-, frašagird*, see Bailey (1971: vii–xvi). A useful discussion of Zoroastrian eschatology is found in Molé (1963: 86–100, 412–418).

26. Compare the parallels between eschatology in Zoroastrianism (Bundahišn 34: 1–33) and in the Bible (Revelation 20: 1–21: 27).

27. The most elaborate description of this sacred history is found in the Bundahišn (1: 1–72, 33: 1–34: 33). The Zoroastrian apocalyptic is preserved in the Zand ī Wahman Yašt (1: 1–9: 23).

28. The English word *paradise* is simply a translation of the Old Persian and Avestan *pairi.daēza-*, "walled garden." It was assimilated into Greek as *paradeisos* and Latin as *paradisus* and appeared in Middle English as *paradis*.

29. The fortress of the sky is also mentioned in the Bundahišn (1*a:* 6, 26: 76).

30. On the nature of the sky, see Bailey (1971: 120–148). For the connections among stones, rock crystals, and metals, see chapter 1.

31. See the Bundahišn (1*a:* 8), the Wizīdagīhā ī Zādspram (34: 20), and the Škand Gumānīg Wizār (4: 75).

32. See also Zaehner (1972: 88–89) and Bailey (1971: 147–148).

33. The theories of macrocosm and microcosm are preserved in a wide variety of non-Zoroastrian sources more ancient than the Pahlavi literature; see Lincoln (1986: 1–40).

34. An important discussion of real time and mythic time is found in Wagner (1986: 81–95).

35. See Wagner (1986: 199–206) for a useful critique of Lévi-Strauss' theories.

36. Lévi-Strauss (1987: 204) reached this conclusion for the relationship between myth and ritual in general.

37. See also Ṣaddar Bondahesh (12: 3–4).

Appendix

1. An analysis of the problems involved in interpretation of the Ahunawar prayer is found in Insler (1975*b*).

2. See Boyce (1975: 262 and n. 48) for references to other interpretations.

3. See the Persian Rivāyats (108, l. 16–109, l. 9) for variations of the Dastūrī.

4. See Boyce (1975: 253–256) for an analysis of this profession of faith. Because there is no evidence for the practice of *xvaētvadaθa* among the ancient Iranians, it is likely that this term is a later interpolation. See also chapter 4 and note 20.

5. Gray (1929: 124–129, 132–133, 156–157, 162–163, 169–170) provides a concise analysis of each deity mentioned in this passage. Zaehner (1972: 87–89, 202) examines the nature of Θwāša, in addition to elucidating the concepts encompassed by Zurvan.

6. See Dhabhar (1963: 10–17) and Kreyenbroek (1985: 145–148).

SELECTED GLOSSARY

Important Zoroastrian terms in Avestan, Pahlavi, New Persian, Pāzand, Dari, and Parsi Gujarati are listed in this glossary under their original forms. All transcribed terms also have been defined where they first appear in the text.

āb (Phl. and N.P.): see *āp-*
Abestāg (Phl.) (variant: Avesta): Pure Instruction, the Zoroastrian scriptures
Ahreman (Phl.): see Aŋra Mainyu
Ahura Mazdā (Av.) (variant: Ohrmazd): Lord Wisdom
aiwayāhan (Pz.): see *aiwyāŋhana-*
aiwyā̊ŋhana-(Av.) (variant: *aiwayāhan*): sacred girdle
amahraspand (Phl.): see *aməša.spənta-*
Amərətāt (Av.) (variant: Amurdād): Immortality, a beneficent immortal
aməša.spənta-(Av.) (variant: *amahraspand*): beneficent immortal(s)
Amurdād (Phl.): see Amərətāt
Aŋra Mainyu (Av.) (variant: Ahreman): Destructive or Evil Spirit
āp-(Av.) (variants: *āb, āw*): water
ardā (Phl.): see *aša-*
Ardwahišt (Phl.): see Aša Vahišta
aša-(Av.) (variant: *ardā*): righteousness
Aša Vahišta (Av.) (variant: Ardwahišt): Best Righteousness, a beneficent immortal
Ašō Zušta (Av.): Friend of Righteousness, the owl
Avesta (Pz.) see Abestāg
āw (P.Gj.): see *āp-*
bāj (N.P. and P.Gj.): see *vāk-*
Barašnūm-Gāh (Phl.) (variant: Barsingō): site of purification
Barašnūm ī nō šab (Phl.) (variants: Bareshnūm-i noh shab nāhn, Noh Shva): Purification of the Nine [Days and] Nights

Bareshnūm-i noh shab nāhn (P.Gj.): see Barašnūm ī nō šab

Barsingō (P.Gj.): see Barašnūm-Gāh

bhasam (P.Gj.): fire ash

bī-namāz (D. and P.Gj.): without prayer

daēva- (Av.) (variant: *dēw*): demon

daštān (Phl.): menstruation

daštānestān (Phl.): place for menstruating women

dastūr (P.Gj.): high priest

daxma- (Av.) (variants: *daxmag, dokhma*): funerary tower

daxmag (Phl.): see *daxma-*

dēw (Phl.): see *daēva-*

dokhma (P.Gj.): see *daxma-*

drug- (Av.) (variants: *druǰ, druz*): lie

druǰ (Phl.): see *drug-*

druǰō.dəmāna- (Av.): hell

Druxš Nasuš (Av.) (variant: Druz ī Nasuš): Corpse Demoness

druz (Phl.): see *drug-*

Druz ī Nasuš (Phl.): see Druxš Nasuš

dušhūxt (Phl.): evil word(s)

dušmat (Phl.): evil thought(s)

dušox (Phl.): hell

dušxwaršt (Phl.): evil deed(s)

framān (Phl.): a minor degree of sin

frašagird (Phl.): see *frašō.kərəti-*

frašō.kərəti- (Av.) (variant: *frašagird*): final renovation of the universe

gaēiϑya- (Av.) (variant: *gētīg*): corporeal, material

gāh (Phl.): place, site, space

Gannāg Mēnōg (Phl.): Destructive or Evil Spirit

gaomaēza- (Av.) (variant: *gōmēz*): unconsecrated bull's urine

garō.dəmāna- (Av.) (variant: *garōdmān*): heaven, paradise

garōdmān (Phl.): see *garō.dəmāna-*

Gāthā (Av.): Hymn(s) or Song(s), a part of the Avesta

gētīg (Phl.): see *gaēiϑya-*

gētīg astišnīh (Phl.): material existence

ghusl (Ar. and P.Gj.): ablution, washing

gōmēz (Phl. and P.Gj.): see *gaomaēza-*

gōwišn (Phl.): (good) word(s)

graom nava pixəm (Av.) (variant: *graw kē pixag*): nine-knotted stick

graw kē pixag (Phl.): see *graom nava pixəm*

gumēzišn (Phl.): mixture

gunza-i punidun (D.): place for menstruating women

hamēstagān (Phl.): limbo

haoma (Av.): plant from which ritual drink is prepared

Haurvatāt (Av.) (variant: Hordād): Wholeness or Perfection, a beneficent
  immortal

hixr (Phl.): see *hixra-*

hixra- (Av.) (variant: *hixr*): bodily refuse or excrement

Hordād (Phl.): see Haurvatāt

humat (Phl.): see *humata-*

humata- (Av. and Pz.) (variant: *humat*): good thought(s)

huwaršt (Phl.): see *hvaršta-*

hūxt (Phl.): see *hūxta-*

hūxta- (Av. and Pz.) (variant: *hūxt*): good word(s)

hvaršta- (Av. and Pz.) (variant: *huwaršt*): good deed(s)

ijār (P.Gj.): leggings

iristō.kaša (Av.): see *nasu.kaša*

J̌ahī (Av.): see J̌ahikā

J̌ahikā (Av.) (variants: J̌ahī, Jeh, J̌eh): Whore Demoness

Jeh (N.P. and P.Gj.): see J̌ahikā

J̌eh (Phl.): see J̌ahikā

karša- (Av.) (variants: *kiš, kash*): furrow(s)

kash (N.P. and P.Gj.): see *karša-*

khāk (N.P. and P.Gj.): see *xāk*

khūb (N.P. and P.Gj.): see *xūb*

kiš (Phl.): see *karša-*

kunišn (Phl.): (good) deed(s)

kustī (N.P. and P.Gj.): see *kustīg*

kustīg (Phl.) (variant: *kustī*): sacred girdle

lard (N.P.): place of nails

maγ (Phl.): see *maya-*

maya- (Av.) (variant: *maγ*): pit(s) for ritual ablutions

magu- (O.P.) (variants: *mōbad, mōbed, mowbed*): Magus

mainyava- (Av.) (variant: *mēnōg*): spirit, spiritual

mānsr (Phl.): see *mąϑra-*

mąϑra- (Av.) (variant: *mānsr*): holy utterance(s) or word(s)

menišn (Phl.): (good) thought(s)

mēnōg (Phl.): see *mainyava-*

mōbad (N.P.): see *magu-*

mōbed (P.Gj.): see *magu-*

motī khūb (P.Gj.): greater ritual power

mowbed (Phl.): see *magu-*

mōy (Phl.): hair

nāhn (P.Gj.): ritual bath

nākhondān (N.P.): place of nails

nasā (Phl.): see *nasu-*

nasā-sālār (Phl., N.P., and P.Gj.): corpse bearer

nasav- (Av.): see *nasu-*

nasu- (Av.) (variants: *nasā, nasav-*): carrion

nasu.kaša (Av.) (variant: *iristō.kaša*): corpse bearer

navgirē (P.Gj.): nine-knotted stick

Navjote (P.Gj.): Newborn Ceremony, initiation into the Zoroastrian faith

nāxun (Phl.): nails

nērang (Phl.) (variants: *nīrang, nīrangdīn*): consecrated bull's urine, incantations

nīrang (N.P. and P.Gj.): see *nērang*

nīrangdīn (P.Gj.): see *nērang*

Niyāyish (N.P. and P.Gj.): see Niyāyišn

Niyāyišn (Phl.) (variant: Niyāyish): praise ceremony

Noh-Shūy (N.P. and P.Gj.): Nine [Night] Baths

Noh Shva (D.): see Barašnūm ī nō šab

Ohrmazd (Phl.): see Ahura Mazdā

padām (Phl.): see *paitidāna-*

padān (P.Gj.): see *paitidāna-*

pādyāb (Phl.) (variant: *pājōw*): unconsecrated bull's urine

Pādyāb (Phl., N.P., and P.Gj.): ritual ablution

Pādyāb-Kustī (N.P. and P.Gj.): ritual ablution, followed by untying and retying the sacred girdle

pahādyun (P.Gj.): stone mounts

paitidāna- (Av.) (variants: *padām, padān, panām*): mouth and nose mask

pājōw (D.): see *pādyāb*

pāk (Phl.) (variant: *pāw*): pure

panām (N.P.): see *paitidāna-*

pāw (P.Gj.): see *pāk*

pāwī (P.Gj.): pure space

paywand (Phl.): connection, contact

rēman (Phl.) (variant: *rīman*): pollution, polluted

rēmanīg (Phl.) (variant: *rīmanī*): polluted person

rīman (N.P. and P.Gj.): see *rēman*

Rīman (P.Gj.): ritual ablution against carrion

rīmanī (N.P. and P.Gj.): see *rēmanīg*

šabīg (Phl.) (variant: *shabī*): sacred white undershirt or vest

Sade Nāhn (P.Gj.): Simple Ritual Bath

sagdīd (Phl.): rite of being seen by a dog

Šahrewar (Phl.): see Xšaθra Vairya

saošyant- (Av.) (variant: *sōšāns*): the three saviors, name of the final saviour

ṣedra (D.): see *ṣudra*

Ṣedra Pushun (D.): ceremony of putting on the sacred undershirt, initiation into the Zoroastrian faith

shabī (N.P.): see *šabīg*

Sī-Shūr (N.P.): see Sī-Shūy

Sī-Shūy (N.P.) (variants: Sī-Shūr, Sī-Shūz, Sī-Shyū): Thirty Washings

Sī-Shūz (D.): see Sī-Shūy

Sī-Shyū (P.Gj.): see Sī-Shūy

Šnūman (Phl.): see Xšnūmaine

sōšāns (Phl.): see *saošyant-*

Spendarmad (Phl.): see Spənta Ārmaiti

Spēnōg Mēnōg (Phl.): see Spənta Mainyu

Spənta Ārmaiti (Av.) (variant: Spendarmad): Holy Devotion, a beneficent immortal

Spənta Mainyu (Av.) (variant: Spēnōg Mēnōg): Beneficent Spirit

srū (Phl.): see *srū-*

srū- (Av.) (variants: *srvā-, srū*): nails

srvā- (Av.): see *srū-*

ṣudra (N.P. and P.Gj.) (variants: *ṣedra, sudre*): sacred white undershirt or vest

sudre (P.Gj.): see *ṣudra*

tanāpuhl (Phl.): a sin that disables a soul from crossing the Bridge of the Separator after death

urwar (Phl.): plant(s), vegetation

urwarām (P.Gj.): pomegranate leaves

vāk- (O.P. and Av.) (variants: *bāj, vāz, wāz*): framing prayer or speech, suppressed tone

varəsa- (Av.) (variant: *wars*): hair

vāz (Pz.): see *vāk-*

Vohu Manah (Av.) (variant: Wahman): Good Mind, a beneficent immortal

wahišt (Phl.): heaven, paradise

Wahman (Phl.): see Vohu Manah

wars (Phl.): see *varəsa-*

wāz (Phl.): see *vāk-*

wizārišn (Phl.): separation

xāk (Phl.) (variant: *khāk*): dust, earth

xrafstar (Phl.): see *xrafstra-*

xrafstra- (Av.) (variant: *xrafstar*): noxious creature(s)

Xšaθra Vairya (Av.) (variant: Šahrewar): Desirable Dominion, a beneficent immortal

Xšnūmaine (Av.) (variant: Šnūman): prayer of propitiation

xūb (Phl.) (variant: *khūb*): ritual power

xvaētvadaθa- (Av.) (variant: *xwēdōdah*): consanguineous marriage

xwēdōdah (Phl.): see *xvaētvadaθa-*

yaozdāthrya (P.Gj.): see *yaoždāθrya-*

yaoždāθrya- (Av.) (variants: *yaozdāthrya, yōĭdāhrgar, yozhdāsragar*): purifier

yashte (P.Gj.): consecrated

Yasna (Av.): part of the Avesta, a sacrifice service

Yašt (Av.): part of the Avesta, hymns

yōjdāhrgar (Phl.): see *yaoždāϑrya-*

yozhdāsragar (N.P.): see *yaoždāϑrya-*

Zand (Phl.): Pahlavi commentary to the Avesta

Zaraϑuštra (Av.) (variant: Zarduxšt): Zarathushtra, Zoroaster

Zarduxšt (Phl.): see Zaraϑuštra

BIBLIOGRAPHY

Complete bibliographical information for the following can be found under the name of the editor or translator.

Agathias: ed. R. Keydell.
Ammianus Marcellinus: ed. and trans. J. C. Rolfe.
Ardā Wīrāz Nāmag: ed. and trans. M. Ph. Gignoux.
Aristotle, *Metaphysics:* ed. and trans. H. Tredennick.
Avesta (Vidēvdāt, Visparad, Yašts, Yasna): ed. K. F. Geldner.
al-Balādhurī, *Ansāb:* ed. M. Ḥamīdullāh.
Bible: King James Version.
al-Bukhārī, *Kitāb al-jāmiᶜ aṣ-ṣaḥīḥ:* ed. M. L. Krehl and T. W. Juynboll.
Bundahišn: ed. T. D. Anklesaria.
Čīdag Handarz ī Pōryōtkēšān: ed. and trans. M. F. Kanga.
Čīm ī Kustīg: ed. and trans. H. F. J. Junker.
Dādestān ī Dēnīg: ed. T. D. Anklesaria, chaps. 1–40; ed. P. K. Anklesaria, chaps.
   41–92.
Dēnkard: ed. D. M. Madan.
Farziyāt-nāma: ed. and trans. J. J. Modi.
Gāthās: ed. and trans. S. Insler; see also Avesta.
Gizistag Abāliš: ed. and trans. H. F. Chacha.
Haδōxt Nask: ed. and trans. M. Haug and H. J. Asa.
Handarz ī Xusrō Kawādān: ed. and trans. P. B. Sanjana.
Herodotus: ed. and trans. A. D. Godley.
Hesiod, *Works and Days:* ed. and trans. H. G. Evelyn-White.
J̌āmāspī: ed. and trans. J. J. Modi.
Josephus, *Antiquities:* ed. and trans. H. St. J. Thackeray.
Jubilees: trans. R. H. Charles.
Mādayān ī Hazār Dādestān: ed. J. J. Modi, vol. 1; ed. T. D. Anklesaria, vol. 2.

Mēnōg ī Xrad: ed. P. Sanjana.

Nāmagīhā ī Manuščihr: ed. B. N. Dhabhar.

Nīrangistān: ed. P. Sanjana, ms. HJ; ed. F. M. Kotwal and J. W. Boyd, ms. TD.

Pahlavi Ĵāmāspī: see Ĵāmāspī.

Pahlavi Rivāyat Accompanying the Dādestān ī Dēnīg: ed. B. N. Dhabhar.

Pahlavi Rivāyat of Ādurfarnbay and Farnbaysrōš: ed. B. T. Anklesaria.

Pahlavi Texts: ed. J. M. Jamasp-Asana.

Pahlavi Vidēvdāt: ed. and trans. B. T. Anklesaria.

Pāzand Ĵāmāspī: see Ĵāmāspī.

Persian Ĵāmāspī: see Ĵāmāspī.

Persian Rivāyats: ed. M. R. Unvala.

Plato, *Alcibiades:* ed. and trans. W. R. M. Lamb.

Plutarch, *Lives: Artaxerxes:* ed. and trans. B. Perrin.

Pursišnīhā: ed. and trans. K. M. Jamaspasa and H. Humbach.

Qurʾān: text and trans. M. M. Pickthall.

Ṛg Veda: ed. S. Th. Aufrecht.

Rivāyat ī Ēmēd ī Ašawahištān: ed. B. T. Anklesaria.

Ṣaddar Bondahesh: ed. B. N. Dhabhar.

Ṣaddar Nasr: ed. B. N. Dhabhar.

Šāyest nē Šāyest: ed. and trans. J. C. Tavadia.

Shāhnāma: trans. A. G. Warner and E. Warner.

Škand Gumānīg Wizār: ed. and trans. P. P. J. de Menasce.

Strabo, *Geography:* ed. and trans. H. L. Jones.

Supplementary Texts to Šāyest nē Šāyest: ed. and trans. F. M. Kotwal.

at-Tibrīzī, *Mishkāt:* ed. and trans. J. Robson.

Vaeϑā Nask: ed. and trans. H. Humbach and K. M. Jamaspasa.

Vidēvdāt (Vendīdād): ed. H. Jamasp; see also Avesta.

Visparad: see Avesta.

Wizīdagīhā ī Zādspram: ed. B. T. Anklesaria.

Xenophon, *Cyropaedia:* ed. and trans. W. Miller.

Yasna: see Avesta.

Yašts: see Avesta.

Zand ī Wahman Yašt: ed. and trans. B. T. Anklesaria.

Zand ī Xwurdag Abestāg: ed. B. N. Dhabhar.

References in the text are to the most recent date of publication or reissue. Spelling variations often occur in the transcriptions of the titles of Zoroastrian texts.

Anklesaria, Behramgore T., ed. and trans. 1949. *Pahlavi Vendīdād.* Bombay: K. R. Cama Oriental Institute.

———, ed. and trans. 1957. *Zand-ī Vohūman Yasn and Two Pahlavi Fragments.* Bombay: K. L. Bhargava.

———, ed. 1962. *Rivāyat-i Hēmīt-ī Asavahistān.* Vol. 1. Bombay: K. R. Cama Oriental Institute.

———, ed. 1964. *Vichitakiha-i Zatsparam.* Pt. 1. Bombay: Parsi Panchayet.

———, ed. 1969. *The Pahlavi Rivāyat of Āturfarnbag and Farnbag-Sröš.* Vol. 1. Bombay: M. F. Cama Athornan Institute.

Anklesaria, Pishotan K., ed. 1958. "A Critical Edition of the Unedited Portion of the Dātestān-i Dīnīk." Ph.D. diss., School of Oriental and African Studies, University of London.

Anklesaria, Tahmuras D., ed. 1899. *The Datistan-i Dinik.* Pt. 1. Bombay: Fort Printing Press.

———, ed. 1908. *The Būndahishn.* Bombay: British India Press.

———, ed. 1913. *Madigān-i-Hazār Dādistān.* Pt. 2. Bombay: Fort Printing Press.

Aufrecht, S. von Theodor, ed. [1861–1863] 1877. *Die hymnen des Rigveda.* 2 vols. Bonn: Adolph Marcus.

Axelrod, Paul. 1974. "A Social and Demographic Comparison of Parsis, Saraswat Brahmins, and Jains in Bombay." Ph.D. diss., Department of Anthropology, University of North Carolina.

Bailey, Harold W. 1970. "A Range of Iranica." In *W. B. Henning Memorial Volume,* ed. M. Boyce and I. Gershevitch, 20—36. London: Lund Humphries.

———. [1943] 1971. *Zoroastrian Problems in the Ninth-Century Books.* Oxford: Oxford University Press.

———. 1985. "Apastāk." In *Papers in Honour of Professor Mary Boyce,* Acta Iranica 24, 9–14. Leiden: E. J. Brill.

Bartholomae, Christian. [1904] 1979. *Altiranisches Wörterbuch.* Berlin: Walter de Gruyter.

Benveniste, Émile. 1970. "Que signifie Vidēvdāt?" In *W. B. Henning Memorial Volume,* ed. M. Boyce and I. Gershevitch, 37–42. London: Lund Humphries.

Beskow, Per. 1978. "The Routes of Early Mithraism." In *Études Mithriaques,* Acta Iranica 17, 7–18. Leiden: E. J. Brill.

Boas, Franz. 1940. "The Limitations of the Comparative Method of Anthropology." In *Race, Language, and Culture,* ed. F. Boas, 270–280. New York: Macmillan.

Bousquet, Georges H. 1960. "Ghusl." In *The Encyclopaedia of Islam.* 2d ed. Leiden: E. J. Brill.

Boyce, Mary. 1970. "Zoroaster the Priest." *Bulletin of the School of Oriental and African Studies* 33(1): 22–38.

———. 1971. "Zoroastrianism." In *Historia Religionum: Handbook for the History of Religions.* Vol. 2, ed. C. J. Bleeker and G. Widengren, 211–236. Leiden: E. J. Brill.

———. 1975. *A History of Zoroastrianism.* Vol. 1. Handbuch der Orientalistik, ed. B. Spuler. Leiden: E. J. Brill.

————. 1977. *A Persian Stronghold of Zoroastrianism*. Oxford: Clarendon Press.

————. 1979. *Zoroastrians: Their Religious Beliefs and Practices*. London: Routledge and Kegan Paul.

————. 1982. *A History of Zoroastrianism*. Vol. 2. Handbuch der Orientalistik, ed. B. Spuler. Leiden: E. J. Brill.

Boyce, Mary, and Firoze M. Kotwal. 1971*a*. "Zoroastrian Bāj and Drōn-I." *Bulletin of the School of Oriental and African Studies* 34(1): 56–73.

————. 1971*b*. "Zoroastrian Bāj and Drōn-II." *Bulletin of the School of Oriental and African Studies* 34(2): 298–313.

Browne, Edward G. 1893. *A Year among the Persians*. London: A. and C. Black.

Burrow, T. 1973. "The Proto-Indoaryans." *Journal of the Royal Asiatic Society* 123–140.

Burton, John. 1988. "The Qur'ān and the Islamic Practice of *wuḍū'*." *Bulletin of the School of Oriental and African Studies* 51(1): 21–58.

Camus, Albert. [1951] 1975. *The Rebel*. Trans. A. Bower. Harmondsworth: Penguin Books.

Carstairs, G. Morris. 1958. *The Twice-Born: A Study of a Community of High-Caste Hindus*. Bloomington: Indiana University Press.

Chacha, H. F., ed. and trans. 1936. *Gajastak Abālis*. Bombay: Parsi Panchayet.

Charles, Robert H., trans. 1917. *The Book of Jubilees or the Little Genesis*. New York: Macmillan.

Choksy, Jamsheed K. 1986*a*. "An Annotated Index of the Greater or Iranian Bundahišn (TD 2)." *Studia Iranica* 15(2): 203–242.

————. 1986*b*. "Purity and Pollution in Zoroastrianism." *Mankind Quarterly* 27(2): 167–191.

————. 1987*a*. "The Zoroastrian Nāhn Purification Rituals." *Journal of Ritual Studies* 1(2): 59–74.

————. 1987*b*. "Zoroastrians in Muslim Iran: Selected Problems of Coexistence and Interaction during the Early Medieval Period." *Iranian Studies* 20(1): 17–30.

————. 1988. "Parsis." *Encyclopedia of Asian History*. New York: The Asia Society and Charles Scribner's.

Christensen, Arthur. 1917. *Le premier homme et le premier roi dans l'histoire légendaire des Iraniens*. Vol. 1. Stockholm: Boktrycheriet.

Cumont, Franz. [1903] 1956. *The Mysteries of Mithra*. Trans. T. J. McCormack. New York: Dover Publications.

Darmesteter, James. 1892. *Le Zend-Avesta: traduction nouvelle avec commentaire historique et philologique*. Vol. 2. Annales du Musée Guimet. Paris: Ernest Leroux.

————. 1895. *The Zend-Avesta*. Pt. 1. Sacred Books of the East, vol. 4, ed. F. Max Müller. Oxford: Clarendon Press.

Dhabhar, Bamanji N., ed. 1909. *Saddar Naṣr and Saddar Bundehesh: Persian Texts Relating to Zoroastrianism*. Bombay: Parsi Panchayet.

————, ed. 1912. *The Epistles of Manushchihar.* Bombay: Fort Printing Press.

————, ed. 1913. *The Pahlavi Rivāyat Accompanying the Dādistān-ī Dīnīk.* Bombay: Parsi Panchayet.

————, ed. 1927. *Zand-i Khūrtak Avistāk.* Bombay: Parsi Panchayet.

————, trans. 1963. *Translation of Zand-i Khūrtak Avistāk.* Bombay: K. R. Cama Oriental Institute.

Dhalla, Maneckji N. 1938. *History of Zoroastrianism.* Oxford: Oxford University Press.

Douglas, Mary. 1968. "Pollution." In *International Encyclopedia of the Social Sciences,* ed. D. L. Sills. 12: 336–342. New York: Macmillan and the Free Press.

————. [1966] 1969. *Purity and Danger: An Analysis of the Concepts of Pollution and Taboo.* London: Routledge and Kegan Paul.

————. [1970] 1973. *Natural Symbols: Explorations in Cosmology.* New York: Vintage Books.

Dresden, Mark J., ed. 1966. *Dēnkart: A Pahlavi Text.* Wiesbaden: Otto Harrassowitz.

Dubash, Sorabji E. 1906. *The Zoroastrian Sanitary Code.* Bombay: British India Press.

Duchesne-Guillemin, Jacques. 1983. "Zoroastrian Religion." In *The Cambridge History of Iran.* Vol. 3, Pt. 2, ed. E. Yarshater, 866–908. Cambridge: Cambridge University Press.

Dumézil, Georges. 1958. *L'idéologie tripartie des indo-européens.* Brussels: Collection Latomus.

————. 1969. *Idées romaines.* Paris: Gallimard.

Durkheim, Émile. [1912] 1957. *The Elementary Forms of the Religious Life.* Trans. J. W. Swain. London: George Allen and Unwin.

Eliade, Mircea. 1965. *The Sacred and the Profane.* Trans. W. R. Trask. New York: Harper Torchbooks.

————. [1954] 1974. *The Myth of the Eternal Return: Cosmos and History.* Trans. W. R. Trask. Princeton: Princeton University Press.

————. [1958] 1975. *Rites and Symbols of Initiation: The Mysteries of Birth and Rebirth.* Trans. W. R. Trask. New York: Harper Torchbooks.

————. 1976. *Myths, Rites, and Symbols.* Vol. 1. Ed. W. C. Beane and W. G. Doty. New York: Harper and Row.

Ellis, William. [1842] 1965. "The Tabu." In *Reader in Comparative Religion: An Anthropological Approach.* 2d ed., ed. W. A. Lessa and E. Z. Vogt, 262–265. New York: Harper and Row.

Evans-Pritchard, Edward E. 1965. *Theories of Primitive Religion.* Oxford: Clarendon Press.

Evelyn-White, Hugh G., ed. and trans. 1914. *Hesiod.* Loeb Classical Library. London: William Heinemann.

Fischer, Michael M. J. 1973. "Zoroastrian Iran between Myth and Praxis." Ph.D. diss., Department of Anthropology, University of Chicago.

———. 1978. "On Changing the Concept and Position of Persian Women." In *Women in the Muslim World,* ed. Lois Beck and Nikki Keddie, 189–215. Cambridge, Mass.: Harvard University Press.

———. 1980. *Iran: From Religious Dispute to Revolution.* Cambridge, Mass.: Harvard University Press.

Frazer, James G. [1890] 1955. *The Golden Bough: A Study in Magic and Religion.* 3d ed. Vol. 3. London: Macmillan.

Freud, Sigmund. 1973. *The Pelican Freud Library.* 15 vols. Harmondsworth: Penguin Books.

Frye, Richard N. 1984*a. The History of Ancient Iran.* Munich: C. H. Beck.

———. 1984*b.* "Religion in Fars under the Achaemenids." In *Orientalia J. Duchesne-Guillemin Emerito Oblata,* Acta Iranica 23, 171–178. Leiden: E. J. Brill.

———. 1985. "Zoroastrian Incest." In *Orientalia Iosephi Tucci Memoriae Dicata,* ed. Gherardo Gnoli and Lionello Lanciotti, 445–455. Rome: Istituto Italiano per il Medio ed Estremo Oriente.

Geertz, Clifford. 1966. "Religion as a Cultural System." In *Anthropological Approaches to the Study of Religion,* ed. M. Banton, 1–46. New York: Frederick A. Praeger.

———. [1968] 1971. *Islam Observed: Religious Developments in Morocco and Indonesia.* Chicago: University of Chicago Press.

———. 1973*a.* "Thick Description: Toward an Interpretive Theory of Culture." In *The Interpretation of Cultures: Selected Essays by Clifford Geertz,* 3–30. New York: Basic Books.

———. 1973*b.* "Ethos, World View, and the Analysis of Sacred Symbols." In *The Interpretation of Cultures: Selected Essays by Clifford Geertz,* 126–141. New York: Basic Books.

———. 1976. "'From the Native's Point of View': On the Nature of Anthropological Understanding." In *Meaning in Anthropology,* ed. K. H. Basso and H. A. Selby, 221–237. Albuquerque: University of New Mexico Press.

———. 1983. "Found in Translation: On the Social History of the Moral Imagination." In *Local Knowledge: Further Essays in Interpretive Anthropology by Clifford Geertz,* 36–54. New York: Basic Books.

———. 1988. *Works and Lives: The Anthropologist as Author.* Stanford: Stanford University Press.

Geldner, Karl F., ed. [1886–1895] 1982. *Avesta: The Sacred Books of the Parsis.* 3 vols. Stuttgart: W. Kohlhammer.

Gennep, Arnold van. [1909] 1960. *The Rites of Passage.* Trans. M. B. Vizedom and G. L. Caffee. Chicago: University of Chicago Press.

Gershevitch, Ilya. 1964. "Zoroaster's Own Contribution." *Journal of Near Eastern Studies* 23(1): 12–38.

Gignoux, M. Philippe, ed. and trans. 1984. *Le Livre d'Ardā Vīrāz.* Paris: Editions Recherche sur les Civilisations.

Gnoli, Gherardo. 1980. *Zoroaster's Time and Homeland*. Seminario di Studi Asiatici, Series Minor, vol. 7. Naples: Istituto Universitario Orientale.

Göbl, Robert. 1971. *Sasanian Numismatics*. Trans. P. Severin. Brunswick: Klinkhardt and Biermann.

Godley, A. D., ed. and trans. 1920–1924. *Herodotus*. 4 vols. Loeb Classical Library. London: William Heinemann.

Goeje, M. J. de, ed. 1904–1940. *Kitāb aṭ-ṭabaqāt al-kabīr*, by Ibn Saʿd. 8 vols. Leiden: E. J. Brill.

Gonda, J. 1980. *Vedic Ritual: The Non-Solemn Rites*. Handbuch der Orientalistik, ed. B. Spuler. Leiden: E. J. Brill.

Goody, Jack. 1961. "Religion and Ritual: The Definitional Problem." *British Journal of Sociology* 12(2): 142–164.

Gray, Louis H. 1929. *The Foundations of the Iranian Religions*. Bombay: K. R. Cama Oriental Institute.

Grimes, Ronald L. 1982. *Beginnings in Ritual Studies*. Washington: University Press of America.

Ḥamīdullāh, Muḥammad, ed. 1959. *Ansāb al-ashrāf*, by Aḥmad b. Yaḥyā al-Balādhurī. Vol. 1. Cairo: Dār al-Maʿārif.

Harvey, Van A. 1966. *The Historian and the Believer: The Morality of Historical Knowledge and Christian Belief*. New York: Macmillan.

Haug, Martin, and Hoshangji J. Asa, ed. and trans. 1872. "Hadokht-Nask." In *The Book of Arda Viraf*, ed. and trans. M. Haug and H. J. Asa, 267–316. London: Trübner and Co.

Henning, Walter B. 1951. *Zoroaster: Politician or Witch-doctor?* Oxford: Oxford University Press.

Herzfeld, Ernest. 1947. *Zoroaster and His World*. 2 vols. Princeton: Princeton University Press.

Hinnells, John R. 1974. "The Iranian Background of Mithraic Iconography." In *Acta Iranica* 1, 242–250. Leiden: E. J. Brill.

———. 1975. "Aspects of the Mithraic Bull-Slaying." In *Mithraic Studies*, ed. J. Hinnells, 290–312. Manchester: Manchester University Press.

Hodivala, Shahpurji K. 1925. *Indo-Iranian Religion*. Bombay: British India Press.

Hodivala, Shahpurshah H. 1920. *Studies in Parsi History*. Bombay: Bahauddin College.

Hoffmann, Karl. 1965. "Av. daxma-." *Zeitschrift für vergleichende Sprachforschung* 79(3–4): 238.

Humbach, Helmut. 1985. "About Gōpatšāh, His Country, and the Khwārezmian Hypothesis." In *Papers in Honour of Professor Mary Boyce*, Acta Iranica 24, 327–334. Leiden: E. J. Brill.

Humbach, Helmut, and Kaikhusroo M. Jamaspasa, ed. and trans. 1969. *Vaeϑā Nask: An Apocryphal Text on Zoroastrian Problems*. Wiesbaden: Otto Harrassowitz.

Insler, Stanley. 1975*a*. *The Gāthās of Zarathustra*. Acta Iranica 8. Leiden: E. J. Brill.
———. 1975*b*. "The Ahuna Vairya Prayer." In *Monumentum H. S. Nyberg* 1, Acta Iranica 4, 409–421. Leiden: E. J. Brill.
Irani, Kaikhosrov D. 1980. "Reflections on the Zoroastrian Religion: The Philosophy of Belief and Practice." *Parsiana* 3(8): 13–23, 43–51.
Jackson, A. V. Williams. 1906. *Persia Past and Present: A Book of Travel and Research*. New York: Macmillan.
Jamasp, Hoshang, ed. 1907. *Vendīdād*. Vol. 1. Bombay: Government Central Book Depot.
Jamaspasa, Kaikhusroo M., and Helmut Humbach, ed. and trans. 1971. *Pursišnīhā: A Zoroastrian Catechism*. Pt. 1. Wiesbaden: Otto Harrassowitz.
Jamasp-Asana, Jamaspji M., ed. 1913. *The Pahlavi Texts*. Bombay: Fort Printing Press.
Jensen, Adolf E.[1951] 1963. *Myth and Cult among Primitive Peoples*. Trans. M. T. Choldin and W. Weissleder. Chicago: University of Chicago Press.
Jones, Horace L., ed. and trans. 1917–1932. *The Geography of Strabo*. 8 vols. Loeb Classical Library. London: William Heinemann.
Junker, Heinrich F. J., ed. and trans. 1959. *Der wissbegierige Sohn: Ein mittelpersischer Text uber das Kustik*. Leipzig: Otto Harrasowitz.
Kanga, Maneck F., ed. and trans. 1960. *Čītak Handarž ī Pōryōtkēšān: A Pahlavi Text*. Bombay: Dorab H. Kanga.
Karaka, Dosabhai F. 1884. *History of the Parsis: Including Their Manners, Customs, Religion, and Present Position*. 2 vols. London: Macmillan.
Keydell, Rudolfus, ed. 1967. *Agathiae Myrinaei: Historiarum Libri quinque*. Berlin: Walter de Gruyter.
The King James Version / New International Version Parallel Bible. 1983. Grand Rapids, Mich.: Zondervan Bible Publishers.
Kotwal, Firoze M., ed. and trans. 1969. *The Supplementary Texts to the Šāyest nē-šāyest*. Copenhagen: Munksgaard.
Kotwal, Firoze M., and James W. Boyd. 1977. "The Zoroastrian Paragnā Ritual." *Journal of Mithraic Studies* 2(1): 18–52.
———, ed. 1980. *Ērbadistān ud Nīrangistān*. Cambridge, Mass.: Harvard University Press.
Krehl, M. L., and T. W. Juynboll, ed. 1862–1908. *Kitāb al-jāmiʿ aṣ-ṣaḥīḥ*, by Abū ʿAbd Allāh Muḥammad al-Bukhārī. 4 vols. Leiden: E. J. Brill.
Kreyenbroek, G. 1985. *Sraoša in the Zoroastrian Tradition*. Leiden: E. J. Brill.
Lamb, W. R. M., ed. and trans. 1927. *Alcibiades*, by Plato. Loeb Classical Library. London: William Heinemann.
Leach, Edmund R. 1958. "Magical Hair." *Journal of the Royal Anthropological Institute* 88: 147–164.
———. 1968. "Ritual." In *International Encyclopedia of the Social Sciences*, ed. D. L. Sills, 13: 520–526. New York: Macmillan and the Free Press.

Lévi-Strauss, Claude. [1958] 1963. *Structural Anthropology*. Trans. C. Jacobson and B. G. Schoepf. New York: Basic Books.

———. 1968. *L'origine des Manières de Table*. Paris: Plon.

———. 1977. *Tristes Tropiques*. Trans. J. Weightman and D. Weightman. New York: Washington Square Press.

———. 1985. *The View from Afar*. Trans. J. Neugroschel and P. Hoss. New York: Basic Books.

———. [1984] 1987. *Anthropology and Myth*. Trans. R. Willis. Oxford: Basil Blackwell.

Lévy-Bruhl, Lucien. [1910] 1926. *How Natives Think*. Trans. L. A. Clare. London: George Allen and Unwin.

Lincoln, Bruce. 1975. "The Indo-European Myth of Creation." *History of Religion* 15(2): 121–145.

———. 1977. "Treatment of Hair and Fingernails among the Indo-Europeans." *History of Religions* 16(4): 351–362.

———. 1986. *Myth, Cosmos, and Society: Indo-European Themes of Creation and Destruction*. Cambridge, Mass.: Harvard University Press.

Littleton, C. Scott. 1982. *The New Comparative Mythology: An Anthropological Assessment of the Theories of Georges Dumézil*. 3d ed. Berkeley: University of California Press.

MacKenzie, David N. 1971. *A Concise Pahlavi Dictionary*. London: Oxford University Press.

Madan, Dhanjishah M., ed. 1911. *The Complete Text of the Pahlavi Dinkard*. 2 vols. Bombay: Society for the Promotion of Researches into the Zoroastrian Religion.

Malinowski, Bronislaw. [1925] 1948. *"Magic, Science, and Religion," and Other Essays*. Glencoe, Ill.: The Free Press.

———. 1962. *Sex, Culture, and Myth*. New York: Harcourt, Brace, and World.

Menasce, P. Pierre J. de, ed. and trans. 1945. *Škand-Gumānīk Vičār: La Solution Décisive des Doutes*. Fribourg: L'Université de Fribourg en Suisse.

Miller, Walter, ed. and trans. 1914. *Cyropaedia*, by Xenophon. 2 vols. Loeb Classical Library. London: William Heinemann.

Mistree, Khojeste P. 1982. *Zoroastrianism: An Ethnic Perspective*. Bombay: Zoroastrian Studies.

Modi, Jivanji J., ed. 1901. *Mādigān-i-Hazār Dādīstān*. Bombay: Parsi Panchayet.

———, ed. and trans. 1903. *Jāmāspi: Pahlavi, Pāzend, and Persian Texts*. Bombay: Education Society.

———. 1922. *The Religious Ceremonies and Customs of the Parsees*. Bombay: British India Press.

———, ed. and trans. 1924. *The Persian Farziāt-Nāmeh and Kholāseh-i Din of Dastur Darab Pahlan*. Bombay: Fort Printing Press.

———. 1932. Darab Hormazdyar's Rivāyat: A Few Notes on an Early Part of Its Contents. *Journal of the K. R. Cama Oriental Institute* 23: 109–238.

————. 1962. *A Catechism of the Zoroastrian Religion*. Bombay: Parsi Panchayet.

Molé, Marijan. 1963. *Culte, mythe et cosmologie dans l'Iran ancien: Le problème zoroastrien et la tradition mazdéenne*. Paris: Presses Universitaires de France.

Monro, J., ed. 1957. *The London Shakespeare*. 6 vols. New York: Simon and Schuster.

Morony, Michael G. 1984. *Iraq After the Muslim Conquest*. Princeton: Princeton University Press.

Musallam, Basim F. 1983. *Sex and Society in Islam: Birth Control before the Nineteenth Century*. Cambridge: Cambridge University Press.

Neumann, Erich. 1954. *The Origins of History of Consciousness*. New York: Harper and Row.

Neusner, Jacob. 1973. *The Idea of Purity in Ancient Judaism*. Leiden: E. J. Brill.

————. 1975. "The Idea of Purity in the Jewish Literature of the Period of the Second Temple." In *Monumentum H. S. Nyberg,* Acta Iranica 5, 123–138. Leiden: E. J. Brill.

————. 1977. *The Mishnaic System of Uncleanness: Its Context and History*. Leiden: E. J. Brill.

Niebuhr, Carsten. 1792. *Travels through Arabia and Other Countries*. Vol. 2. Trans. R. Heron. Edinburgh: R. Morison and Sons.

Nietzsche, Friedrich. [1891–1892] 1980. *Thus Spoke Zarathustra*. Trans. W. Kaufmann. Harmondsworth: Penguin Books.

Nyberg, Henrik S. [1938] 1970. "Die altiranische soziale Religion II: Die Gathagemeinde." In *Zarathustra,* Wege der Forschung 169, ed. B. Schlerath, 53–96. Darmstadt: Wissenschaftlich Buchgesellschaft.

————. 1974. *A Manual of Pahlavi*. Pt. 2. Wiesbaden: Otto Harrassowitz.

Obeyesekere, Gananath. 1984. *The Cult of the Goddess Pattini*. Chicago: University of Chicago Press.

Parsiana. 1986. Vol. 9(6). Bombay: Parsiana Publications.

————. 1987. Vol. 10(1). Bombay: Parsiana Publications.

"Parsi Marriage and Divorce Act 3 of 1936." *Acts of India 1936*.

"Parsi Marriage and Divorce Act 15 of 1865." *Acts of India 1865*.

Parsons, Talcott. 1949. *Essays in Sociological Theory: Pure and Applied*. Glencoe, Ill.: The Free Press.

Pavry, Cursetji. [1926] 1929. *The Zoroastrian Doctrine of a Future Life: From Death to the Individual Judgment*. 2d ed. New York: Columbia University Press.

Penner, Hans H. 1985. "Language, Ritual, and Meaning." *Numen* 32(1): 1–16.

Perrin, Bernadotte, ed. and trans. 1914–1926. *Plutarch's Lives*. 11 vols. Loeb Classical Library. London: William Heinemann.

Pickthall, Muhammad M. 1977. *The Glorious Qur'ān: Text and Explanatory Translation*. New York: Muslim World League.

Polomé, Edgar C. 1980. "The Gods of the Indo-Europeans." *Mankind Quarterly* 21(2): 151–164.

————. 1985. "The Study of Religion in the Context of Language and Culture: A

Prospect for the Coming Decade, with Focus on Germanic and Indo-European." *Mankind Quarterly* 26(1): 5–18.

Poole, Fitz J. P. 1986. "Metaphors and Maps: Towards Comparison in the Anthropology of Religion." *Journal of the American Academy of Religion* 54(3): 411–457.

Power, Eileen. 1975. *Medieval Women*. Ed. M. M. Postan. Cambridge: Cambridge University Press.

Pritchard, James B., ed. [1950] 1969. *Ancient Near Eastern Texts Relating to the Old Testament*. 3d ed. Princeton: Princeton University Press.

Radcliffe-Brown, A. R. 1952. *Structure and Function in Primitive Society*. Glencoe, Ill.: The Free Press.

Ricoeur, Paul. 1969. *The Symbolism of Evil*. Trans. E. Buchanan. Boston: Beacon Press.

Riencourt, Amaury de. 1983. *Woman and Power in History*. Bath: Honeyglen Publishing.

Robson, James, ed. and trans. 1963–1965. *Mishkāt al-Maṣābih,* by Walī ad-Dīn Muḥammad b. ʿAbd Allāh at-Tibrīzī. 4 vols. Lahore: M. Ashraf.

Rolfe, John C., ed. and trans. (1935–1940) 1950–1952. *Ammianus Marcellinus*. 3 vols. Loeb Classical Library. London: William Heinemann.

Roll, Israel. 1977. "The Mysteries of Mithras in the Roman Orient: The Problem of Origin." *Journal of Mithraic Studies* 2(1): 53–68.

Sanjana, P. Behramji, ed. and trans. 1885. *Ganjeshayagan, Andarze Atrepat Maraspandan, Madigane Chatrang and Andarze Khusroe Kavatan*. Bombay: Duftar Ashkara.

Sanjana, Peshotan, ed. 1894. *Nirangistan*. Bombay: Parsi Panchayet.

———, ed. 1895. *The Dīnā ī Maīnū ī Khrat*. Bombay: Education Society.

Schacht, Joseph. 1913. "Wuḍū'." In *The Encyclopaedia of Islam*. 1st ed. Leiden: E. J. Brill.

Schmidt, Hans-Peter. 1960. "The Sixteen Sanskrit Ślokas of Ākā Adhyāru." *Bulletin of the Deccan College Research Institute* 21: 157–196.

Schwartz, Martin. 1985a. "The Religion of Achaemenian Iran." In *The Cambridge History of Iran*. Vol. 2, ed. I. Gershevitch, 664–697. Cambridge: Cambridge University Press.

———. 1985b. "Scatology and Eschatology in Zoroaster: On the Paronomasia of Yasna 48.10 and on Indo-European h^2eg 'to make taboo' and the Reciprocity Verbs *kwsen(w)* and *megh*." In *Papers in Honour of Professor Mary Boyce*, Acta Iranica 25, 473–496. Leiden: E. J. Brill.

Seervai, Kh. N., and B. B. Patel. 1899. "Gujarat Parsis from Their Earliest Settlement to the Present Time." *Gazetteer of the Bombay Presidency* 9(2): 208–219.

Shahbazi, A. Shapur. 1977. "The 'Traditional Date of Zoroaster' Explained." *Bulletin of the School of Oriental and African Studies* 40(1): 25–33.

Shaked, Shaul. 1971. "The Notions *mēnōg* and *gētīg* in the Pahlavi Texts and Their Relation to Eschatology." *Acta Orientalia* 33: 59–107.

Smith, Morton. 1971. *Palestinian Parties and Politics That Shaped the Old Testament.* New York: Columbia University Press.

Spiro, Melford E. 1966. "Religion: Problems of Definition and Explanation." In *Anthropological Approaches to the Study of Religion,* ed. M. Banton, 85–126. New York: Frederick A. Praeger.

Staal, Frits. 1979. "The Meaninglessness of Ritual." *Numen* 26(1): 2–22.

———. 1986a. "The Sound of Religion (I)." *Numen* 33(1): 33–64.

———. 1986b. "The Sound of Religion (II)." *Numen* 33(2): 185–224.

Stavorinus, Johan S. 1798. *Voyages to the East Indies.* Vol. 1. Trans. S. H. Wilcocke. London: G. G. Robinson and J. Robinson.

Steiner, Franz. 1956. *Taboo.* New York: Philosophical Library.

Stevenson, M. Sinclair. 1971. *The Rites of the Twice-Born.* 2d ed. Delhi: Munshiram Manoharlal.

Stronach, David. 1984. "Notes on Religion in Iran in the Seventh and Sixth Centuries B.C.E." In *Orientalia J. Duchesne-Guillemin Emerito Oblata,* Acta Iranica 23, 479–490. Leiden: E. J. Brill.

Tafazzoli, Ahmad. 1975. "Elephant: A Demonic Creature and a Symbol of Sovereignty." In *Monumentum H. S. Nyberg,* Acta Iranica 5, 395–398. Leiden: E. J. Brill.

Tambiah, Stanley, J. 1968. "The Magical Power of Words." *Man* 3(2): 175–208.

———. 1979. "A Performative Approach to Ritual." *Proceedings of the British Academy* 65: 113–169.

Tavadia, Jehangir C., ed. and trans. 1930. *Šāyast-nē-šāyast: A Pahlavi Text on Religious Customs.* Hamburg: Walter de Gruyter.

Thackeray, H. St. J., ed. and trans. 1930. *Josephus: Jewish Antiquities, Books I–IV.* Loeb Classical Library. London: William Heinemann.

Thompson, G. 1949. *The Prehistoric Aegean.* Vol. 1. London: Lawrence and Wishart.

Tredennick, Hugh, ed. and trans. [1933–1935] 1936. *Aristotle: The Metaphysics.* 2 vols. Loeb Classical Library. London: William Heinemann.

Turner, Victor W. 1967. *The Forest of Symbols: Aspects of Ndembu Ritual.* Ithaca: Cornell University Press.

———. 1968. "Myth and Symbol." In *International Encyclopedia of the Social Sciences,* ed. D. L. Sills, 10: 576–582. New York: Macmillan and the Free Press.

———. 1977a. "Symbols in African Ritual." In *Symbolic Anthropology: A Reader in the Study of Symbols and Meanings,* ed. J. L. Dolgin, D. S. Kemnitzer, and D. M. Schneider, 183–194. New York: Columbia University Press.

———. 1977b. *The Ritual Process: Structure and Anti-structure.* Ithaca: Cornell University Press.

———. 1982. *From Ritual to Theatre: The Human Seriousness of Play.* New York: Performing Arts Journal.

Tylor, Edward B. [1871] 1958. *Primitive Culture: Researches into the Development of Mythology, Philosophy, Religion, Art, and Custom.* Vol. 1. Gloucester, Mass.: Smith.

Unvala, Manockji R., ed. 1922. *Dārāb Hormazyār's Rivāyats*. Vol. 1. Bombay: British India Press.

Van Ess, Dorothy. 1961. *Fatima and Her Sisters*. New York: John Day.

Wagner, Roy. 1986. *Symbols That Stand for Themselves*. Chicago: University of Chicago Press.

Warner, A. G., and E. Warner, trans. 1905–1925. *Shāh-nāma of Firdausī*. 9 vols. London: Trubner.

Wayman, Alex. 1982. "The Body as a Microcosm in India, Greek Cosmology, and Sixteenth-Century Europe." *History of Religions* 22: 172–190.

Wensinck, Arend J. 1913. "Tayammum." In *The Encyclopaedia of Islam*. Leiden: E. J. Brill.

Widengren, Geo. 1980. "Microcosmos-Macrocosmos." *Archivio di Filosofia* 1980: 297–312.

Windfuhr, Gernot L. 1976. "Vohu Manah: A Key to the Zoroastrian World-Formula." In *Michigan Studies in Honor of George G. Cameron*, ed. L. L. Orlin, 269–310. Ann Arbor: University of Michigan Department of Near Eastern Studies.

———. 1984. "The Word in Zoroastrianism." *Journal of Indo-European Studies* 12(1–2): 133–178.

———. 1987. "The Zoroastrian Yasna Ritual." Paper presented at the American Oriental Society Meeting, Los Angeles, March 1987.

Zaehner, Robert C. 1961. *The Dawn and Twilight of Zoroastrianism*. London: Weidenfeld and Nicolson.

———. [1955] 1972. *Zurvan: A Zoroastrian Dilemma*. New York: Biblo and Tannen.

———. [1956] 1976. *The Teachings of the Magi: A Compendium of Zoroastrian Beliefs*. New York: Oxford University Press.

INDEX

40–50, 128, 149 n.28; primitive
fears and prohibitions, 51; purifier,
24, 29, 34, 42–46; requirement for
crossing Bridge of the Separator,
128; similar rituals in other religions, 47–50; vitiation of, 50–
52, 93; vs. Rīman ritual, 71–72
bedding, pollution of, 106
beliefs and practices. *See* religious
beliefs
beneficent immortals, 4–5, 10, 124–
125, 137. *See also names of particular
beneficent immortals*
birds, exposure of corpses to, 7, 17
blood, 94, 95. *See also* menstruation
Boas, Franz, xxx, 146 n.10
body. *See* human body
bovines, 117, 118, 119
Boyce, Mary, xx, xxi
breath and saliva, 14, 84–85
Bridge of the Separator, 127–128
Buddhist beliefs, 94
bull, primordial, 116–118, 129, 131
bull's urine, consecrated: purificatory
use of, 20, 116–119, 134; used in rituals, 35, 48, 49, 63, 66, 67, 69, 73–
74, 76
—unconsecrated: associated with immortality, 117–118; purificatory use
of, 11, 20, 116–117, 119; ritual use of,
81, 91, 98, 100, 105; used in rituals,
27, 28, 38, 45, 48, 49, 53–54, 56, 58,
63, 66, 67, 69, 74, 76
Bundahišn ("Book of Primal Creation"), 5, 95–96, 97, 116, 119, 125, 129

Camus, Albert, xxvi
carrion: difference from excrement,
78; pollution from, 12, 13, 16–17;
purification for contact with, 24,
67, 69, 71. *See also* corpses; personal
property, pollution of
celibacy, discouragement of, 88–89

childbirth, 70, 91, 99–102. *See also*
menstruation
Čīdag Handarz ī Pōryōtkēšān ("Select Counsels of the Ancient
Sages"), 4
confessional prayer. *See* Petīt
Pašēmānīh
consanguineous marriage, 89–90,
153 n.20
converts to Zoroastrianism, 41,
149 nn.26, 27
corn and fodder, pollution of, 106
corpse bearers, 69, 70, 76, 107–110,
152 n.29
Corpse Demoness: and corpses, 16–
17, 108; expulsion of, 20, 25, 27, 28,
74–75; pollution of blood by, 94,
95; semen seized by, 91
corpses, 7, 16–17, 24, 104–107
cosmos, 3, 21, 116, 124–126, 133–137,
156 n.20
creation, xxvi, xxxi, 4
creation myths, 116–118, 128, 155 nn.5,
6, 8
creatures. *See* animals and plants
creed, Zoroastrian, 21, 45, 112, 134
Cyrus II the Great, 85

Dādestān ī Dēnīg ("Book of Reli-
gious Judgments"), 9, 55, 89, 121
Daēna, the, 127–128
Dante Alighieri, 9
Dārāb Hormazyār, Rivāyats of, 9
Darius III, 15
Darmesteter, James, xx
Dastūrī, 109, 139
Davāzdah Hamast, 98, 99
death, 16, 67, 127–128, 156 n.21. *See
also* corpses; suffering and death
defecation. *See* urine and feces
demons, xxi, xxvi, 6, 95, 127–128. *See
also* Aŋra Mainyu
Dēnkard ("Acts of the Religion"), 4,